ARKANSAS VOICES

ARKANSAS VOICES

Revised Edition

Edited by
Sarah M. Fountain

University of Central Arkansas Press
1989

Copyright 1989 by UCA Press
All rights reserved
Manufactured in the United States of America

Designer: Robert E. Lowrey
Illustrator: Gary Floden

LIBRARY OF CONGRESS CATALOGING IN PUBLICATION DATA
Main entry under title:

Arkansas Voices
    I. American literature—Arkansas-

I. Fountain, Sarah Jane, 1927-

ISBN 0-944436-09-9

CONTENTS

Preface	xiii
Acknowledgements	xv
Prologue	xvii

I. LEGENDS FROM THE RED MAN

Anonymous
Boka, the Evil Bird	2
Dardanelle	2
The Magawana	2
The Ozarks	3
"Forked Top" Mountain Is Landmark	3

Fred W. Allsopp
The Footprints on the Rock	4
Teponah's Fatal Wooing	5
How Sequoyah Got His Wife	7
The Legend of the Valley of Vapors	8

John R. Swanton
How Day and Night were Divided	11
Thunder Helper	12
The Origin of Corn	13
The Orphan and the Origin of Corn	14
The Orphan and the Origin of Corn (Second Version)	17
The Tar Baby	20
The Language of Animals	21
The Origin of Races	22
The Origin of Races (Second Version)	22
The Creation of the Earth	23
Alabama Stories	
The Flood	25
Thunder	25
The Ordering of the Months and Seasons	26

Dee Brown
"The Bear Man"	27
How Day and Night were Divided	30

How Rabbit Brought Fire to the People	31
How Rabbit Fooled Wolf	32
Buffalo Woman, A Story of Magic	35

II. "BIG WINDYS" AND OTHER YARNS

Weldon Stone
Devil Take A Whittler	41

Charles F. M. Noland
Pete Whetstone	50
Pete Whetstone's Bear Hunt	50
Pete Whetstone Alive and Kicking	52
Letter From Pete Whetstone	54
Letter from Pete Whetstone	56
Letter from Pete Whetstone	57

James Masterson
The Arkansas Traveler	58
A Traverler, A Cabin, and a Fiddle	59

Ruth McEnery Stuart
An Arkansas Prophet	63

Thomas Bangs Thorpe
The Big Bear of Arkansas	83

James Masterson
A Fight	94

Wayman Hogue
Newt Shafer, Candidate	98

Cassius M. Johnson
Change the Name of Arkansas	101

William T. Porter
An Arkansas Storm, Or the Screecher's fight with a painter	103
A Day's Sport in Arkansas	104
"Bar" Hunting in Arkansas	108
The Old Bear of Tironga Bayou, Arkansas, Tarney's Hunt	110
A Bear Hunt	113
Fishing in Arkansas	116

Marion Hughes
    Fishing in Arkansaw   120

III. THE FOLKLORE TRADITION

Otto Rayburn
    The Fighting Parson   124

Vance Randolph
    Sticks in the Knapsack   127
    What Candy Ashcraft Done   128
    Big Knives in Arkansas   130
    Tobe Killed a Bear   131
    The Well Digger   132
    You Ain't Coming Back   133
    Yellow Bread   134
    Stiff as a Poker   135
    Casting Out the Devil   137
    The Boy that Made Up Songs   138
    The Big Old Giant   140
    Three Little Pigs   141
    Uncle Johnny's Bear   143
    The Banjo-Picking Girl   144

Folk Tales of Black Folks
    A "Dry-Clean" Baptizing   146
    A Darkey "Draps" A Talking Turtle   147
    Animal and Bird Stories
        Stealing the Butter   148
        Bear and Buzzard   151
        Tar Baby   152
        Mr. Rabbit and Mr. Frog Make
            Mr. Fox and Mr. Bear Their Riding Horses   153
    Old Marster and John Stories
        John and the Horse   155
        Master Gone to Philly-Me-York   156
        Talking Turtle   157
        John Praying   158
        A Dime for the Sack   159
        John's Courtship   160
    Jocular Tales: Tales of haunted houses, ghosts and the frights.
        Waiting for Martin   161
        On the Cooling Board   164

Who Darket de Hole?	164
Dividing Souls	165
I'm Going to Fall	166
Eating Farther Down the Hog	166
I'm Sopping My Own Gravy Now	167
Informants	168

IV. ARKANSAS VOICES SING

Songs of the Hills

The Cambric Shirt	171
The Miller's Daughter	173
Johnny Randolph	175
Barbara Allen	177
On the Banks of Sweet Dundee	179
The Pretty Mohee	180
The Blackbird	181
The Frog's Courtship	183

Songs of the Black Folks	186
The Musical "Quill"	196

V. THE POETIC VOICE OF ARKANSAS

Albert Pike

Ode to the Mocking-bird	200
Sunset in Arkansas	202
Night on the Arkansa	204

Fay Hempstead

A New Bethesda	205
Ichabod	207
The Night-Watch	209

Fred W. Allsopp

Fancy and I	211
David O. Dodd	212
Lines to the "Old Lady"	214
Petit Jean	215

John Gould Fletcher

Late Summer	220

Spring	221
The Swan	222

Glenn Ward Dresbach
An Old Mill	223
I Would Build Myself A House	224
A Vagabond At The Gates	224
I Have Always Said I Would Go	225
Mail Box	225

Rosa Zagnoni Marinoni
Hot Springs	226
Winter Dusk in the Ozarks	227
Standing Chimneys	228
Christmas in the Ozarks	228
Native	229

Edsel Ford
Everyman	230
White River Float	231
Contingent	231
At the Museum Again	232
Low Tide At Fire Island	233

Booker T. Jackson
Of People and Power	234
Theme for Dignity	234
Soul Democracy	235
The Crisis of 57	235

Richard Hudson
Kite	237
Theoretical Problems of the Piano	237
On Going to Wars	238
Telegraph Road, "On Pea Ridge"	239
Retreat to Calico Rock	240

Maya Angelou
I Almost Remember	242
Southeast Arkanasia	243
My Arkansas	244
Still I Rise	245

Jack Butler
    The Ant-Hill   247
    Three   248
    The Frustration of Simple Desires   249
    In Love's Way   251

James Whitehead
    Domains   252
    Tornadoes (for H.R.T.)   253
    The Opinion of an Interesting Old Man   254

Miller Williams
    Main Street   255
    The News   256
    For Rebecca, For Whom Nothing has Been Written
        Page After Page   257
    About the Airplane, Then   258
    Normandy Beach   258
    The Muse   260
    Rebecca at Play   261

Lily Peter
    The Green Linen of Summer   261
    For an Autumn Night   262
    from: "The Cypress Bayou"   263

Terry Wright
    Narcissus   264
    WELL,   265
    from: Recording   266

William Mills
    Rituals Along the Arkansas, For Robert Lowrey   269

Mike Nichols
    For Grandfather's Want To Go Up Home   271
    Untitled   272

Newcomers
    Flatrock Creek (Dorthy Jones)   274
    Beds (Judd Mann)   275
    Aerobics Class (Tammy J. Marshall)   275
    Traffic (Jennifer Miller Methvin)   276
    Tiny Infant (Deedre Colquitt)   277

False Faces (Jerri Hutcheson)	279
Frustration (Mark Overton)	279
Pursuits (Trudy Walker)	280
The Unicorn (Elizabeth West)	281
The Wedding Guest (Floyd Collins)	282
Skinny Dipper (Julia Guernsey)	283
Henry Samuel Chesser Tours His Farm (Judy Ruiz)	283
If I Should Live a Thousand Years (Japhet N. Makia)	285
Remembering Highways (Tony Gifford)	285
Coma (Bob Child)	286
Compelling Little Moments of Forward Motion Vertigo (E. E. Eller)	287

PREFACE

Tracing the development of mankind's cultlure has occupied man since the beginning of recorded history. Once man had a language, he began to record his actions for his posterity. This recorded development has taken many forms. Historians turn to official documents, court records, journals, and diaries. Here they find data which reveal pertinent facts as to when things occurred and why. Artists and archeologists study paintings, architecture, and sculpture to discover styles of expression and tastes. Sociologists pore over census reports, income figures and expenditures to determine the mode and standard of living in a given period. Each of these examinations provides illuminating details which are necessary to the understanding of man's development through the ages. However, to know the facts of existence is not to know the man himself. There is only one source which can offer a glimpse into that most important ingredient of culture— the man. To obtain this glimpse, one must hear the voice of the man as he relates his own story.

Man's voice is heard in the tales he tells; his chuckles and laughter ring in his jokes and in the yarns he spins. Ballads and poetry give vent to his emotions and to his dreams. Man verbalizes his deepest feelings, found in the private depths of his soul, through his stories, his poems, and his songs. These revelations comprise what we know as literature. It is this form of recorded development that affords future generations the opportunity to look INTO the man. Literature then can be accurately labeled as "the voice of man's spirit."

Arkansas voices have been speaking for two hundred years or more to form a bulk of literature which reflects a culture and heritage peculiar to our state. We have an abundance of storytellers, balladeers, and poets. It is sad, indeed, that their efforts are not made more available to our students in Arkansas schools. The voices of Arkansas, both past and present, have much to offer. It is hoped that this volume will in some small way serve to alleviate what for too long has been neglected.

When the first edition of *Arkansas Voices* was released in 1976, I felt that I had done my part to promulgate the Arkansas heritage. Now, twelve years later, I realize that I only scratched the proverbial surface. Having recently edited *Authentic Voices*, a collection of historical material, I am compelled to try once again to put the literary talent of Arkansans before the reading public. The general situation has improved somewhat since my first effort.

There exist today more outlets for literary talent than ever before. Societies of literary art have emerged and are flourishing; journals and magazines dedicated to the literary arts now enjoy favor among literary groups. All of these efforts are commendable, but there seems to be the same timidity within the general reading public to delve into this treasure of Arkansas literary talent. Hopefully my efforts in this revision will bring a desire for such delving.

Much of the first edition is retained in this volume, for if the material was valuable in 1976, it has the same value today. However, a search of other, more recent volumes has yielded a bountiful harvest. A totally new and exciting addition, albeit a somewhat dangerous one, is the section on young, talented poets, writing in Arkansas today. To imagine that this source is definitive is ludicrous, but the addition does indicate that poetry is alive, well, and in our midst today.

The Ozark folktales, as collected by Vance Randolph, are sill a delight to read. Some have been deleted and others have been substituted. Some new yarns, or "Big Windys," have been unearthed to provide more merriment. New and more authentic Indian legends are included. Additional tales of Black Folks have been added for the reader's entertainment. All in all this revised edition of *Arkansas Voices* is much more satisfying to the editor. I hope it will be to the reader.

Once again I am indebted to Robert Lowery and Jeff Henderson for their encouragement. Tom Dillard, Archivist at UCA, has been most helpful, and I am grateful. To Tom Coates and Henry Smiley, who put the first edition into the computer, I say "Thanks!" Without the patient assistance of Barbara Whisnant and Charlene Bland, the copyright letters would not have been mailed. I should also like to acknowledge the fine art work done by Gary Floden. The illustrations add much to this volume. And of course, without the support of my other half, Bill, I would not have undertaken this revision at all. To all of these people and to some whom I am sure I have overlooked, I extend my heartfelt gratitude.

ACKNOWLEDGMENTS

Maya Angelou: From *Oh Pray My Wings Are Gonna Fit Me Well* by Maya Angelou. Copyright © 1975 by Maya Angelou. Reprinted by permission Random House, Inc.

Maya Angelou: From *And Still I Rise* by Maya Angelou. Copyright © 1978 by Maya Angelou. Reprinted by permission of Random House, Inc.

Dee Brown: from *Tepee Tales of the American Indian retold for Our Times* by Dee Brown. Copyright © 1979 by Dee Brown. Reprinted by permission of Henry Holt and Company, Inc.

Jack Butler: from *West of Hollywood: Poems from a Hermitage* by Jack Butler. August House Poetry Series. Copyright © 1980 by Jack Butler. Reprinted by permission of August House, Inc. Little Rock.

Jack Butler: from *The Kid Who Wanted to be a Spaceman and Other Poems* by Jack Butler. Copyright © 1984 by Jack Butler. Reprinted by permission of August House, Inc. Little Rock.

Richard Dorson: from *Negro Tales from Pine Bluff, Arkansas, and Calvin, Michigan* by Richard M. Dorson. Copyright © 1958 by Richard M. Dorson. Reprinted by permission of Indiana University Press.

Glenn W. Dresbach: from *Collected Poems* by Glenn W. Dresbach. Copyright 1950 by Glenn W. Dresbach. Reprinted by permission of The Caxton Printers, Ltd.

John Gould Fletcher: from *Selected Poems* by John Gould Fletcher. Copyright © 1938 by John Gould Fletcher. Reprinted by permission of Ethel C. Simpson, Trustee, Literary Estate of John Gould Fletcher, University of Arkansas, Fayetteville, Arkansas.

Edsel Ford: Reprinted from *Looking for Shiloh: Poems* by Edsel Ford, by permission of the University of Missouri Press. Copyright 1968 by Edsel Ford.

Richard W. Hudson: Unpublished. Printed by permission of Richard W. Hudson.

Booker T. Jackson: from *Needs World The* by Booker T. Jackson. Copyright © 1972 by Booker T. Jackson. Reprinted by permission of Booker T. Jackson.

James Masterson: from *Arkansas Folklore*. Copyright © 1974. Reprinted by permission of Rose Publishing Co. Little Rock.

William Mills: Reprinted by permission of Louisiana State University Press from *The Meaning of Coyotes* by William Mills. Copyright © 1984 by William Mills.

Mike Nichols: Unpublished. Printed by permission of Mike Nichols.

Lily Peter: from *The Green Linen of Summer and Other Poems*. Copyright 1964 by Lily Peter. Reprinted by permission of Lily Peter.

Vance Randolph: from *The Devil's Pretty Daughter* by Vance Randolph. Copyright © 1955. Columbia University Press. Used by permission.

Vance Randolph: from *Who Blowed Up the Church House*, Copyright 1952; from *Sticks in the Knapsack*, Copyright 1958; from *The Talking Turtle*, Copyright 1957. Reprinted by permission of Frances B. Lott, Trustee, Vance Randolph Estate, Columbia, South Carolina.

Vance Randolph: Reprinted from *Ozark Folksongs* by Vance Randolph, by permission of the University of Missouri Press. Copyright 1980 by the Curators of the University of Missouri.

James Whitehead: from *Domains* by James Whitehead. Copyright 1966 by James Whitehead. Reprinted by permission of James Whitehead.

Miller Williams: Reprinted by permission of Louisiana State University Press from *Distractions* by Miller Williams. Copyright © 1981 by Miller Williams.

Miller Williams: Reprinted by permission of Louisiana State University Press from *The Boys on Their Bony Mules* by Miller Williams. Copyright © 1983 by Miller Williams.

Terry Wright: Unpublished. Printed by permission of Terry Wright.

PROLOGUE

The term "hillbilly" has been for many years a term that Arkansans react to with resentment and ignominy. Today's sophisticated society and the trend toward urbanization has moved us even farther from the "hills" and the respect for a unique lifestyle. While the term in its most strict application refers only to those people of the Ozark country, to the rest of the nation all Arkansans have been "hillbillies." Perhaps it is this generalization that rankles most; in the more cosmopolitan areas where there are manifestations of culture, there is a tendency to consider the "hillbilly" an ignorant man, a barefoot moonshiner. In 1932, Karr Shannon, in Hillbilly Philosophy, *defined the "hillbilly" in a most pleasing manner. The life style he describes incites pure envy for the Arkansan caught in the mad pursuit of progress today. Perhaps being a "hillbilly" is not so bad; perhaps such a label is one of charm and fascination. Arkansans might well be proud to be "Hillbillies."*

BEING A HILLBILLY

I am a hillbilly—admittedly so. I am a hillbilly because I was born, reared and still live near a little village which nestles among the foothills of the beautiful Ozark Mountains, in North Arkansas. I enjoy being a hillbilly because I love to have neighbors for miles around, know everybody in the home town by the first name and know who to trust and how far. I like to lie flat on my back in the front yard on a summer's night and, unhampered by electric street signs and searchlights, gaze into the open starry sky for hours and hours. I enjoy standing on my front porch as the sun rises over the eastern horizon and drink in the pure morning air fresh from the dew-covered meadows and green hillsides. The ringing echoes of the call of the cows and low moos in answer, the grunting of the pigs and the hoot of the owl at twilight are all music to my ears.

In the land of the hillbilly you may spring astride a prancing pony and ride across green fields, see the young plants push their way to maturity, observe new life in everything, and listen to the broken silence of "gee" and

Hillbilly Philosophy (LittleRock: ParkeHarper Co., 1932).

"haw." You may turn down long shady lanes and across green pastures dotted with contented cows. And you are made to laugh at the young bull calf as he hoists his tail high in the air and scampers down the hillside and out of sight. Or you can go into the woods, lose yourself in the thick forests unchanged by advancing civilization and listen for hours to barking squirrels, cooing doves, chirping crickets, and a native orchestra of a hundred feathered throats.

If you had rather take advantage of more modern conveniences (and we have them in the hills to the great surprise of many) you may feed the gas over well-surfaced highways that wind their way through the hills and across high and low mountain ranges. At each bend of the road is a panorama that would rival the most carefully selected scenes of the city theaters. The traveler may gaze across twenty-five miles of rolling mountain ranges cut by valleys and ravines. Wild honeysuckles along the way sweeten each breath of mountain air and fresh green leaves of lofty oaks wave a gentle greeting to the stranger. The picturesque scenes include distant streams of a silvery luster and nearby springs to quench the thirst.

Now and then may be seen a little farm home on the mountain side, and here and there small fields and truck patches. The tinkle of cowbells comes from green pastures below to mingle with the chorus of chirping birds and the rat-tat-tat of the yellow hammer drumming his bill against a dead limb. You may shift a gear and motor to the top of one of the high peaks along White River. On top nature seems to unfold in all her glory. If you are so fortunate as to be here in the spring time you would find the hill sides all around sprinkled with dogwood blossoms and other wild flowers. You may view the beautiful river for miles as it winds a rugged course among the hills toward the flats of the Mississippi. Here are many cascades that would be celebrated in song and poetry were they in some New England gorge. A view of clear streams flowing into the White River may be seen and traced almost to their source as they rush on over gravel beds to form emerald pools and shallow runs before joining the waters of the river.

To enjoy the life of a real hillbilly you should try your hand at rowing up the river in a boat or put on your bathing suit and splash into the clear warm waters in mid stream. But the average mountain stream in these parts runs clear and cold the whole year round, and many fish loll at ease in the deep holes under rapids, or play hide-and-seek around rocks and water-soaked logs in the shoals. Such ideal places for casting lure many miles away from the sultry offices in the large cities.

I have been to the city and had my fill of the so-called luxurious ease and artificial pleasures and am back in the hills to stay until the trumpet call. It is said you can get the boy out of the country, but you can't get the country out of the boy. I am glad that is true. The hillbilly is made for the hills and it goes against the grain to put him down on concrete streets and close him up between marble walls. He is native to the hills as a rabbit is native to the woods, and too much handling and culturing destroys his happiness. He is labeled as "green" by the city dude, which is true, and when he is transplanted from his native soil to the sidewalks of a city he will dwindle away and die if some of his environment is not created about him. But on the other hand, the city guy is nothing but a hot-house plant who cannot adapt himself to the elements of a country life and will soon wilt and die if he is cut off from all his artificial means of existence.

The hillbilly has every reason to live close to God. The little weatherworn church in the grove beacons to him throughout the year, and hardy preachers in fiery oratory preach hell fire and damnation under green arbors during the summer. The old family Bible occupies chief place in most every home. This the hillbilly takes as the inspired writing of Almighty God. But he has another volume at his command by the same author. His natural surroundings of hill and dale, woodlands and singing streams, and all that nature gives is the pure unadulterated handwriting of God.

> At night, he observes the twinkling stars on
>   every side,
> During the days, sees the beautiful plants of
>   God's pride,
> He considers in the spring earth's covering of
>   green
> And gleaming lakes and streamlets of purest
>   sheen,
> Watches the little insect sport in his sunlit
>   beam,
> Lists' to the birds' sweet song and beasts'
>   victorious scream,

And then knows the love and might of the
One Supreme.

There is sorrow for the man who is cooped up in a two-by-four office in a city. In spite of all his modern conveniences, about all he knows about *freedom* is what he reads as the definition of the word in the dictionary. He is just about as comical when he comes up here as one of us fellows would be in his society. While he is playing the market, we are playing checkers and pitching horseshoes at the country store. And we know about as much about his Wall Street as he knows about our cherished Happy Hollow. While he is running his fingers through his hair under an electric light by an electric fan trying to balance his budget, I am sitting on my porch under the moonlight watching the gentle breeze carry the smoke from my cob pipe, and as content and free as an Indian chief before his wigwam in the pre-civilization days.

In the winter time I, a hillbilly, can sit by my fireside with my wife and our five-year-old hillbilly son in peaceful bliss. We keep in touch with the civilized world through two daily papers, magazines and the latest books. Or we can intermingle the joys of city life and the country fireside by turning on the radio and listening to music, sermons and lectures from the most cultured centers, interrupted now and then by the bay of a hound or the lonely call of the hunter's horn.

In conclusion, I wish to say that the city man may continue to enjoy his brick house, paved streets, electric appliances, sewer system, tap water, theaters, golf clubs, limousine, milk wagons, fire alarms, pipe organs, and all the shrieking and rumbling noises. But give me the dandelions of the field and daisies thereof with the right to play among them and to gather them. Allow me to keep the yellow shores of the country creeks and the yellow sands beneath their waters, with the dragon flies that skim the surface. Let mine be the odors of bending willows that dip into the waters of broad ponds and lazy streams. Leave me the useful idle fields to tramp over and all snowclad hills where one may coast. And all meadows, with the clover blooms and butterflies thereof; and all woods, with their appurtenances of squirrels and whirring birds and echoes and strange noises. And let me continue to breathe the fragrance of new mown hay and autumn's ripening grain. Give me the paved flats and skyscrapers of a city for a day, but let me keep my hills for the rest of my life.

CHAPTER 1

LEGENDS FROM THE RED MAN

Regional literature of the United States, regardless of its specific locale, has a common beginning with the original American—the Indian. The legends of the red man have attracted the attention of various collectors throughout the years. The Federal Government early in this century recognized the value of the stories and legends coming from these first Americans and began to systematically record their literature for posterity. From these records we are able to discern a lifestyle and culture, a personality that lends itself to an understanding of a people in the days before "civilization" began to take its toll.

The Osages and the Quapaws, two great tribes native to Arkansas, contributed heavily to the legends. The Cherokees, who made their painful migration along the "Trail of Tears," gave to Arkansas literature the great chief Sequoyah and the many legends which surround him, as well as other delightful stories and legends. Other migrating tribes, crossing the area in search of a home, left romantic tales behind them. The following legends come from several sources and comprise only a small portion of the material to be found in special collections around the state.

Rarely do Indian legends and stories encompass great length. Like the people who gave them life, the tales are simple, direct, and uncluttered by extraneous verbiage. Some are quite brief, as illustrated in the first of the legends to follow. Still others develop their romantic narratives in more depth. Regardless of length, the tales provide interesting reading.

Boka, the Evil Bird

The following short legends were taken from the *Morrilton Headlight* of August 7, 1936.

Once upon a time a tribe of Indian Pygmies inhabited the valley which is now known as Hot Springs. They lived on bugs and beetles and never harmed anyone.

Their one enemy was a large bird that flew down every day and caught some of them. One day these small men asked the fairies to help them.

They worked all day and by night they built a huge wall over which they put leaves and grass. Then bent a cedar tree over it ready to fall. When Boka came the people ran for the wall. As Boka followed, the cedar fell and killed him. His carcass blew away and where it fell springs which produced hot water bubbled up and made the Indians happy.

Dardanelle

Dardanelle, Cherokee Indian chief, while recovering from a wound, fell in love with a beautiful maiden of the Choctaw Tribe. Often at midnight he went to see her, for the two tribes were at war. One day he told her to ask her father if she could marry him. If she could she was to wave her mantle, if the mantle did not wave he would jump from a high rock into the river. As she did not give the signal, he sprang into the river. This rock from which he jumped has ever since been called Dardanelle.

The Magawana

The Magawana is a roll of deer skin tied up in a buck skin. The Great White Spirit told the Chief to get Magawana and that when he wanted his advice he would find it written on the skies. When the Chief grew old he was told by the Great White Spirit to return to Magawana. This grieved the old Chief so much that he was found dead. The mountain on which he lived and was buried is called Magawana or Mt. Magazine.

The Ozarks

Long, long ago the Mas-sa-tow-qua Tribe of Indians lived in Arkansas. There was only one thing the Great White Spirit would not let them do and that was to visit a cave in which the wise men said gold could be found. This made the people more anxious to go to the cave and when they were inside the Great White Spirit sent an earthquake and closed the cave. This earthquake caused the Ozark Mountains.

"Forked Top" Mountain Is Landmark

South of State Highway 10, in Perry County, amid a panorama of tangled mountains, there is a mountain peak more conspicuous than any around it. The natives call it Old Forked Top Mountain, and according to an ancient legend, this is how it got its name:

This legend was found in the Arkansas Gazette, dated May 20, 1962

The Quapaws and Osage Indians, hereditary enemies, considered the area neutral because of the large number of ailing Indians who passed that way enroute to the thermal waters in the Valley of Vapors to the South.

Once an Osage youth and a Quapaw maiden met in the neutral valley in quest of rest and recreation. The maiden was sweet and demure; the warrior, strong and brave. Although their tribes had been enemies for ages, the young couple wandered together in the sequestered labyrinths of the unchallenged domain. Love entered their hearts and they whispered the old, old story. Knowing the Quapaw father of the maiden would never permit her union with a hated Osage, the lovers eloped and hid away in the deep, lonely mountains to the north. The father of the girl pursued them. Perceiving that they were being followed, the lovers ascended to the top of a mountain high above its less lordly neighbors. The father reached the base of the mountain and sent messengers to demand the return of his daughter. The lovers only laughed and drew closer together, while the Ouachita mists hid them from view. Highly incensed, the father appealed to the Great Spirit for help. With no divine intervention apparent, the Quapaw father and his warriors began to climb to the top. Realizing it could not condone disrespect for parental authority by the youths, and unwilling to see them torn apart, the Great Spirit caused a bolt from heaven to descend upon the mountain and rend it asunder.

Clasped in a loving embrace, the Osage warrior and the Quapaw maiden died together and the mountain stands with a great forked top as a monument to their love, and a perennial warning to clandestine lovers throughout the ages.

Fred W. Allsopp, the collector of these and many other legends and stories, was not a native Arkansan, though he spent most of his life in the state. He was born in England on June 25, 1867. His family migrated to Toronto when he was only an infant. Several years later the family entered the United States and settled in 1880 in Prescott, Arkansas. At the age of 17, Allsopp traveled to Little Rock, where he began his journalistic career as a mailing clerk with the Arkansas Gazette. *This unobtrusive beginning led to a most brilliant career in the field of journalism. After working his way up to advertising manager, he became managing editor and part owner of the* Gazette. *He held this position for many years, during which time the newspaper flourished. Besides his profession in journalism, Allsopp gained wide recognition as a business and civic leader in Little Rock and in literary circles.*

The Footprints on the Rock

Fred W. Allsopp, *Folklore of Romantic Arkansas,* Vol. I. (Grolier Society, 1931).

Near Clarksville there is a large stone, four feet high, six feet wide, and ten feet long, in which are very plain imprints of human feet—one supposed to be that of a man and the other that of a woman.

Osage Indians lived there before the coming of the Cherokees, and an Indian legend is current in regard to the peculiarly marked rock. The legend is that Water Lily, the daughter of a chief, was loved by a warrior named Shooting Star, whose passion was not reciprocated.

One day a white stranger arrived at the Indian village. He was welcomed and decided to make his home among these friendly Indians. Eventually he fell in love with Water Lily, and she with him.

Shooting Star was angered and determined to get rid of his rival. He played upon the susceptibilities of the old Indian Chief and other Indians in the village, until he succeeded in turning their friendly feelings for the white man into distrust and hatred.

The poor white man was tried on some trumped up charge, was condemned to die, and, tied hand and foot, was placed on the rock.

But Lily's regard for her lover was intensified, and she determined to save him. She consulted a medicine man supposed to be able to heal the sick or raise the dead. He gave her an enchanted arrow and instructed her in its use.

The white man was standing on the rock, when the Indians began to torture him before putting him to death. Since she could not contend with a multitude, Water Lily fitted the mystic arrow to her bow and shot at her lover to end his suffering. Immediately a mighty upheaval of the earth shook the village, and the rock was thrown up out of the ground, while Water Lily stood by her lover's side.

The arrow intended for the captive had been turned by some mysterious power toward Shooting Star and was found embedded in his heart.

The Indians, believing that the Great Spirit was displeased, at once freed the white man, and he and Water Lily were united.

The footprints of the white man and the Indian maiden who stood by his side on the great rock remain, and perhaps have been there for hundreds of years, in memory of these lovers. How the rock came to receive the impressions is unexplained, unless the legendary upheaval caused a softening of the concreted mass.

Teponah's Fatal Wooing

Teponah, the son of Wild Eagle, chief of the Minetarees, a branch tribe of the Southern Sioux, was a handsome youth, and a mighty athlete. His muscles were like the sturdy oak, and his arrows flew straight and swift. He was loved by all the maidens, for soft was his voice and cunning were his ways. He devoted his wooing to evil purpose and many a flower that bloomed to shed fragrance in the camp of fond parents was plucked from its stem and crushed by the sensual Teponah. Like the siren that sits on the beach and plays sweet melodies to entice admirers to their destruction was the handsome son of Wild Eagle, whose eyes were like flashes of love and whose tongue was as musical as the trills of the woods' sweetest songster, but whose heart was as black as night and as cold as the blister of winter.

Once at eventide, when the sun had fallen behind the mountain, Teponah repaired to the brook which babbles its way down the valley to the trysting place of Happy Hollow, to meet Monetah, the beautiful daughter of old Shewaugan, whose eyesight was lost in defending Wild Eagle in a fight with the Dekotahs. Monetah came not, for she saw a strange light when she approached the mouth of the valley and, frightened, ran away from her ruin.

While he awaited the coming of the beautiful Monetah, darkness climbed down the valley, and Teponah was shrouded with night. Casting his eyes to the heavens, he saw a troop of sorrowing maidens, clad in robes of white gossamer. On their heads were leaves of autumn, and in their hands were brown twigs from the pine trees. They circled down towards him, and he saw the pale faces of those he had mocked with deception. Then the shadowy forms disappeared, but the light in the valley became much brighter, until it seemed to bask in delight o'er the mountains. From the head of the valley Teponah saw coming toward him a being whose beauty bewitched him. His eyes were dazzled by the light of her face and his heart leapt with emotion. She came like the measure of song, with rhythm in every footstep, and when she spoke it was with a voice whose cadence was sweeter than music. She approached Teponah and sat down by his side. He saw that her form was ethereal, and the charm of her presence was confusing to his senses. The robes she wore were like the hues of the rainbow, and her beautiful hair, which trailed at her feet, was unmatched by that of the angels.

With melody that falls on the ear like the sound of a distant flow of waters, mingling its musical splashing with the songs which float through the forests, thus spoke the Bright Being to the handsome Teponah:

"From my home in the happiest grounds for hunting; from the fields where bloom the merriest maidens; from the land where flows the purest water, have I come, to seek your favor. Take my hand, O handsome, brave, Teponah. Let me follow in your footsteps. Let your sweet voice woo and win me, for I cannot be without you."

Then she clasped her arms about him, and her breath she poured upon him till the woods were filled with incense. Overcome, he answered:

"Bright Being, my heart leaps out toward you; I will follow in your footsteps; I will woo you as you have won me, and will be a husband to you."

Giving her hand to Teponah, she led him up the Hot Springs mountain, the while a pathway opened up before them, and her light shone like a sunbeam—her touch was warm and thrilling. Thus they climbed the sloped mountain-side till they gained its rugged summit and stood upon the rocks which overlooked the valley. Then before his raptured vision dropped a golden ladder with its base resting on a large stone upon the summit and its top reaching to the heavens. Ascending it, she beckoned him to follow. But, alas! when he raised his foot, the golden mirage faded from his vision, and headlong he was flung from the crag down the valley. When the hot sun came upon his corpse, the carrion birds that search the valley found Teponah's bloody remains, and they made a feast upon it, till only the blistered bones were left to mark the lover's fatal step.

How Sequoyah Got His Wife

Se-quo-yah was proclaimed a warrior from the door of the council lodge, and his first quest was for a wife. Selecting the Indian maid of his choice, he painted himself in the finest Indian style, blending together every color of the rainbow. He greased his hair, smoothed out his locks, and adorned them with Indian jewels, and, enveloping himself in a buffalo hide, repaired to the lodge of his chosen one. Hours he stood there by the wigwam door, ever smiling, never speaking, and day after day he continued this silent courtship until the old Indians fixed a price on the girl. Then the Indian girl gave him the first demure smile of encouragement. Before this, neither had spoken a word to the other in private. Se-quo-yah hastened home to obtain the horses and robes, which were to be exchanged for his bride. He tied the horses near her wigwam, and went home in doubt and fear. Even before the sun arose the next morning, he hastened to the wigwam of his love, and joyfully found the horses stabled, and that she had neatly packed the robes away. Thus he knew his suit was not rejected. No other ceremony of marriage was performed. The gifts were made and accepted, and the girl was Se-quo-yah's wife.

This wife was no common Indian maiden. In form she was like the women of her race; she was tall, erect, and of a delicate frame; her features

Adapted from George E. Foster, *Life of Se-quo-yah*, 1885.

were formed with perfect symmetry, and her countenance was cheerful and amiable. But in her soul and in Se-quo-yah's was a higher intuition than that bestowed on any other of the Cherokees. Their sympathies were one and their lives were markedly happy, for nature spoke to them what it only whispered to others. Every bird that sang, every scene of nature awakened new aspirations in Se-quo-yah. Even the wind playing melodies on the leaves seemed like words of the Great Spirit, which Se-quo-yah's sensitive nature translated into words of wisdom.

The Legend of the Valley of the Vapors

"The Legend of the Valley of the Vapors" was taken from the *Arkansas Democrat*, March 20, 1949.

The many thousands of people who flock to Hot Springs, Arkansas, each year seeking health and happiness are following the traditional pattern set by both Indians and white men many centuries ago.

When Ponce de Leon landed on the coast of Florida on that memorable Easter Sunday, 1513, he was searching for the "Fountain of Youth," not that he wanted to be a boy again, but because he was an old man broken in health and grown weary with the duties of the governorship of Puerto Rico.

While exploring the region that is now Arkansas, Hernando de Soto became seriously ill and was taken by a friendly Indian chief to a "lake of healing water" where he bathed and rested and was healed. The chief probably called it "No-wa-say-lon, Breath of Healing" or "Man-a-tak-a, Palace of Peace." But to us, it is the "Valley of Vapors" of the world-famous Hot Springs, Arkansas.

The Indians' Great Spirit was your God and mine, and they reverenced Him to the extent that the "Valley of Vapors" was dedicated to the spirit of healing. Hostile and warring tribes laid aside their weapons, smoked the pipe of peace, and shared equally in the health-giving waters of the hot springs. No act of violence was permitted in the "Palace of Peace," and no bird or animal could be killed for fear of provoking the anger of the Great Spirit, causing it to desert the valley forever.

No American legend could be more beautiful or told in more childish simplicity than the Indian legends of how the "Valley of Vapors" came into being.

Hundreds and hundreds of years before white men knew about America and Arkansas and the Valley of Vapors, the Kanawagas Indians were so brave and powerful that they were permitted to rule the vast area lying between the Great Plains and the Father of Waters.

Another Indian tribe, in its attempt to explain the formation of Hot Springs, paid tribute to their Great Spirit with the legend, "Bakka, the Evil Bird."

Long, long before the memory of man, a race of Indian pygmies, the Pinnetahs, made their home in the Valley of Vapors. These little people ate birds and beetles but were very brave and hardy. The peace and tranquillity of their beautiful valley came to an end one day with the appearance of Bakka, the Evil Bird, who came to nest on a nearby mountain.

Bakka had a beak as long and sharp as a deer's antlers, the head of a bear, the claws of a lion, and a face like the sun. Its great wings darkened the sun, and it made a noise like storm as it swooped down each day and bore some unfortunate struggling pygmy away to its nest. The Bakka had a great feast, but the pygmies were heartbroken to see their number diminishing so rapidly.

Near the Pinnetahs lived a friendly tribe of Indian pixies . . . fairy people, with clothes of spider webs and coats of dandelion hair. The pixies dared not battle the mighty Bakka, but they were cunning little folks and helped the pygmies perfect a plan.

Together, the pixies and pygmies worked days making a huge trap. A high stone wall was built, over which were spread leaves and branches covered with pine trees, bent in such a manner that they would fall when a trigger was pulled.

Next day the Bakka came, and the Pinnetahs lured the great bird to their trap by rushing into the stone enclosure. The Pinnetahs escaped by a secret passageway, sprung the trigger and the Bakka was crushed to death by the falling trees.

The carcass of the evil bird was blown away by the wind, and great was the rejoicing when the pinnetahs discovered that the Great Spirit had caused the earth to be broken where the great bird's body had lain, bringing forth hot, healing water as atonement for their troubles and terrors.

The whole of this beautiful region was theirs to have and to hold. They roamed over its beautiful hills and valleys, winning victories over all their enemies until they sincerely believed themselves the favorites of the Great Spirit, or perhaps his equal. But they forgot him as the giver of success and happiness, and he finally became offended.

Then a great plague descended upon the Kanawagas and they feared that the whole tribe might die of the awful disease. They could no longer hunt the wild animals or defend themselves against their enemies, and were brokenhearted to see strong warriors and innocent children snatched away.

The wise men, whose advice had been scorned, called together the entire tribe and begged them to make restitution to the Great Spirit, and by ceremonies and sacrifices, secure his forgiveness. This they did, even to the extent of self-inflicted wounds, and the Great Spirit in his mercy, forgave them.

Their bodies were still fever-racked; therefore, they camped in a peaceful valley whose cluster of clear, cool springs quenched their burning thirsts. Late one afternoon while they were sitting around their campfires, thin spirals of vapor began rising from the springs. They paid little attention until the vapor became very dense and rose with such force that it made a loud hissing sound. They rushed to the springs, felt the water, and discovered it was exceedingly hot. They were almost terror stricken in their belief that the Great Spirit had suddenly become angry and had made the water of the springs so hot that they would perish of thirst.

Again, the wise men of the tribe came to their rescue and explained that the Great Spirit had fully forgiven them, and as a token, had breathed his healing breath upon the waters so that the people might drink and bathe in them and be healed.

They believed the words of their wise men, did as they advised, and were soon well and happy.

They promised to never disobey the Great Spirit, and in appreciation, named the sacred grounds "No-wa-say-lon, or Breath of Healing" and dedicated it to Him whose breath was ever present over the springs in the beautiful Valley of Vapors.

Between 1908 and 1914, John R. Swanton traveled extensively in the Southeastern regions of the United States, collecting Indian tales and legends for the Bureau of American Ethnology, a division of the Smithsonian Institution. The Bureau, realizing that much of this literature would be lost when the older Indians died, commissioned Swanton, as well as other ethnologists, to visit the various reservations throughout the country, recording the oral literature as it was dictated. The effort was an arduous undertaking, since at that time there were no tape recorders for the subjects to speak into. Each tale had to be transcribed, as it was being told, on paper with a pen or pencil. Another factor of difficulty was the labeling of each tale; by the turn of the century, the tribes were closely intermingled within the confines of a given reservation so one tribe had adopted into its store of tales and legends those which had possibly originated in another tribe, or perhaps even another nation. All of them are, however, Indian and Swanton's collection does come from tribes of the Southeast. The stories which follow come from Swanton's Creek Stories and are appropriate for a collection of Arkansas literature because the Creeks did for a time live in Arkansas prior to the last great removal which took them into the Oklahoma Territory.

How Day and Night were Divided

The animals held a meeting and No-koos-see (Nokosi), the Bear, presided.

The question was, how to divide day and night.

Some desired the day to last all the time; others wished it all night. After much talk, Chew-thlock-chew (Tciloktco), the ground squirrel, said:

"I see that Woot-Kew (Wotko), the Coon, has rings on his tail divided equally, first a dark color then a light color. I think day and night ought to be divided like the rings on Woot-Kew's tail."

The animals were surprised at the wisdom of Chew-thlock-chew. They

John R. Swanton, *Myths and Tales of the Southeastern Indians*, Smithsonian Institution, Bureau of American Ethnology, Bulletin 88, United States Government Printing, 1929.

adopted his plan and divided day and night like the rings on Woot-Kew's tail, succeeding each other in regular order.

No-koos-see from envy scratched the back of Chew-thlock-chew and thus caused the stripes on the back of all his descendants, the ground squirrels.

Thunder Helper

A boy went along on a hunting party with three of his uncles. While they were away from camp he took charge of it, prepared sofki for them and did any other work that was necessary. The camp was on a small stream and one day he heard a kind of roaring in this stream. He went in the direction of the sound and saw something standing up over the water, part way up which another creature had wrapped itself. The latter was white about the neck. The thing it was wrapped about was quivering and making a thundering noise. This was Thunder and the creature coiled about it was a Tie-snake or Strong-snake (Stahwanaia). Each of the contestants asked the boy to help him, saying, "My friend, help me."

The boy did not know at first which being to assist, but finally he aimed an arrow at the white neck and pierced it, whereupon the snake loosened its

Sofki is a native dish made from corn, possibly a gruel

coils and fell into the water dead. The Thunder said, "You are just a boy, but you shall always be my friend."

Then the boy went back to camp, and presently his uncles returned from hunting. Thunder had told him that when they all went home from their camp he must walk behind his uncles, and he did so. He added, "When you get home, ask your oldest uncle to give you a medical course (a fast for four days), and if he refuses ask the others in turn." So the boy asked the oldest uncle, but he said, "You are too young." He asked the next younger and he refused. The youngest, however, said he supposed he had better do so, and he did. In those days the Indians were always going on war expeditions and when the fast was over the boy said to his uncle, "Let us travel," meaning, "Let us go to war." When they got close to the enemy's town the boy told his uncle to remain where he was for a while. Then he went off into the woods a short distance and made a circle and came back in the form of a rainbow. His uncle followed him and the boy went along making it thunder and lighten until by his powers his uncle saw him destroy the entire town. After that they returned home.

The Origin of Corn

It is said that corn was obtained by one of the women of the Tamalgi clan. She had a number of neighbors and friends, and when they came to her house she would dish some sofki (a native dish made from corn) into an earthen bowl and they would drink it. They found it delicious, but did not know where she got the stuff of which to make it. Finally they noticed that she washed her feet in water and rubbed them, whereupon what came from her feet was corn. She said to them, "You may not like to eat from me in this way, so build a corncrib, put me inside and fasten the door. Don't disturb me, but keep me there for four days, and at the end of the fourth day you can let me out." They did so, and while she was there they heard a great rumbling like distant thunder, but they did not know what it meant. On the fourth day they opened the door as directed and she came out. Then they found that the crib was well stocked with corn. There was corn for making bread, hard flint corn for making sofki, and other kinds. She instructed them how to plant grains of corn from what she had produced. They did so, the corn grew and reproduced and they have had corn ever since.

The Orphan and the Origin of Corn

An old woman was living in a certain place. One time, when it was raining, she found a little blood in the water, laid it aside carefully and covered it up. Some time afterwards she removed the cover and found a male baby under it. She started to raise him, and when he was old enough to talk he called her his grandmother.

When the child was 6 or 7 years old his "grandmother" made a bow and arrows for him and he began going out hunting. The first time he came back from the hunt he said to her, "What is the thing which jumps on the ground and goes flopping along?" "It is a grasshopper," she said. "Go and kill it and bring it to me," and he did so.

The next time he came in from hunting he said, "What was the thing I saw flying from tree to tree?" "It is a bird. Go and kill it and bring it to me to eat."

Next time he returned from hunting he said, "What is the shiny thing with long legs and slender body which I saw run away?" "That is a turkey," she said. "Go and kill it and bring it to me. It is good to eat."

Next time he said, "What is the thing with a wooly tail which I saw climbing a tree?" "It is a squirrel. It is good to eat," she said, so he killed it and brought it in.

The next time he said, "What is the thing with long legs, short body and tail, a blackish nose and long ears?" "It is a deer. Go and kill it and bring it in. It is good to eat." This is how he found out the names of all the creatures.

The next time he returned from hunting he said, "I saw something with big feet, a big body loping forward, and big round ears but looking as if it had no tail. What is it?" "It is a bear," she replied. "Go out and kill it and bring it in, for it is good to eat." And so he did.

The next time he said, "I saw a big thing which has long hair halfway down the shoulders but nowhere else except at the end of the tail. It had its head close to the ground and when it raised it I saw that it had short horns and big eyes. What is it?" "That must be a bison," she said. "Go and kill it and bring it in. It is good to eat." So he killed it and brought it in.

After that he stopped questioning his grandmother regarding the animals because he had learned about all of them, and he could now hunt by himself and so make his living. He went out hunting all of the time.

The old woman warned him, however, not to go to a big mountain which they could see in the distance.

The old woman provided corn and beans for them but did not tell him where she got them and after a while he became curious. One time when she was out of corn and beans and he was about to go hunting she told him that she would cook sofki and blue dumplings against his return. He started off but instead of going hunting slipped back to the house and peeked through a crack. Then he saw his grandmother place a riddle on the floor, stand with one foot on each side of it and scratch the front of one her thighs, whereupon corn poured down into the riddle. When she scratched the other thigh beans poured into the riddle. In that way the orphan learned how she obtained the corn and beans.

Afterwards the orphan went off hunting, but when he came back he would not touch the food. His grandmother asked him if he was in pain or if anything else was the matter with him, urging him to eat. When she could not persuade him, she said, "You must have been spying upon me and have learned how I get the corn and beans. If you do not want to eat the food I prepare, you must go away beyond the mountain which I forbade you to pass." Then she told him to bring her some live jays and some live rattlesnakes with which she made a kind of headdress, and she also made a flute for him. As he walked along wearing the headdress and blowing upon the flute the birds would sing and the snakes shake their rattles.

Then his grandmother said to him, "Now, all is ready for you. Start along on this trail, but before you leave lock me up in this log cabin and set it on fire. After you have been gone for some time come back to look at this place, for here you were raised." She had provided in advance that he was to marry the first girl whom he encountered.

The orphan did as his grandmother had directed, and when he reached the other side of the mountain he came upon numbers of people playing ball. When they saw him all were pleased with his headdress of jays and rattlesnakes and stopped to look at him.

Rabbit was among these people, and when he saw how all were attracted by the orphan he wanted to be like him, so he persuaded the orphan to let him travel along in company. Before they had gone far they came to a sheet of water, and Rabbit said, "There are many turtles here. Let us go down into the water and get a lot of them." The youth agreed and Rabbit said, "When I shout 'all ready' we will dive in." But, at the appointed word, instead of diving into the water, Rabbit went to where his companion's headdress and flute were lying and prepared to run off with them. Before he could get away, however, the youth came out and called. "Why are you doing that?" "It is so pretty that I was just looking at it. When I say 'Ready' let us dive again." The youth did as had been agreed, but Rabbit jumped out of the water, seized the headdress and flute and ran off with them.

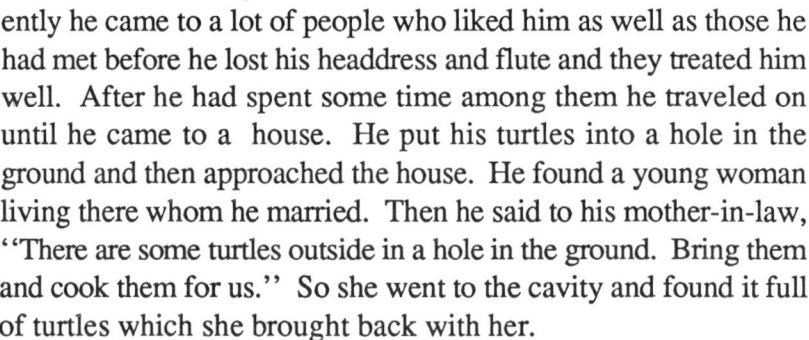

The youth collected many turtles and started on carrying them. Presently he came to a lot of people who liked him as well as those he had met before he lost his headdress and flute and they treated him well. After he had spent some time among them he traveled on until he came to a house. He put his turtles into a hole in the ground and then approached the house. He found a young woman living there whom he married. Then he said to his mother-in-law, "There are some turtles outside in a hole in the ground. Bring them and cook them for us." So she went to the cavity and found it full of turtles which she brought back with her.

After they had finished eating, someone came to them and said that Rabbit had been arrested for stealing the youth's property. The youth went to the place and as soon as he came up the jays and the rattlesnakes, who had been absolutely silent while they were in Rabbit's possession, began to make a noise, the jays to sing and the snakes to rattle. He put on his headdress once more, took his flute, and started home, the birds and snakes singing and rattling for joy at being restored to him. The people who held Rabbit threw him down among a lot of dogs but the dogs were asleep and he ran off. The dogs awoke at once and began smelling around but they could not catch him.

After the youth had gotten home he said to his wife, "Let us go down to the creek. I want to swim. By crossing four times I can poison all of the fish there." His wife told him to do so and, as he was able to accomplish everything which he undertook, he performed this feat also. He killed all of the fish in that stream. Then he told his wife to call all of the townspeople, and they came down in a crowd and had a great meal off of fish.

After the youth and his wife had gotten home the former said that since he was feeling happy she must wash her head and comb her hair and part it in the middle. When she had done so, he told her to go into the house and stand perfectly still in a window looking out. Thereupon he seized an ax and struck her in the parting, splitting her into two women who looked just alike.

When Rabbit heard what the other man had done, he wanted to imitate him, and said to his wife, "Let us go down to the creek. I want to swim and when I cross four times the fish will come to the surface." "Well, go and do so," she said. So Rabbit swam across four times. When he dived he struck a minnow and stunned it, so that when he came out he found it mulling about as if it had been poisoned. He told his wife to call all of her people down to get fish. She did so, but, finding only one minnow lying at the edge of the water, they became angry with Rabbit and went home.

As soon as Rabbit and his wife returned from the creek, Rabbit said, "Wash you head, part your hair and stand in the window." She did this; he struck her on the parting with an ax and killed her.

Some time later the youth said to his wife, "Let us go over to the place where I grew up, for I want to see it." They went there, and when they had arrived found that all sorts of Indian corn and beans had grown up in it. That was where the corn came from. So the corn was a person, that old woman, and if it is not treated well it will become angry. If one does not "lay it by," i.e., heap up the soil about it in cultivation, it calls for its underskirt. The laying by of the corn is the underskirt of old lady corn.

The Orphan and the Origin of Corn
(Second Version)

In early days the Indians lived in camps, and when they got tired of one place they moved off to another. The men would go out hunting and the women would go to dig mud potatoes. One time, while they were living this way, each clan encamped by itself, an old woman came to one of the camps and said, "I would like to to warm myself on the other side of your fire." They said they had no place for her and added "Maybe they will give you a place at the next camp." But the people at the next camps said the same thing, and so it was with all of them until she came to the last, which was the Alligator camp. There they said to her "Why, there is plenty of room here. You can stay here." Next morning the men started out hunting and the

Told by Big Jack of Hilibi.

The Alligator, Tamalgi, and Turkey clans were considered as practically identical.

women went for potatoes, leaving the children at home. Now this woman was Corn itself and, while they were away, she made hominy out of herself and fed the children with it. When the grown people came home the children said "Why, this woman had plenty of food. She fed us all while you were gone." Then the leading man said "Tell her to have plenty of food and I will eat when I come back." So the children told her, and she made blue dumplings and all kinds of food made from corn. The children said "Why, she shelled it off from those sores," but he answered "All right, I will be hungry and eat it." When he returned he feasted with the old woman and thought the new food good. Then she told him to build two cribs with an entry between them, and she said "At night, just at dark, put me at the door of one and push me in, and come right away." He did so and could hear a roaring that night. Next morning, when he went to the cribs, they were both filled with corn. It was in this way that flour corn and flint corn originated. The same old woman also told the man not to drop the corn around or waste it.

One time some people were living in a certain place, and they noticed that the dripping from the eaves of the house (I do not know whether this was during a rainstorm or not) were red. So they picked up some old pieces of pottery which had been dripped upon (called paski') and put them under the bed. During that night they heard something under the bed crying like a child, so they drew out what they had placed there and found it was a baby. The old woman who found him took care of him and nursed him until he grew up. When he got to be about four feet tall, she made a bow and arrows for him, and he wandered about shooting. A long way off from where they lived was some rising ground, and the boy was told never to go to that and look beyond it. When the boy went out hunting for the first time he came in and said to the old woman," Some things with blue heads came running." "Those were turkeys," she said; "We can eat them. Kill them. They are game." The next time he came in he said, "I saw some things with white tails." "We eat those. They are good," said the old woman. When he got back with these various things he would find the old woman with white dumplings and other corn foods, and he wondered how she got them. One time he came back and, instead of entering the house, peeked through a crack. Then he saw the old woman shake her body, and when she shook it the grain poured out of her.

By and by the young man went over the rising ground which he had been warned not to cross and looked over. On the other side he saw people playing ball. When he came back the old woman offered him some food but he would not eat and she said, "You scorn me, then." He had seen men and women on the other side of the hill, and he did not care for her any more. Then the old woman told him to find a rattlesnake and a blue jay. Out of these she made him a fife (flute).

That was to be an ornament for the top of his head. Then she told him to kill the trees all about to make a field. "When you get through," she said, "take me and drag me all around over that place and burn me up, and after three months come over and look at me."

The boy did as the old woman had told him, and afterwards he put on the headdress she had made for him and crossed the rising ground again. There he met a Rabbit who made friends with him. They went on together and presently they came to a pond where there were turtles, and Rabbit said, "Let us go in and get some turtles." So they got ready, and when Rabbit said, "Dive" they dived together under water. Rabbit, however, instead of remaining down there getting turtles, came out right away, seized the youth's headdress and ran away with it. Meanwhile the youth collected a number of turtles which he tied to a cord and brought ashore. He found that Rabbit had disappeared with his headdress, but he took the turtles he had caught and went along until he came to a house. Putting his turtles into a hole which had been dug near by he went to the door and said to the old woman who lived there, "You had better make a fire and cook those turtles, and send round to invite all of your neighbors." She did so and had a feast. After the feast all met at the square ground. When Rabbit came there wearing his red coat (?) and headdress, the rattlesnake and jay called out, "The rumor is the Pasakola has stolen that man's cap." He struck them with his flute to make them stop, but they kept on calling just the same and trying to get to their true master, so the people took them away and gave them to him.

After that the youth took the old woman's daughter as his wife. One day he went down to the river with her and washed his head in the stream, and all of the fish floated up intoxicated. Then he said to his wife, "You had better tell your mother to come down and cook this fish." So the old woman went down to the creek and found lots of big fish there, and she told the young men to go all around the edge of the town and notify everybody to come to the feast. All did so. By and by the youth told his wife to comb her hair in the center, and when she had done it he seated her on the doorstep, took an ax, and with one blow cut her in two so cleverly that he made two women out of her.

After that Rabbit thought that he could do the same things. So he went down to the creek and washed his head and told his wife (who was sister to the wife of the other man) to tell her mother to go down and get the big fish there. She went down, but there was nothing there. Then Rabbit had his wife comb and part her hair, seated her on the doorstep and struck her on the head, killing her instantly.

By and by the youth recalled what the first old woman had told him about going back to see where he had dragged her about, and he did so. He found the whole place covered with red silk corn (probably yellow corn). Wormseed and cornfield beans were also growing in this field. So he used the wormseed as a "cold bath" (medicine) before he ate the corn and the beans, and that is why they now take it before eating corn in husking time.

(Editor's Note: The following story is traditionally attributed to Joel Chandler Harris, so I was somewhat taken aback when I came across it among Swanton's Indian transcriptions. Swanton notes, however, that by the time the transcribing of Indian tales began, there had been much amalgamation of cultures, so accurate sources were impossible to determine. Harris could have gotten the story from the Indian culture, or the Indians could have adapted Harris' story into their culture. Whatever the circumstance, the tale of The Tar Baby is a part of Indian culture.)

The Tar Baby

A man missed peas from his garden and, after vain efforts to catch the thief, he made a tar-person and put it in the garden near the peas.

A Rabbit had been coming every night for the peas and the tar-person was quickly discovered by him. Stopping near, he said: "Who's that? What's your name?" and, receiving no reply, he hopped close to the figure and said: "If you don't speak I will hit you." He struck the tar-person and his paw stuck. Again he asked, "Why don't you speak? Let go of my foot or I will hit you harder," but the second paw stuck as he hit him again. "I have got another foot, stronger than these, and I'll hit you still harder," and the third time he hit the tar-person. "I have got one more foot and I will have to kill you if you don't let go of my feet." He kicked with the last foot and that stuck fast. The Rabbit then struck with his head and it stuck.

Next morning the man came into the garden and, when the Rabbit saw him, he called out "Oh, I have caught the thief who's been stealing your peas. Here he is."

"Yes, I see the thief," replied the man, "and I intend to kill him." Seizing the Rabbit he pulled him away from the tar-person and carried him to a stake near a pigpen. There he securely fastened the Rabbit, saying:

"I will go to the house and get some boiling water to scald you."

As soon as the man had left a Wolf come along and, seeing the Rabbit tied, asked him what it meant.

"Oh, this man wanted me to eat up all these pigs in the pen and because I could not do so he tied me here."

"I can eat them for him," said the Wolf, "let me take your place." "All right," responded the Rabbit, so the Wolf untied him and took his place at the stake and was in turn tied by the Rabbit, who ran away and crawled into a hollow tree. When the man returned and saw the Wolf, "So," he said, "you are at your old tricks and have changed yourself so as to look like a wolf. Well, I will scald you anyway." He poured the boiling water on the Wolf, who howled in pain and finally broke the string and ran off. Then he sat at the foot of the very tree in which the Rabbit was concealed and as he licked his scalded hide the Rabbit reached down and stuck a splinter into him. Jumping up, the Wolf exclaimed, "I wish the ants would stop biting me and adding to my afflictions!"

The Language of Animals

Formerly men and animals talked to one another and later they lost the ability to do so, but the great medicine men had the gift. One time an old woman was much frightened at the sight of a yearling Bull coming toward her bellowing and she tried to escape. The Bull reassured her, however, in language she could understand, saying, "Don't be afraid of me. I am just enjoying myself singing." He added that she must not tell of her experience or she would die.

After that the old woman knew the language of the animals and listened to them as they talked together. She was blind in one eye, and once when she was shelling corn she heard the Chickens say to one another, "Get around on her blind side and steal some of the corn." She was so much tickled at this that she laughed out loud. Just then her husband, who was a very jealous man, came in and believed she must be thinking of some other man, so he said, "Why do you get so happy all by yourself?" Then she related her adventure with the Bull and told him what the Chickens had just been saying, but the moment she finished her story she fell over dead.

The Origin of Races

There is an old story to the effect that some people once came to a very small pool of water to bathe. The man who entered this first came out clean and his descendants, the white people, have the same appearance. He had, however, dirtied the water a little and so the next man was not quite so clean, and his descendants are the Indians. By this time the water was very dirty and so the last man came out black and his people are the negroes.

The Origin of Races
(Second Version)

Three Indians were once out hunting. One went after water and found a nice hole of water but was afraid to drink. Another went down to it, dipped his fingers in, and said, "It is good. Let us go into it." So he dived in and came out. When he came out he was white. From him came the white people. The second dived in and came out darker because the water was somewhat roily. From him came the Indians. The third dived in and came out black because the water was now very roily. From him came the negroes. Just before the first man dived he felt of the rocks and they rattled. He did not tell the others that this was gold. They went on from there and the Indian found something else. The white man was told about this and he picked it up. It was a book. He asked the Indian to read this but he could not. The white man, however, could read it, and it was to tell him about this gold. The book gave him this advantage. "The Nokfilas (whites) were terrible people to take the lead."

The Creation of the Earth

In the beginning the waters covered everything. It was said "Who will make the land appear?"

Lock-chew, the Crawfish, said: "I will make the land appear."

So he went down to the bottom of the water and began to stir up the mud with his tail and hands. He then brought up the mud to a certain place and piled it up.

The owners of the land at the bottom of the water said:

"Who is disturbing our land?" They kept watch and discovered the Crawfish. Then they came near him, but he suddenly stirred the mud with his tail so that they could not see him.

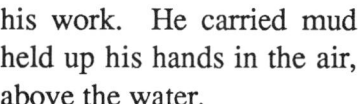

Lock-chew continued and piled it up until at last he held up his hands in the air, and so the land appeared above the water.

The land was soft. It was said: "Who will spread out the land and make it dry and hard?" Some said: "Ah-yok, the Hawk, should spread out the soft land and make it dry." Others said "Yah-tee, the Buzzard, has larger wings; he can spread out the land make it dry and hard."

Yah-tee undertook to spread out and dry the earth. He flew above the earth and spread out his long wings over it. He sailed over the earth; he spread it out. After a long while he grew tired of holding out his wings. He began to flap them, and thus he caused the hills and valleys because the dirt was still soft.

"Who will make the light?" it was said. It was very dark.

Yohah, the Star, said, "I will make the light."

It was so agreed. The Star shone forth. It was light only near him.

"Who will make more light?" it was said.

Shar-pah, the Moon, said: "I will make more light." Shar-pah made more light, but it was still dark.

T-cho, the Sun, said: "You are my children, I am your mother, I will make the light. I will shine for you."

She went to the east. Suddenly light spread over all the earth. As she passed over the earth a drop of blood fell from her to the ground, and from this blood and earth sprang the first people, the children of the Sun, the Uchees.

The people wished to find their medicine. A great monster serpent destroyed the people. They cut his head from his body. The next day the body and head were together. They again slew the monster. His head again grew to his body.

Then they cut off his head and placed it on top of a tree, so that the body could not reach it. The next morning the tree was dead and the head was united to the body. They again severed it and put it upon another tree. In the morning the tree was dead and the head and body were reunited.

The people continued to try all the trees in the forest. At last they placed the head over the Tar, the cedar tree, and in the morning the head was dead. The cedar was alive, but covered with blood, which had trickled down from the head.

Thus the Great Medicine was found.

Fire was made by boring with a stick into a hard weed.

The people selected a second family. Each member of this family had engraved on his door a picture of the sun.

In the beginning all the animals could talk, and but one language was used. All were at peace. The deer lived in a cave, watched over by a keeper and the people were hungry. He selected a deer and killed it. But finally the deer were set free and roved over the entire earth.

All animals were set free from man, and names were given to them, so that they could be known.

ALABAMA STORIES

The Flood

When this world was almost lost in the waters a frog predicted it. One man seized the frog and threw it into the fire, but another said, "Don't do that." He took it, cared for it, and healed it, and it said to him, "The land will almost disappear in the waters. Make a raft and put a thick layer of grass underneath so that the beavers can not cut holes through the wood." So he cut long dry sticks of wood and tied them together and put a quantity of grass underneath.

When other people saw this they said, "Why did you make it?" He answered, "A flood is going to cover the whole country." "Nothing like that can happen," they said. Some persons stayed about laughing at him. After some time he finished his raft and the flood came. When it arrived fish came with it and some of the people killed them and said, "We are having a good time." The man and his family got upon the raft along with the frog.

When the water rose the raft went up also, and some of the people said, "We want to get on," but no one got on. When it rose higher all of the other people were drowned. Then those on the raft floated up with it. The flying things flew up to the sky and took hold of it, with their tails half in the water. The ends of their tails got wet. The red-headed woodpecker was flat against the sky and said, "My tail is half in the water."

Thunder

A certain woman had four sons and one daughter. One rainy day the daughter went after wood and came upon a track made by lightening. Presently she met a man who seized her and carried her home to his house. Her mother and her brothers began hunting for her but they did not know where she had gone. One day her oldest brother started out after her and reached the house where she lived, but he did not come back. The same thing happened to the second and the third. Then the youngest started, and while he was going along a big star came out of the water which he put inside of his clothes. By and by he reached the house where his sister lived and remained for four days. When they invited him to sit down he saw that the chair on which they wished to place him was an alligator. They asked him to sit down on another chair, but he saw that this was a turtle. Next Thunder, who had carried off his sister, sent him after water. As he approached the spring, however, he saw that there were two snakes by it, one on each side. He took his bow and arrows and shot both of them. Then he got some water and came back. Next morning Thunder went out early to hunt, and when he was gone the youth took his sister and carried her off, though she did not want to go. As he approached a small creek he heard Thunder coming after him and when he reached the bank Thunder overtook him and was going to kill him. The youth, however, took the star out from under his clothes and dropped it upon the ground, when it ran at Thunder and after a struggle beat him and drove him back. The youth then took his sister back to their mother, who was very glad to see her.

The Ordering of the Months and Seasons

All things were made at the same time. The earth, sun, moon—all things—got ripe and were left to man. The creatures having assembled, any who liked a certain month took it and ran off. They pursued but did not catch him. He threw it down on the ground as he ran and it started a new moon. If a variety of bird wanted a month, when it was put down, he took it and ran off with it. When the months were all divided up, they were left to the various creatures. When the Horse was brought forth he said he would have grass to eat and they left it to him. Just so the Bear said he would eat acorns to get fat and they were left to him. The Birds said they wanted to eat insects which come out of the ground when it is hot and they took them. Whatever month one made a gobbling noise for he took. The Horse said, "I will pull heavy things for people." The Cow said, "I am going to raise children for people." And the summer was made. Winter, spring, and summer were made together. Winter said, "Man is going to roast his leg around me." When it was summer the Humming Bird said, "I will stay about and kiss the flowers." When summer was too hot and it was not good to work, the luminaries changed places, the sun and moon. The sun turned into the moon.

Meaning that in winter people keep close to the fires.

Dee Brown is a native Arkansan, residing in Little Rock. Mr. Brown has for many years written about the American West with an emphasis on the American Indian. His work Bury My Heart at Wounded Knee *details the treatment of some Indians who were actively rebelling against the policy of keeping native Americans on reservations. Another of his works,* The Gentle Tamers, *tells the stories of pioneer women who helped to settle the great prairies of the middle west. In the volume from which these stories are taken,* Tepee Tales of the American Indian, *Brown has chosen some of the tales and legends collected by the early ethnologists and has rewritten them, placing them in a more easily read form for today's reader. The two tales of "How Day and Night Were Divided" are examples. Swanton's recording from the Indian interview is restructured by Brown.*

The other selections from Brown were chosen to illustrate the red man's love of animal tales and of magic.

"The Bear Man"

One springtime morning a Cherokee named Whirlwind told his wife goodbye and left his village to go up in the Smoky Mountains to hunt for wild game. In the forest he saw a black bear and wounded it with an arrow. The bear turned and started to run away, but the hunter followed, shooting one arrow after another into the animal without bringing it down. Whirlwind did not know that this bear possessed secret powers, and could talk and read the thoughts of people.

At last the black bear stopped and pulled the arrows out of his body and gave them to Whirlwind. "It is of no use for you to shoot at me," he said. "You can't kill me. Come with me and I will show you how bears live."

"This bear may kill me," Whirlwind said to himself, but the bear read his thoughts and said: "No, I will not hurt you."

"How can I get anything to eat if I go with this bear?" Whirlwind thought, and again the bear knew what the hunter was thinking, and said: "I

Dee Brown, *Tepee Tales of the American Indians.* New York: Holt, Rinehart and Winston, 1979 have plenty of food."

Whirlwind decided to go with the bear. They walked until they came to a cave in the side of a mountain, and the bear said: "This is not where I live, but we are holding a council here and you can see what we do." They entered the cave, which widened as they went farther in until it was as large as a Cherokee townhouse. It was filled with bears, old and young, brown and black, and one large white bear who was the chief. Whirlwind sat down in a corner beside the black bear who had brought him inside, but soon the other bears scented his presence.

"What is that bad smell of a man?" one asked, but the bear chief answered: "Don't talk so. It is only a stranger come to see us. Let him alone."

The bears began to talk among themselves and Whirlwind was astonished that he could understand what they were saying. They were discussing the scarcity of food of all kinds in the mountains, and were trying to decide what to do about it. They had sent messengers in all directions, and two of them had returned to report on what they had found. In a valley to the south, they said, was a large stand of chestnuts and oaks, and the ground beneath them was covered with mast. Pleased at this news, a huge black bear named Long Hams announced that he would lead them in a dance. While they were dancing, the bears noticed Whirlwind's bow and arrows, and Long Hams stopped and said, "This is what men use to kill us. Let us see if we can use them. Maybe we can fight them with their own weapons."

Long Hams took the bow and arrows from Whirlwind. He fitted an arrow and drew back the sinew string, but when he let go, the string caught in his long claws and the arrow fell to the ground. He saw that he could not use the bow and arrows and gave them back to Whirlwind. By this time, the bears had finished their dance, and were leaving the cave to go to their separate homes.

Whirlwind went out with the black bear who had brought him there, and after a long walk they came to a smaller cave in the side of the mountain. "This is where I live," the bear said, and led the way inside. Whirlwind could see no food anywhere in the cave, and wondered how he was going to get something to satisfy his hunger. Reading his thoughts, the bear sat up on his hind legs and made a movement with his forepaws. When he held his paws out to Whirlwind they were filled with chestnuts. He repeated this magic and his paws were filled with huckleberries which he gave to Whirlwind. He then presented him with blackberries, and finally some acorns.

"I cannot eat acorns," Whirlwind said. "Besides you have given me enough to eat already."

For many moons, through the summer and winter, Whirlwind lived in the cave with the bear. After a while he noticed that his hair was growing all over his body like that of a bear. He learned to eat acorns and act like a bear, but he still walked upright like a man.

On the first warm day of spring the bear told Whirlwind that he had dreamed of the Cherokee village down in the valley. In the dream he heard the Cherokees talking of a big hunt in the mountains.

"Is my wife still there waiting for me?" Whirlwind asked.

"She awaits your return," the bear replied. "But you have become a bear man. If you return you must shut yourself out of sight of your people for seven days without food or drink. At the end of that time you will become like a man again."

A few days later a party of Cherokee hunters came up into the mountains. The black bear and Whirlwind hid themselves in the cave, but the hunters' dogs found the entrance and began to bark furiously.

"I have lost my power against arrows," the bear said. "Your people will kill me and take my skin from me but they will not harm you. They will take you home with them. Remember what I told you if you wish to lose your bear nature and become a man again."

The Cherokee hunters began throwing lighted pine knots inside the cave.

"They will kill me and drag me outside and cut me in pieces," the bear said. "Afterwards you must cover my blood with leaves. When they are taking you away, if you look back you will see something."

As the bear had foretold, the hunters killed him with arrows and dragged his body outside and took the skin from it and cut the meat into quarters to carry back to their village. Fearing that they might mistake him for another bear, Whirlwind remained in the cave, but the dogs continued barking at him. When the hunters looked inside they saw a hairy man standing upright, and one of them recognized Whirlwind.

Believing that he had been a prisoner of the bear, they asked him if he would like to go home with them and try to rid himself of his bear nature. Whirlwind replied that he would go with them, but explained that he would have to stay alone in a house for seven days without food or water in order to become as a man again.

While the hunters were loading the meat on their backs, Whirlwind piled leaves over the place where they had killed the bear, carefully covering the drops of blood. After they had walked a short distance down the mountain, Whirlwind looked behind him. He saw a bear rise up out of the leaves, shake himself, and go back into the cave.

When the hunters reached their village, they took Whirlwind to an empty house, and obeying his wishes barred the entrance door. Although he asked them to say nothing to anyone of his hairiness and his bear nature, one of the hunters must have told of his presence in the village because the very next morning Whirlwind's wife heard that he was there.

She hurried to see the hunters and begged them to let her see her long missing husband.

"You must wait for seven days," the hunters told her. "Come back after seven days, and Whirlwind will return to you as he was when he left the village twelve moons ago."

Bitterly disappointed, the woman went away, but she returned to the hunters each day, pleading with them to let her see her husband. She begged so hard that on the fifth day they took her to the house, unfastened the door, and told Whirlwind to come outside and let his wife see him.

Although he was still hairy and walked like a bear on hind legs, Whirlwind's wife was so pleased to see him again that she insisted he come home with her. Whirlwind went with her, but a few days later he died, and the Cherokees knew that the bears had claimed him because he still had a bear's nature and could not live like a man. If they had kept him shut up in the house without food until the end of the seven days he would have become like a man again. And that is why in that village on the first warm and misty nights of springtime, the ghosts of two bears—one walking on all fours, the other walking upright—are still seen to this day.

How Day and Night were Divided

After the world was made, some of the animals wanted the day to last all the time. Others preferred that it be night all the time. They quarreled about this and could come to no agreement. After a while they decided to hold a meeting, and they asked Nokosi the Bear to preside.

Nokosi proposed that they vote to have night all the time, but Chew-thlock-chew the Ground Squirrel said: "I see that Wotko the Raccoon has rings on his tail divided equally, first a dark color then a light color. I think day and night ought to be divided like the rings on Wotko's tail."

The animals were surprised at the wisdom of Chew-thlock-chew. They voted for his plan and divided day and night like the dark and light rings on Wotko the Raccoon's tail, succeeding each other in regular order.

But Nokosi the Bear was so angry at Chew-thlock-chew for rejecting his advice that he thrust out a paw and scratched the Squirrel's back with his sharp claws. This is what caused the thirteen stripes on the backs of all his descendants, the Ground Squirrels.

How Rabbit Brought Fire to the People

In the beginning there was no fire and the earth was cold. Then the Thunderbirds sent their lightning to a sycamore tree on an island where the Weasels lived. The Weasels were the only ones who had fire and they would not give any of it away.

The people knew that there was fire on the island because they could see smoke coming from the sycamore, but the water was too deep for anyone to cross. When winter came the people suffered so much from the cold that they called a council to find some way of obtaining fire from the Weasels. They invited all the animals who could swim.

"How shall we obtain fire?" the people asked.

Most of the animals were afraid of the Weasels because they were bloodthirsty and ate mice and moles and fish and birds. Rabbit was the only one who was brave enough to try to steal fire from them. "I can run and swim faster than the Weasels," he said. "I am also a good dancer. Every night the Weasels build a big fire and dance around it. Tonight I will swim across and join in the dancing. I will run away with some fire."

He considered the matter for a while and then decided how he would do it. Before the sun set he rubbed his head with pine tar so as to make his hair stand up. Then, as darkness was falling, he swam across to the island.

The Weasels received Rabbit gladly because they had heard of his fame as a dancer. Soon they had a big fire blazing and all began dancing around it. As the Weasels danced, they approached nearer and nearer the fire in the center of the circle. They would bow to the fire and then dance backwards away from it.

When Rabbit entered the dancing circle, the Weasels shouted to him: "Lead us, Rabbit!" He danced ahead of them, coming closer and closer to the fire. He bowed to the fire, bringing his head lower and lower as if he were going to take hold of it. While the Weasels were dancing faster and faster, trying to keep up with him, Rabbit suddenly bowed very low so that the pine tar in his hair caught fire in a flash of flame.

He ran off with his head ablaze, and the angry Weasels pursued him, crying, "Catch him! Catch him! He has stolen our sacred fire! Catch him, and throw him down!"

But Rabbit outran them and plunged into the water, leaving the Weasels on the shore. He swam across the water with the flames still blazing from his hair.

The Weasels now called on the Thunderbirds to make it rain so as to extinguish the fire stolen by Rabbit. For three days rain poured down upon the earth, and the Weasels were sure that no fire was left burning except in their sycamore tree.

Rabbit, however, had built a fire in a hollow tree, and when the rain stopped and the sun shone, he came out and gave fire to all the people. After that whenever it rained, they kept fires in their shelters, and that is how Rabbit brought fire to the people.

How Rabbit Fooled Wolf

Two pretty girls lived not far from Rabbit and Wolf. One day Rabbit called upon Wolf and said, "Let's go and visit those pretty girls up the road."

"All right," Wolf said, and they started off.

When they got to the girls' house, they were invited in, but both girls took a great liking to Wolf and paid all their attention to him while Rabbit had to sit by and look on. Rabbit of course was not pleased by this, and he soon said, "We had better be going back."

"Let's wait a while longer," Wolf replied, and they remained until late in the day. Before they left, Rabbit found a chance to speak to one of the girls so that Wolf could not overhear and he said, "The one you've been having so much fun with is my old horse."

"I think you are lying," the girl replied.

"No, I am not. You shall see me ride him up here tomorrow."

"If we see you ride him up here," the girls said with a laugh, "we'll believe he's only your old horse."

When the two left the house, the girls said, "Well, call again."

Next morning Wolf was up early, knocking on Rabbit's door. "It's time to visit those girls again," he announced.

Rabbit groaned, "Oh, I was sick all night," he answered, "and I hardly feel able to go."

Wolf kept urging him, and finally Rabbit said, "If you will let me ride you, I might go along to keep you company."

Wolf agreed to carry him astride on his back. But then Rabbit said, "I would like to put a saddle on you so as to brace myself." When Wolf agreed to this, Rabbit added: "I believe it would be better if I should also bridle you."

Although Wolf objected at first to being bridled, he gave in when Rabbit said he did not think he could hold on and manage to get as far as the girls' house without a bridle. Finally Rabbit wanted to put on spurs.

"I am too ticklish," Wolf protested.

"I will not spur you with them," Rabbit promised. "I will hold them away from you, but it would be nicer to have them on."

At last Wolf agreed to this, but he repeated: "I am very ticklish. You must not spur me."

"When we get near the girls' house," Rabbit said, "we will take everything off you and walk the rest of the way."

And so they started up the road, Rabbit proudly riding upon Wolf's back. When they were nearly in sight of the house, Rabbit ranked his spurs into Wolf's sides and Wolf galloped full speed right by the house.

"Those girls have seen you now," Rabbit said. "I will tie you here and go up to see them and try to explain everything. I'll come back after a while and get you."

And so Rabbit went back to the house and said to the girls: "You both saw me riding my old horse, did you not?"

"Yes," they answered, and he sat down and had a good time with them.

After a while Rabbit thought he ought to untie Wolf, and he started back to the place where he was fastened. He knew that Wolf must be very angry with him by this time, and he thought up a way to untie him and get rid of him without any danger to himself. He found a thin hollow log and began beating upon it as if it were a drum. Then he ran up to Wolf as fast as he could go, crying out: "The soldiers are hunting for you! You heard their drum. The soldiers are after you."

Wolf was very much frightened of soldiers. "Let me go, let me go!" he shouted.

Rabbit was purposely slow in untying him and had barely freed him when Wolf broke away and ran as fast as he could into the woods. Then Rabbit returned home, laughing to himself over how he had fooled Wolf, and feeling satisfied that he could have the girls to himself for a while.

Near the girls' house was a large peach orchard, and one day they asked Rabbit to shake the peaches off the tree for them. They went to the orchard together and he climbed up into a tree to shake the peaches off. While he was there Wolf suddenly appeared and called out: "Rabbit, old fellow, I'm going to even the score with you. I'm not going to leave you alone until I do."

Rabbit raised his head and pretended to be looking at some people off in the distance. Then he shouted from the treetop: "Here is that fellow, Wolf, you've been hunting for!" At this, Wolf took fright and ran away again.

Some time after this, Rabbit was resting against a tree-trunk that leaned toward the ground. When he saw Wolf coming along toward him, he stood up so that the bent tree-trunk pressed against his shoulder.

"I have you now," said Wolf, but Rabbit quickly replied: "Some people told me that if I would hold this tree up with the great power I have they would bring me four hogs in payment. Now, I don't like hog meat as well as you do, so if you take my place they'll give the hogs to you."

Wolf's greed was excited by this, and he said he was willing to hold up the tree. He squeezed in beside Rabbit, who said, "You must hold it tight or it will fall down." Rabbit then ran off, and Wolf stood with his back pressed hard against the bent tree-trunk until he finally decided he could stand it no longer. He jumped away quickly so the tree would not fall upon him. Then he saw that it was only a leaning tree rooted in the earth. "That Rabbit is the biggest liar," he cried. "If I can catch him I'll certainly fix him."

After that, Wolf hunted for Rabbit every day until he found him lying at a nice grassy place. He was about to spring upon him when Rabbit said, "My friend, I've been waiting to see you again. I have something good for you to eat. Somebody killed a pony out there in the road. If you wish I'll help you drag it out of the road to a place where you can make a feast off it."

"All right," Wolf said, and he followed Rabbit out to the road where a pony was lying asleep.

"I'm not strong enough to move the pony by myself," said Rabbit, "so I'll tie its tail to yours and help you by pushing."

Rabbit tied their tails together carefully so as not to awaken the pony. Then he grabbed the pony by the ears as if he were going to lift it up. The pony woke up, jumped to its feet, and ran away, dragging Wolf behind. Wolf struggled frantically to free his tail, but all he could do was scratch on the ground with his claws.

"Pull with all your might," Rabbit shouted after him.

"How can I pull with all my might," Wolf cried, "when I'm not standing on the ground?"

By and by, however, Wolf got loose, and then Rabbit had to go into hiding for a long, long time.

Buffalo Woman, A Story of Magic

Snow Bird, the Caddo medicine man, had a handsome son. When the boy was old enough to be given a man's name, Snow Bird called him Braveness because of his courage as a hunter. Many of the girls in the Caddo village wanted to win Braveness as a husband, but he paid little attention to any of them.

One morning he started out for a day of hunting, and while he was walking along looking for wild game, he saw someone ahead of him sitting under a small elm tree. As he approached, he was surprised to find that the person was a young woman, and he started to turn aside.

"Come here," she called to him in a pleasant voice. Braveness went up to her and saw that she was very young and very beautiful.

"I knew you were coming here," she said, "and so I came to meet you."

"You are not of my people," he replied. "How did you know that I was coming this way?"

"I am Buffalo Woman," she said. "I have seen you many times before from afar. I want you to take me home with you and let me stay with you."

"I can take you home with me," Braveness answered her, "but you must ask my parents if you can stay with us."

They started for his home at once, and when they arrived there Buffalo Woman asked Braveness's parents if she could stay with them and become the young man's wife. "If Braveness wants you for his wife, we will be pleased," said Snow Bird, the medicine man. "It is time that he had someone to love."

And so Braveness and Buffalo Woman were married in the custom of the Caddo people and lived happily together for several moons. One day she asked him, "Will you do whatever I may ask of you, Braveness?"

"Yes," he replied, "if what you ask is not unreasonable."

"I want you to go with me to visit my people."

Braveness said that he would go, and the next day they started for her home, she leading the way. After they had walked a long distance they came to some high hills, and all at once she turned round and looked at Braveness and said: "You promised me that you would do anything I say."

"Yes," he answered.

"Well," she said, "my home is on the other side of this high hill. I will tell you when we get to my mother. I know there will be many coming there to see who you are, and some may provoke you and try to make you angry, but do not allow yourself to become angry with any of them. Some may try to kill you."

"Why should they do that?" asked Braveness.

"Listen to what I am about to tell you," she said. "I knew you before you knew me. Through magic I made you come to me that first day. I said that some will try to make you angry, and if you show anger at even one of them, the others will join in fighting you until they have killed you. They will be jealous of you. The reason is that I refused many who wanted me."

"But you are now my wife," Braveness said.

"I have told you what to do when we get there," Buffalo Woman continued. "Now I want you to lie down on the ground and roll over twice."

Braveness smiled at her, but he did as she had told him to do. He rolled over twice, and when he stood up he found himself changed into a Buffalo.

For a moment Buffalo Woman looked at him, seeing the astonishment in his eyes. Then she rolled over twice, and she also became a Buffalo. Without saying a word she led him to the top of the hill. In the valley off to the west, Braveness could see hundreds and hundreds of Buffalo.

"They are my people," said Buffalo Woman. "This is my home."

When the members of the nearest herd saw Braveness and Buffalo Woman coming, they began gathering in one place, as though waiting for them. Buffalo Woman led the way, Braveness following her until they reached an old Buffalo cow, and he knew that she was the mother of his beautiful wife.

For two moons they stayed with the herd. Every now and then, four or five of the young Buffalo males would come around and annoy Braveness, trying to arouse his anger, but he pretended not to notice them. One night, Buffalo Woman told him that she was ready to go back to his home, and they slipped away over the hills.

When they reached the place where they had turned themselves into Buffalo, they rolled over twice on the ground and became a man and a woman again. "Promise me that you will not tell anyone of this magical transformation," Buffalo Woman said. "If people learn about it, something bad will happen to us."

They stayed at Braveness's home for twelve moons, and then Buffalo Woman asked him again to go with her to visit her people. They had not been long in the valley of the Buffalo when she told Braveness that the young males who were jealous of him were planning to have a foot-race. "They will challenge you to race and if you do not outrun them they will kill you," she said.

That night Braveness could not sleep. He went out to take a long walk. It was a very dark night without moon or stars, but he could feel the presence of the Wind spirit.

"You are young and strong," the Wind spirit whispered to him, "but you cannot outrun the Buffalo without my help. If you lose, they will kill you. If you win, they will never challenge you again."

"What must I do to save my life and keep my beautiful wife?" asked Braveness.

The Wind spirit gave him two things. "One of these is a magic herb," said the Wind spirit. "The other is dried mud from a medicine wallow. If the Buffalo catch up with you, first throw behind you the magic herb. If they come too close to you again, throw down the dried mud."

The next day was the day of the race. At sunrise the young buffalo gathered at the starting place. When Braveness joined them, they began making fun of him, telling him he was a man-buffalo and therefore had not the power to outrun them. Braveness ignored their jeers, and calmly lined up with them at the starting point.

An old Buffalo started the race with a loud bellow, and at first Braveness took the lead, running very swiftly. But soon the others began gaining on him, and when he heard their hard breathing close upon his heels, he threw the magic herb behind him. By this time he was growing very tired and thought he could not run any more. He looked back and saw one Buffalo holding his head down and coming very fast, rapidly closing the space between him and Braveness. Just as this Buffalo was about to catch up with him, Braveness threw down the dried mud from the medicine wallow.

Soon he was far ahead again, but he knew that he had used up the powers given him by the Wind spirit. As he neared the goal set for the race, he heard the pounding of hooves coming closer behind him. At the last moment, he felt a strong wind on his face as it passed him to stir up dust and keep the Buffalo from overtaking him. With the help of the Wind spirit, Braveness crossed the goal first and won the race. After that, none of the Buffalo ever challenged him again, and he and Buffalo Woman lived peacefully with the herd until they were ready to return to his Caddo people.

Not long after their return to Braveness's home, Buffalo Woman gave birth to a handsome son. They named him Buffalo Boy, and soon he was old enough to play with the other children of the village. One day while Buffalo Woman was cooking dinner, the boy slipped out of the lodge and went to join some other children at play. They played several games and then decided to play that they were Buffalo. Some of them lay on the ground and rolled like Buffalo, and Buffalo Boy also did this. When he rolled over twice, he changed into a real Buffalo calf. Frightened by this, the other children ran for their lodges.

About this time his mother came out to look for him, and when she saw the children running in fear she knew that something must be wrong. She went to see what had happened and found her son changed into a Buffalo calf. Taking him up in her arms, she ran down the hill, and as soon as she was out of sight of the village she turned herself into a Buffalo and with Buffalo Boy started off toward the west.

Late that evening when Braveness returned from hunting he could find neither his wife nor his son in the lodge. He went out to look for them, and someone told him of the game the children had played and of the magic that had changed his son into a Buffalo calf.

At first, Braveness could not believe what they told him, but after he had followed his wife's tracks down the hill and found the place where she had rolled he knew the story was true. For many moons, Braveness searched for Buffalo Woman and Buffalo Boy, but he never found them again.

CHAPTER 2

"BIG WINDYS" AND OTHER YARNS

Man's capacity for spinning yarns is, I think, an innate characteristic. This is not to imply that man is an innate liar, but to recognize that his imagination and his desire to entertain are his second nature. He wants his audience to enjoy his experiences. Because the experiences he recounts are HIS and will be of little interest to others unless he can instill in his audience a feeling of "being there," he tends to embellish the story with exaggerations and colorful descriptions. It is these embellishments that turn mere stories into yarns. The larger the embellishment, the closer the yarn comes to the "Big Windy," that delightful story which borders on pure fantasy.

Man's interest in telling stories falls generally into two broad categories: oral and written. The oral category comes from a long heritage and is labeled Folklore. The written category represents man's desire to entertain on the printed page. While Folklore reflects the influence of the past and has common progenitors regardless of locale, written tales reveal the character and spirit peculiar to the teller and his particular region. Arkansas has produced a vast number of written tales through which the reader can gain not only enjoyment, but also a feel for the colorful expression of narration. The pieces included in this chapter should not be confused with the traditional folktales, which are included in a separate chapter, nor with the modern short story. The tales presented here are of an earlier age when humor of a more simple entertainment is found in spinning a yarn and in the hyperbole of the "Big Windy."

That hunting and fishing stories lend themselves to the exaggeration of yarns is common knowledge even today. Rarely do we hear a hunter or fisherman recount his experiences without elaborating somewhat on the details. We call them "whoppers," "fish tales," and sometimes just plain lies, but in truth they constitute nothing less than yarns and sometimes "Big Windys."

Devil Take A Whittler

Weldon Stone was born on a cotton farm in Texas. After attending Baylor University and Southern Methodist University, he held teaching positions at Texas A & M, Louisiana Polytechnic, the University of Oklahoma, and the University of Louisville. He spent eleven summers in the Arkansas Ozarks, collecting material for his Whittler characters. In addition to Devil Take a Whittler, *Stone has written several plays and short stories.*

Weldon Stone. *Devil Take a Whittler* (New York: Rinehart, 1948).

In one of the several years pitchforks and alligators rained on Arkansas, on a certain fine morning in spring, Old Hawk, wheeling high and handsome over Breakshin Holler, noted with his usual satisfaction something of a commotion down around the Turtle, that colossal river bluff of granite between the Big Bend and Fool's Cap Mountain. A lusty, copper-headed young woman was standing on the tip-point of the Turtle's nose throwing rocks and chunks of her mind in the general direction of a canoe already out of range but still going downstream at a rapid rate. The man putting the power to the canoe was Lem Skaggs. With him, squatting in the prow and piping a gay ditty on his pretty silvery flute, was Old Nick, the Devil himself, Lem's twin and bosom crony. Delighted with the sight and sound of it all, Old Hawk cut a fancy dido and screamed, adding his aery bit to the earthy turmoil below. It was indeed a sight to behold, even in Breakshin Holler.

With Old Nick's turkey-red cape flaring out behind and the prow of the canoe spatting the water like a running mud hen, Lem was counting his strokes aloud and throwing an extra charge of fire and vinegar into each succeeding one up to twenty-four, warping his tough hickory paddle like a broomstick, notching its lift and dip to the stop and flow of the flute. After the twenty-fourth stroke he would drag his paddle and cut loose a yell, a clean, long blade of sound that laid Little Breakshin open from the Turtle to the Bend. Old Nick, never missing or flatting a note, would bob his head in devilish approval and a long-legged blue heron preceding them down the river would start up and wing off another hundred yards, settle down and cock himself nervously—head, leg, and wing—for the next horrific but fascinating yell.

Lem Skaggs was feeling his oats this fine morning, and he had more reasons than he could shake a stick at. It was springtime, April the First, his twenty-fourth birthday. The jug at his knee was nearly full, the canoe—finished the day before, the first he had ever made—was riding the water perfectly; and Old Nick had just done him another good turn: set him free on the earth again after Kat back yonder on the Turtle had roped and tied him and got the iron hot. Now, with Old Nick's help, his mind was made up; he wasn't going to gee and haw for Kat or any other woman under the sun. He was just going to be himself—a foot-loose, dirty-shaking, woolgathering Skaggs—never settling to any one woman or any one part of the earth. "That's the way, Lem," Old Nick had said, slapping him hard on the back, "the only way for a man to live—specially a Skaggs and a whittler."

"It is, for a fact," Lem had agreed, and reaffirmed it now with an extra-long, extra-powerful yell, then held his breath to listen for the separate echoes he knew would come—one from the Big Bend, one from the Turtle. The Bend reported first and Lem, though he had a feeling it might bring him bad luck, risked a glance behind him. Kat was still standing on the Turtle's nose, still watching him. But she wasn't throwing rocks any more—just standing there flat-footed, wide-legged, with both hands empty. Lem wished he hadn't looked. "Plague take it, Nick. I hate to make aryone suffer—even Kat. Maybe I ought to go back. Tell her why, anyhow." Old Nick's tootling came to a choking stop, and he stared at Lem over his shoulder with an expression of pained chagrin.

"I never thought I'd see the day," he said at last, quietly chiding.

"What day?"

"The day Lem Skaggs would take to bragging—blowing his self up like ary other dirt-common mortal. It hurts me, Lem. Hurts me right where I live at. After all I've done fer ye."

"I wasn't bragging."

"It's what we call it down my way. Why, Lem, don't ye know—ain't I told ye time and again—Kat don't care a whit more for you than she would ary other hickory sapling she could get ahold of?"

"I reckon you have."

"Then it stands to reason it's so."

"Looks thataway."

"Well get on with your paddling then. I'll h'ist another ditty."

"Couldn't I just give her a fare-ye-well—just with my paddle?"

"Shore. 'Twon't do ye no harm from here. Might holp ye."

Raising his paddle high overhead, Lem held it there waiting, hoping Kat wasn't too angry or too hurt with him to see and respond. Apparently she wasn't. Whirling quickly around, Kat bowed low to the Turtle and whipped her skirt over her back in an ancient female gesture of scorn. As Lem jerked his paddle down, Old Nick whinnied like a wild stallion.

"Are ye satisfied now? Are ye, Lem?"

"Seeing it's like that, I reckon I'm more'n satisfied."

Still laughing, but routing it through his nose, Old Nick struck up a fresh tune and Lem knifed his paddle deep in Little Breakshin. It wasn't far now to the Big Bend; once around it, he would be all the way out of the holler, getting on down toward the flat, where the people wore shoes the year round, and store-bought clothes, and lived, some of them in houses built of brought-on lumber. For the Flat was not far from Lebanon, and most of its people aped the hifalutin ways of townfolks and foreigners, drinking their liquor out of bottles, going to preaching every summer—sometimes even in the winter. There would be no tarrying—not for Lem Skaggs—in such a place as the Flat. He had been there once, on sad business, a long time ago. This morning he would sail right on through it without so much as a how-dy-do, no matter who might hail him to stop and chew the willow twig. Though this was not the first sashay he had made to shake the dirt of his birthplace from his feet, he would be tarred and feathered if it wasn't the last.

Strange, anyhow, and hard to fathom, Lem reflected, the circumstance, or whatever it was, that had held him this long in Breakshin Holler, when he had been, for a year at least, as foot-loose and fancy-free as Old Hawk up there in the blue. Certainly it was nothing a man could put his finger on, or touch even with reason. His father Shaw and his mother Lutie had tried that the spring before, done their dead level best to show him the reason in their leaving the Holler.

"All this fine pretty country," Shaw had argued, "is bound for the dogs. The Flatters are coming on, pushing up against us. They'll cut down the trees and plow up the earth, and there'll be hogs awallering ever'wheres, and no deer this side the Rim. Much longer, it won't be fitten for a Skaggs to live in. Ye'd best come along."

But Lem, though he knew Shaw spoke the truth, had not been persuaded.

"I'm figuring on whittling me out a canoe-boat. When it's done, I might be along."

"If it's Kat that's holding ye," Lutie had said, "I reckon she'd be willing to go along."

"'Tain't Kat—nor ary other woman," Lem had denied.

Lutie's last argument, the weakest of all, had come nearest to persuading him.

"We'll miss ye, Lem—feel lonesome and bereft without ye."

"I'm liable to be along one of these days," Lem had said.

But the word *liable*, to any Skaggs, meant maybe so, maybe not; and Lutie had sighed deeply and turned away.

"Anyhow, we'll be looking fer ye."

Then without further waste of words or breath, Shaw and Lutie had set foot up the river trail, headed west over the far rim of the holler, intending to stop only when they had found what they were looking for—country that was not all cluttered up with people, "country fitten fer Skaggses to live in." Lem had watched them go with a queer feeling, and that night he had slept out on the Turtle under a full moon, with his jug beside him.

Why he had done so, and why he had got howling drunk, Lem hadn't known then and didn't know now. But turning it over in his mind, he figured it might have been because he knew in his bones that he had made a mistake, that he should have made tracks with his family. And now, headed down Breakshin rather than up, he reckoned he might be making another and bigger mistake. Nevertheless, there was something that had him by the yingyang, pulling him willy-nilly downstream like a fish tied to a floating log. Lem Skaggs meant to know what that something was if he had to paddle himself and Old Nick clear into the middle of the ocean to find it.

So vowing, Lem plied his paddle without a breathing spell till all the familiar stretch of the Breakshin, all of it he knew as intimately as a fisherman gets to know his favorite trout stream, was far behind him and the Flat just ahead. Here the river widened out, the current ran slow, and Lem began to feel a torturing ache in the muscles of arm, back, and belly. Quietly he eased his paddle athwart the canoe, let it rest there while he stretched his knotting muscles and filched behind Old Nick's back a last look at this part of the world he was seeing for the last time.

It was not, as Lem had thought many times before, much to brag about—nothing to compare with his own Breakshin Holler. The Flat was too flat, so flat it strained a man's eyes to look at it, his mind to recall it. For a mile on either side the river and nearly as far down-stream, there were no hills, no ridges, few trees. Just a fringe along the riverbank of sycamores and willows over whose tops Lem could see wispy spirals of smoke rising from the chimneys of the hard-working, earth-plowing Flatters. For this was rich bottom land, the best in the whole country, Lem had heard tell; and it worked the people who owned it mighty hard. Even now on such a fine morning as this when everybody able to get about should have been fishing, they were at it tooth and toenail. Lem could hear them through Old Nick's tootling, hear the harsh voices of men hollering at their mules, scolding and cursing them for their laziness, and the fretted voices of women tongue-lashing their children, their men, and their mules on to greater industry. A hen cackled, a rooster crowed, and Old Nick stopped tootling.

The canoe was going nowhere, but floating idly as a bean pod out of the sluggish current, drifting before a gentle south wind toward the left bank. Twisting his neck like a wounded, stick-prodded owl, Old Nick stared and glared at Lem's face. But Lem was unaware that Old Nick had stopped his tootling or that he was about to throw a fit of righteous reproof. From some distance downstream, from the left bank beyond the margin of sycamores and willows, came a new sound in the Flat: Lem's ears were tuned to this alone, his eyes and his attention all fixed on the spot it seemed to come from.

"Well, Lem, I cain't do my work and yorn too."

Old Nick's voice was peculiarly grumpy—the voice of a fat man whose dinner is unreasonably late. He had been thinking ever since they rounded the Big Bend of a feast Lem had promised in Lebanon: a dog's bait for them both of store cheese and crackers. Lem's promise and all that tootling had whetted his appetite something terrible. But Lem, apparently, had forgotten such things as cheese and crackers, even what he was supposed to be doing. Glancing briefly at Old Nick, he looked down the river to the left again. Old Nick spoke more sharply.

"You heared me, Lem Skaggs. Here I am tootling my guts out for ye the whole morning long, and what do ye do? Lay off on me, that's what, and let my music go to waste. Didn't even know I'd quit, did ye? And I'm getting hungry."

"I thought I heared something. Listen."

Old Nick listened, heard it too: a sound of hammering—of two hammers out of time striking metal and wood, and of two echoes quarreling up and down Breakshin together. Hastily, Old Nick slapped the flute against his palm, shook the spit out of it, licked his lips.

"It's a house abuilding, ain't it? Brought-on lumber," Lem guessed.

Old Nick was in a swivet, trying to decide whether to argue or tootle. A little of both, maybe, would be best.

"What of it? 'Tain't none of your business, or mine, Grab ahold of that paddle, Lem. I'm the Devil, and I cain't be still. Got to be doing things."

Lem took up the paddle again. It was still wet, the handle with the sweat of his palms. The clean white hickory was already soiled, and Lem sighed ruefully, wishing he had taken the time and trouble to stain it with walnut.

"Now what's the matter?" Old Nick demanded. "What're ye honing fer that y'ain't got?"

"Nary a thing. Just awondering."

"What?"

"Why you cain't ever let a feller rest, or rest your own self—ferget who ye are."

Old Nick snorted.

"Now that'd be a pretty pickle, wouldn't it? You'd best stick to your paddling, Lem Skaggs—let me do the thinking."

"We could swap, couldn't we, take it turn about?"

"We could, but we ain't."

Fearful to risk another word, Old Nick struck up a ditty on his flute, a gay ty-rollicking tune called *The Devil's Dream*, a tune Lem seldom could hear without feeling an immediate and terrific urge to do something about it—throw his weight around in all directions, and stand up on his hind legs and yell down the whole shooting match of the world. But its present effect on him was disappointing to Old Nick. Lem merely began paddling again, and that with a haphazard, lackadaisical stroke barely sufficient to keep the canoe headed downstream. Lem Skaggs, for once in his life, wasn't interested in Old Nick's tootling, wasn't even hearing it. Instead he was listening to that sound of hammering down the river, hearing it clearly through the best of *The Devil's Dream*.

As he listened and speculated, Lem lifted and dipped the paddle more and more lazily, the slow current caught up with and outran the canoe, and Old Nick's pretty cape fell plumb from arm to shoulder, the hem tuckering about his clean polished feet. But Old Nick, now deep in the groove with head lifted to the sun and eyes closed, was unaware of Lem's bemusement; and so, as a matter of fact, was Lem himself. His eyes were fixed again on that screen of sycamores along the downstream left bank, probing and searching through their glancing springtime foliage. From just beyond the sycamores, he knew now, came the sound exciting his curiosity, distracting, enticing him—the striking sound of hammers on nail and wood, the sound of something being made. Like a wandering foot-loose beaver hearing from a distance the slip-slap of hard broad tails on mud and water, Lem was being drawn willy-nilly toward this turmoil of creation. But not, of course, with any purpose—not with the slightest notion of joining in, of lending a hand.

Though he had brought along as precious, inseparable parts of himself all the few tools he owned—adz, hatchet, and saw—Lem had no intention of allowing himself to get a job of work—not any time soon and never, certainly, this near home. Those tools, stuffed for rustproof keeping into the legs of his other pair of pants, were mainly just to have and have along, to keep bright and clean and sharp and always ready to hand like the whittling knife he carried in a sheath of doeskin strapped to his thigh where any other man would have a pocket. Lem's tools were things to look at often, to use only when the spirit, or his belly, moved him. Work at any other time, for any other reason, was a sorry waste of breath and salt, a notion even Old Nick condemned, branded as "downright shiftless and no-'count."

But a difference of opinion was as common between Lem and Old Nick as agreement in spirit, and there had been off and on many a go-round between them, with Lem as likely as not holding his own, even against Old Nick's best argument—his flute and the pretty, dream-making music he could pour out of it to befuddle and dizzy a man beyond reason. That is, if a man listened to it with both ears—the very thing that Lem at the moment was not doing.

By now the canoe, with a little urging from Lem, had drifted in very near the left bank and almost abreast of the sound his ears were keyed to. Through a break in the sycamores he could see bare, skeleton rafters of milled pine, see too the heads and shoulders and uplifted, hammer-wielding arms of two men, one of whom looked very familiar to him. When the man turned round to spit, digging into his pocket for nails, Lem recognized him for certain. It was his cousin Fancher, who had grown up along with Lem but now lived in Lebanon because a couple of years back he had been caught selling liquor from the common Skaggs still—liquor that belonged to him only in the amount he could drink and keep down. Since then Fancher hadn't been very popular with the Skaggses, though he occasionally came up Breakshin to visit and show off what he had learned in Lebanon and tell again the story of the Big Pearl, how but not where he had found it, how he had sold it for hard cash to a man from Hot Springs—the story that always ended with the same words, the same flourish of a little black book: "And here's my bankbook to show ye."

Of the hundred or more people Lem knew—bloodkin, in-laws, and Flatters—Fancher Skaggs was about the last one he cared to see, this morning or any other, and he was just about to dig his paddle deep and hard into Little Breakshin when Fancher, his attention caught by Old Nick's tootling, looked down to the river and saw them. After staring a moment, he raised his hammer in recognition and spoke to the red-faced ox-built man working with him; then the two dropped their hammers and together started down to the river through the sycamores.

The canoe, caught in a gentle eddy, turned slowly around. The stern jarred gratingly on a rocky ledge at the waterline, and Old Nick's music was cut off like the squealing of a stuck pig. The pretty, silvery flute, like an arrow aimed at a fish, hit the water and disappeared. Gripping the gunwales hard, Old Nick peered down at the tiny rings rippling out from the spot where he had seen that last flash of sunlight of silver. Then, his face a sight to behold, a startled mask of anger and fear, of disbelief and despair—the face of a good man tarred and feathered for doing good—he looked at Lem and tried to speak. Instead he began to whimper, and Lem squirmed in a hogs-head of guilt and embarrassment, ashamed for Old Nick, and ashamed for himself for being ashamed. And Fancher and the heavy man were near, he knew without looking, but looked to make sure, and recognized the heavy man. It was Garne Johnson, another person Lem wasn't anxious to see.

"Shut up, plague take it," he scolded. "I didn't aim to do it. Ye want the whole plague-taked shooting match of the world to hear ye, and see ye benastying your face like a two-year-old crying for a sugar-tit? Shut up now. Fancher and that other feller's coming—it's Garne Johnson. If he sees ye watering the earth thataway, he'll tell the parson on ye, shore.

"I'm—trying to stop."

"Well, make haste and do it—or hide your face."

Taking the easier choice, Old Nick bowed his head between his knees, and Lem, feeling like a mangy, suck-egg hound, lifted the hem of the pretty crimson cape and flung it hastily over Old Nick's head. Fancher and Garne Johnson, a moment later emerged from the trees and came sliding down the steep incline to the rocky ledge. Both seemed to be amused, Fancher in particular.

"What's the matter with Old Nick?"

Fancher, Lem saw, hadn't changed for the better, still asked questions a real Skaggs should have kept to himself.

"Nothing much."

"He's bawling, ain't he? What about?"

"He lost his flute."

Old Nick's head came up with a jerk.

"I never done it. It was all your fault, Lem Skaggs. You know it was."

"I never aimed to do it."

"But ye done it."

Fancher was delighted, Garne Johnson puzzled.

"I never heared of such doings," he said, and looked to Fancher for help. "What're they up to?"

"Ain't no telling. What is it, Lem? What're ye doing?"

"Traveling."

Old Nick snorted.

Pete Whetstone

Charles F. M. Noland is considered by many to be the greatest humorist in Arkansas literature. For the first 22 years of her statehood, Arkansas was the subject of sketches by Noland which appeared in The Spirit of the Times. *The first of these sketches was read in 1836.*

Noland emigrated in 1826 to Batesville, where his father was head of the land office. As a young man, he challenged the nephew of Governor John Pope to a duel which resulted in the death of his opponent. In 1836 he was admitted to the bar, and thereafter, was engaged in the practice of law and became active in state politics. He was elected for four consecutive terms to the state House of Representatives. Noland was appointed by the legislature as the special messenger to carry the first state constitution to Washington, a duty for which he is generally remembered. He edited the Batesville Eagle *for several years before his death in 1858.*

Pete Whetstone, Noland's "other personality," compares in a number of ways to Peter Finley Dunne's Mr. Dooley, and both parallel literary inventions of Mark Twain. Whetstone's style is purely colloquial; he indulges in the hyperbole and colorful dialect which are characteristic of the period. Whetstone exemplifies Noland's ability to make his characters lifelike and plausible. His observations were published as letters to the editor of The Spirit of the Times.

Pete Whetstone's Bear Hunt

Charles F. M. Noland. *Pete Whetstone of Devil's Fork*, eds. Ted R. Worley and Eugene A. Nolte (Van Buren, AR: Argus, 1957).

Devil's Fork of Little Red River, (Ark.) Feb. 15th, 1837

Dear Mr. Editor, —Being this is a rainy day, I thought I would write you about the bear hunt. Well, next morning after the fight with Dan Looney, I started out. I was mighty sore I tell you, for Dan had thumped me in the sides until I was as blue as indigo. I saddled my horse, got my wallet, and fetched a whoop, that started my dogs; they knew what I was after, and seemed mightily pleased. I took six with me, as good dogs as ever fought a bear. Sharp-tooth and General Jackson, if there was any difference, were a little the best. I struck for the Big Lick, where Sam Jones and Bill Stout were to meet me. I found them there—they had a good team of dogs. We had heard of great sign up the Dry Fork, and there we determined to go. It was about thirty miles off, and as we did not wish to fatigue our dogs, it took us until the middle of next day to reach it; we rested that evening and put out by day-break next morning.

In about half an hour, old General raised a cry: I knew then we were good for a bear—the other dogs joined him. The track was cold; we worked with him till about ten, when they bounced him. Bill Stout was ahead and raised the yell—such music, oh lord, and such fighting. I got the first shot; my gun made long fire, and I only slightly wounded him. At the crack of the gun the dogs gathered; he knocked two of my young dogs into the middle of next week before you could say Jack Robinson—the others kept him at bay until Bill Stout could shoot; his ball struck him too far back. He was a tremendous bear, and just lean enough to make a good fight. He made two other dogs hear it thunder, shook off the whole pack, and got into a thicket, and the next moment plunged down a steep cliff. I listened only for an instant, to hear the clear shrill note of Sharp-tooth, as he plunged in after him, and then socked the spurs into Dry-bones, and, Bill Stout on Fire-tail, and Sam Jones on Hard-times, dashed around the hill. We rode for our lives, for we knew that many of our dogs would suffer if we did not relieve him. When we overtook them, they had him at bay; two dead, and three crippled dogs told of the bloody fight they had had. Sam Jones fired; the wound was that time mortal. At the crack of the gun, the dogs again clamped him; with a powerful reach of his paw, he grabbed the old General, and the next moment fastened his big jaws on him; this was more than flesh and blood could stand: I sprung at him with a butcher-knife, and the first lick sent it to the handle. He loosened his jaws and Sam Jones caught the old General by the hind legs and pulled him away. I gave him one more stab, and he fell dead.

I examined the old General, and found that he was not much injured. We lost seven dogs that day, and many of the others were so badly crippled, as to render it necessary for us to lay by for a few days. Sam found a bee tree, and I killed some fat turkeys; with them, and the ribs of the old he, we had

fine times. It has stopped raining, so I must stop for the present.
Ever yours,
Pete Whetstone

Pete Whetstone Alive and Kicking

Batesville, (Ark.) May 5th, 1837

Dear Mr. Editor,—Well, here I am, used plum up—as bad off as a small varmint in "Sharptooth's" grab. Old *Sir William* cleared me out—they acted as foul as a buzzard's nest, or I would have been in town with a pocket full of rocks. There is no use to cry over a "lost bear," but I will make some of them think day is breaking next Fall. This here place ain't much for feeding man or brute; the "green tree" finished me—I hadn't enough left to buy a half pint. Dry Bones liked to have had the big head; but I would have had him out or burst a shoe-string.

Well, I have had all sorts of a time since my last letter;—knocked the hind sights off from old bess—used up two painters, and made a mash of lots of little varmints. I tell you, they have had me in a tight place: I tell you how it was—Squire Wood came over to my house, and says he, "Pete, you must run for the legislature." Well, now, the Squire has a hankering that way, and he thought I would say no, and then ask him; but he warnt smart. Says I, "Squire, I don't care if I do." This here sorter took him by surprise; but he acted like a man, and is doing his best for me. Says he, "Pete, you must make a stump speech at the 'log rolling' on the middle park [fork]." "Well," says I, "good." I went to the "log rolling"; I found my opponent there. He was cutting a wide swath among the sovereigns. I guess I used him up; for the moment I rode up I called for a "gallon and sugar." "Hurrah for Pete," shouted the hell-fire chaps, "he is the man who don't care for a dollar." I stirred among the boys; presently some fellow cried out, "A speech from Pete." I tell you I began to have the thumps; says I, "Look here, lawyer McCampbell, arter you is manners." Up jumped lawyer Mac, and bowing low, addressed the crowd:—"Friends and fellow citizens,—I am an unambitious man—I never sought office; I belong to a party that are modest and unassuming,—I am a disciple of the Van Buren, Amos Kendall, Tom Ben-

James M'Campbell of Independence County was a lawyer, who with J. Steele codified Arkansas laws under the title Laws of Arkansas *(Little Rock, 1835)*

ton, Buck Woodruff school. I have been always a democrat—one that loves the many, and hates the few;—I am a professional man. I have spent a patrimony in preparing myself to be useful to mankind, and you ought to elect me. I hold this doctrine to be correct, that a representative should vote as his party directs. I pledge myself to vote as Chester Ashley and Buck Woodruff tell me. Who is Pete Whetstone? Why, he is an uneducated man—he knows nothing of the immortal principles of Lindley Murray—*quem deus vult per dere prinsque dementat*—yes, fellow citizens, I say, *sic transit gloria mundi*—which means the higher a monkey climbs, the plainer he shows his tail."

Down he sat."What larning," says one. "He is a great man," said another. I swallowed a horn of bald face and riz up. "Boys," says I, "Pete's out for the Legislature, Pete is an ambitious man—but his is an honorable ambition. Pete always went for Old Hickory, but can't swallow Martin Van Buren, or Buck Woodruff. Pete's a democrat, according to the old fashion meaning. Lawyer McCampbell says he has spent a fortune to make himself useful. All Pete can say is, that he laid out his money badly. He asked who Pete is?—Why, he is a professional bear-hunter, and a scientific bee-hunter. Pete is no orator; but when it comes to killing a bear, or finding a bee tree, he is there. Pete ain't good at figures, but he can read big print. If he goes to the Legislature, he will do his best for you. Pete tracks no man. As to that strange tongue that lawyer McCampbell speaks, I can say nothing; it ain't Shawnee, Creek, or Cherokee;—maybe it is Dutch. Pete never flies higher than he can roost. You all know him, and if you don't want him to go to the Rock, just say so. Pete has a 'couple of gallons' over at the doggery; step over and drink."

"Hurrah for Pete!"—"He is my chap," shouted about three-fourths. This is the lawyer's stronghold, and I have him safe. I expect he has been taking some pulls on me since I left; but if he has, I will make him think a Rhode-Island jackass has kicked him. To-morrow I put out for Devil's Fork, and I will tell you more about my election when I get home.

Ever yours,
Pete Whetstone

P.S. Look here, don't call me Peter—my name is Pete. I have a monstrous notion of that Mr. John Stevens, and tell him if he wants to have a colt a little

---

Side notes:

William E. Woodruff was editor of the Little Rock *Arkansas Gazette* from the time of its inception in 1819 off and on until the Civil War.

Chester Ashley was a prominent Little Rock lawyer.

Lindley Murray's (1745-1826) *English Grammar*, first published in 1795, was the most widely used text of its day.

A "horn" was a drink, and "bald face" was homemade whiskey.

Noland was at the time a candidate for the Legislature. Whetstone's activities, and his opinions as well, were generally parallel with those of Noland.

faster than Bussing 'coon, why, call him Pete Whetstone.

Letter From Pete Whetstone

Little Rock, (Ark.) Nov. 16, 1837

Dear Mr. Editor,—Pete has been here a week and better, but he has been so busy he couldn't write you. This is a great place, and we can have lots of fun every day. Legislating don't suit Pete's genius—he has found that out. I have been prowling about pretty considerable, and the way I have seen some sights is about right. And would you believe it, the Circus is here. I went last night. I tell you what, that spotted fellow they have along made fun. If they would just go to the Devil's Fork, I reckon they would make money. The way them chaps ride is a caution. I guess they would be great on a bear hunt. Then there was one fellow lifted three great big anvils at once; may be he ain't all horse; I reckon he could knock the filling out of Jim Cole; and they laid an anvil on his belly and hit it with a sledge hammer; Spot said it settled his supper. I guess it did.

But I am going again to-night. Well, they invited me to a party—I didn't like much to go, because I was afraid I wouldn't know how to act—but lawyer McCampbell said I must go. Well, I got me a new coat and spruced up pretty slick, I tell you.

I started about 7—I tell you I never see such sights before—the way there was nice looking ladies was right. The finery Jim Cole carried sister Sal wasn't priming to it—and then such dancing. Says one gentleman, "Mr. Whetstone, don't you dance?" "I reckon I does," says I. "Well," says he, "let me get you a partner." "I am much obliged to you," says I. At that he led me up to the prettiest sort of gal. "My friend Mr. Whetstone, of the Devil's Fork." says he. " I hope you are well, Miss," says I. Oh, Lord, may be she didn't smile sweetly on me. Says she, "Mr. Whetstone, how did you leave your sister Sal?" Says I, "mighty well, Miss, I thank you." Just right at that, up comes a ghost-looking chap, and says he, "Miss, will you allow me the pleasure to dance with you." She bowed, and he led her off, leaving me standing like a widow's pig on a cold morning. Thinks I, you'll catch it, Mr. Ghost, for your smartness, when a fellow tapped me on the back. "Come, Col. Whetstone, (he was a candidate) and take some apple toddy." "I don't care if I do," says I. I told him how Ghost used me. "Oh," says he, "that is a small matter, and you must not get mad." I asked him how I could get to dance, for I wanted to show them a few Devil Fork steps. He said he would introduce me to a partner. "What must I do then?" says I. "Bow to her, and ask the pleasure of dancing with her," says he. Well, he introduced me to a nice little critter, I tell you. Says I, "Miss, will you allow me the extreme pleasure of dancing with you." She said she would. Out we went. Well, the first motion after the fiddlers struck up, showed me I wasn't in the right place. I got scared and couldn't get the figure; says one of them in a whisper, "Mr. Whetstone, ain't you up to "kertillions?" At that says I, "ladies and gentlemen, excuse me if you please, I am in the wrong row now, for I never got higher than a reel in all my life." At that they all commenced giggling; this made me mighty mad. After a while they said supper was ready; I tell you I never set down to such good things before—I just wish Cole could have seen it.

Well, Capt. Brown is going to resign his office in the bank; he has made a good President, and I go in for giving the devil his due. Well, the fuss about the State Bank ain't a priming to what is going on about the Real Estate Bank. B.B. couldn't get to be President, and the way Talleyrand and Buck are mad is awful. It went into the Senate yesterday; Z was preaching agin it was a sin: Wappanocca answered him, and said he, Z was a stockholder, and jist because he couldn't be a director, he got mad. It all won't do; the Bank will flourish, for it has got into honest hands. In a great hurry,

    Your friend,
    Pete Whetstone

Roswell Beebe was a Little Rock land speculator.

"Talleyrand" was Chester Ashley.

Pete is probably referring here to Mark Izard, the senator representing St. Francis and Greene Counties. The old name for the letter Z, as in "A to izzard," would have been the same as the senator's name.

Letter from Pete Whetstone

Devil's Fork of Little Red, (Ark.) Dec. 24, 1837

On December 4, 1837, while the Arkansas House of Representatives was in session, Speaker John Wilson came down from the chair and killed a member, J. J. Anthony of Randolph County, who was contending for his right to the floor. Both men used bowie knives in the fight.

"Dr. Kraft," another of Noland's thinly veiled name-disguises, was Dr. George B. Croft, a member of the Territorial Council from Greene County

"Bitter Mast" was an acorn mast, as distinguished from other forms of mast such as nuts and berries. Acorns have a bitter taste.

My Dear Mr. Editor,—Well, here I am, safe at home. The Legislature adjourned for a month, on account of the small pox. They were tired, and only wanted a good excuse. Well, I ain't writ you for a long time. We had a bloody fight in our house—I tell you it was dreadful slaughtering—the way the big knives were pulled out, and such a slashing—it was awful. But I reckon a man has to pay now for toting a knife, pistol, or other dangerous weapon. Well this here is a mighty fluxible world, as Dr. Kraft said—perhaps you don't know Dr. Kraft. Well he is a perfect crumpification of cases, and the way he figured at Randolph Court was a sin to Moses—lots of inditemens for gambling—just playing a small game. Well, Kraft was a witness in every case, and they do say he and the State's Feliciter were in Cohoot. Kraft made as high as $13 one day by being witness.

Well, what do you think? Some of my enemies up about the blowing cave, are trying to injure me—they say I am too hard on the Methodists, but he scorns a possum wherever he finds him. Pete don't apologise. He wishes to hurt no man, woman, or child's feelings, but like the Jack-ass dancing among the chickens, tells every body to look out for their own toes.

Well, after all, bear-hunting is another sort of legislating, and the way we are going to make the fur fly is funny. I came to Batesvlle, and saw N's rifle—the way she is a slick gun is right—I just wish I had sich a one, for if I had, I'd made the varmint see sights.

Pork is as high as six dollars, and scarce at that—nothing but a little "bitter mast." Lawyer McCampbell is mixing strong among the people. He is bound to be elected.

The New York elections have reached the Devil's Fork—such a gitting off the fence I never did see—Turkies sliding, as Dr. Kraft would say. By the bye, Dr. Kraft used to be in the Legislature—he is a perfect knight of the blue riband, and the way he drank Muscat for Buck when he was at the Rock, was sinful—When they handed him biscuits at a party, says he, "I thank you, sir, these will do me," and the way he handled the sweet bread was awful. He is going to try again—if he fails, he starts for the State of Greene.

To-morrow is Christmas, and I have lots of eggs. The way I'll walk into a bowl of nog in the morning will be nice. Sister Sal and Jim Cole are well, and their boy is a bulger. I forgot to tell you—the citizens gave us a splendid ball at the Rock—it was in the State House—four sets dancing at one time—reels for the benefit of the Sub County Members—the way Pete went it was a caution—he got as high as cotillions are a huckleberry above reels. I am sleepy now, so good night.

    Ever yours,
    Pete Whetstone

Letter from Pete Whetstone

Devil's Fork of Little Red, Dec. 30, 1837

    My Dear Mr. Editor,—Pete's in a passion—the way his dander is up is nothing to nobody. I have just heard from Batesville, that some of the people are mad about that letter what I writ you about my trip to the Springs, way last summer. If any body says I meant a slur on any body, he tells a big lie, and what's more, I'll thrash the ticks off him in a minit, if I can find him out. I know how it is come about. Ever since I talked of leaving the Devil's Fork and settling in Independence, the Van Burenites have been trying to injure me. I reckon I guess I know who they are, although they are cutting deep, they stand mighty far from the blood. One of them tried twenty-seven times hand running to get in the Legislature. He got in once—next to his partner, he is the greatest man in his way, west of White river. He is a perfect thing—lays two eggs every day—on Sunday three, and occasionally drops a nutmeg. Pete would look well making fun of people who treated him as well as they did at the Springs—besides Pete has been on the Devil's Fork these twelve years, and is real Arkansas every inch of him.

    I will start over to Batesville tomorrow, and I will make some of them smell a worse smell than the Kentuckian did.

    Well, I have had one bear fight since I come back—it wasn't much of a fight—Jim's pack nailed in half an hour's run, and pinned it so close that Jim killed it with his butcher knife. It was an old she, not very fat, but tolerable eating. There is but little frost this year, and bear will be scarce, except in spots—the way deer and turkeys are fat is a caution—they always thrive best when there is but little acorn mast.

We are to have a big quarter race on New Year's Day, 'twixt the Biling Pot and the Chawed Bullet. Jim Cole and Dan Looney made it—they carry 100 lbs. on each. The Devil's Fork chaps are going it with a rush on the Biling Pot, though from what I can learn, the Chawed Bullet picks it up like mice a-fighting. I am persuading Jim to pay the forfeit, for the Biling Pot gets so full of wild oats and vinegar, that there is no dependence on him—but Jim won't listen to me, for he says he's a mighty man to bet on horse racing.

Ever yours,
Pete Whetstone

The Arkansas Traveler

James Masterson devoted an entire chapter of his book Arkansas Folklore *to an investigation of the "Arkansas Traveler" story. This story is probably the best-known yarn to come from the spinning tradition found in Arkansas. It has not always met with favor among Arkansans, because many feel that the image of the rustic ignorance of the squatter is derogatory and insulting. On the contrary, the story should be viewed as an example of the colorful wit which makes Arkansas distinctive from her sister states. Like the Ozark folktales, the Traveler story is meant to convey the unique humor of hill people—a point of pride, not ridicule. The story is a vital thread in the fabric of native literature; it is still another voice to be heard. As Masterson indicates, there are several versions of this story. Only one is presented here.*

A Traveler, A Cabin, And A Fiddle

A belated wayfarer in a lonely section of Arkansas wished to pass the night at the log cabin of a squatter whom he found engaged in fiddling and re-fiddling the first part of the jig known as The Arkansas Traveler. But the fiddler was inhospitable. He refused to accommodate the stranger, answered his questions evasively, and interrupted him by playing again the first part of the tune. At length the traveler thought of a question which, he hoped, would arouse the musician's curiosity. "Why," he asked, "don't you fiddle the rest of the tune." Instantly the backwoodsman bristled with attention. "Kin you play the turn of that thar tune?" he inquired. The traveler took the fiddle and performed the second part. At once the squatter invited him to enter, and to enjoy the best that his humble home could afford.

James Masterson. *Arkansas Folklore* (Little Rock: Rose, 1974).

Thus goes the story of the Arkansas Traveler—the most celebrated specimen of Arkansas folklore and humor. "The Arkansas Traveler" is a phrase which has served as the title for a dialogue, a fiddle tune, at least two paintings, several engravings, and a number of plays. The origins and relationships of all these are highly perplexing. In the present chapter we shall introduce the problem by examining the twelve printed versions of the dialogue.

I. The Faulkner Version (printed between 1858 and 1860). The Arkansas Traveler, with both music and words ascribed to Colonel Sandford C. Faulkner, was printed, probably between 1858 and 1860, on both sides of a small sheet. This very rare document is not available, but we may quote a revision published at Little Rock in 1876 as "arranged and corrected by Colonel S.C. Faulkner."

A lost and bewildered Arkansas Traveler approaches the cabin of a Squatter, about forty years ago, in search of lodgings, and the following dialogue ensues:

Dialogue

Traveler.—Halloo, stranger.
Squatter.—Hello yourself.
T.—Can I get to stay all night with you?
S.—No, sir, you can't git to—
T.—Have you any spirits here?

S.—Lots uv'em; Sal seen one last night by that ar ole hollar gum, and it nearly skeered her to death.
T.—You mistake my meaning; have you any liquor?
S.—Had some yesterday, but Ole Bose he got in and lapped all um it out'n the pot.
T.—You don't understand; I don't mean pot liquor. I'm wet and cold and want some whiskey. Have you got any?
S.—Oh, yes—I drunk the last this mornin.
T.—I'm hungry; havn't had a thing since morning; can't you give me something to eat?
S.—Hain't a durned thing in the house. Not a mouffull um meat, nor a dust uv meal here.
T.—Well, can't you give my horse something?
S.—Got nothin' to feed him on.
T.—How far is it to the next house?
S.—Stranger! I don't know, I've never been thar.
T.—Well, do you know who lives here?
S.—Yes zir!
T.—As I'm so bold, then, what might yur name be?
S.—It might be Dick, and it might be Tom; but it lacks right smart uv it.
T.—Sir! will you tell me where this road goes to?
S.—It's never gone any whar since I've lived here; It's always thar when I get up on the mornin'.
T.—Well, how far is it to where it forks?
S.—It don't fork at all; but it splits up like the devil.
T.—As I'm not likely to get to any other house tonight, can't you let me sleep in yours; and I'll tie my horse to a tree, and do without anything to eat or drink?
S.—My house leaks. Thar's only one dry spot in it, and me and Sal sleeps on it. And that thar tree is the ole woman's persimon; you can't tie to it, 'caze she don't want 'em shuk off. She 'lows to make beer out'n um.
T.—Why don't you finish covering your house to stop the leaks?
S.—It's been rainin' all day.
T.—Well, why don't you do it in dry weather?
S.—It don't leak then.
T.—As there seems to be nothing alive about your place but children, how

do you do here anyhow?
S.—Putty well, I thank you, how do you do yourself?
T.—I mean what do you do for a living here?
S.—Keep tavern and sell whisky.
T.—Well, I told you I wanted some whisky.
S.—Stranger, I bought a bar'l more'n a week ago. You see, me and Sal went shars. After we got it here, we only had a bit betweenst us, and Sal she dind't want to use hern fust, nor me mine. You see I had a spiggin in one eend, and she in tother. So she takes a drink out'n my eend, and pays me the bit for it; then I'd take one out'n hern, and give her the bit. Well, we's getting long fust-rate, till Dick, durned skulking skunk, he born a hole on the bottom to suck at, and the next time I went to buy a drink, they wont none thar.
T.—I'm sorry your whisky's all gone; but, my friend, why don't you play the balance of that tune?
S.—It's got no balance to it.
T.—I mean you don't play the whole of it.
S.—Stranger, can you play the *fiddul*?
T.—Yes, a little, sometimes.
S.—You don't look like a fiddlur, but ef you think you can play any more onto that thar tune, you kin just try it.
(The traveler takes the fiddle and plays the whole of it.)
S.—Stranger, tuck a half a duzen cheers and sot down. Sal, stir yourself round like a six-horse team in a mud hold. Go round in the hollar whar I killed that buck this mornin', cut off some of the best pieces, and fotch it and cook it for me and this gentleman, d'rectly. Raise up the board under the head of the bed, and got the ole black jug I hid from Dick, and gin us some whisky; I know thar's some left yit. Til, drive ole Bose out'n the bread-tray, then climb up in the loft and git the rag that's got the sugar tied in it. Dick, carry the gentleman's hoss round under the shead, give him some fodder and corn; much as he kin eat.

Til.—Dad, they ain't knives enuff for to sot the table.
S.—Whar's big butch, little butch, ole case, cob-handle, granny's knife, and the one I handled yesterday! That's nuff to sot any gentleman's table, outer you've lost um. Durn me,

stranger, ef you can't stay as long as you please, and I'll give you plenty to eat and to drink. Will you have coffey for supper?

T.—Yes, sir.

S.—I'll be hanged if you do, tho', we don't have nothin' that way here, but Grub Hyson, and I reckon it's mighty good with sweetnin'. Play away, stranger, you kin sleep on the dry spot to-night.

T.—(After about two hours fiddling.) My friend, can't you tell me about the road I'm to travel to-morrow?

S.—To-morrow! Stranger, you won't git out'n these diggins for six weeks. But when it gits so you kin start, you see that big sloo over thar? Well, you have to git crost that, then you take the road up the bank, and in about a mile you'll come to a two-acre-and-a-half cornpatch. The corn's mitely in the weeds, but you needn't mind that; jist ride on. About a mile and a half or two miles from thar, you'll cum to the damdest swamp you ever struck in all your travels; it's boggy enouff to mire a saddle-blanket. Thar's a fust rate road about six feet under thar.

T.—How am I to get at it?

S.—You can't git at it nary time, till the weather stiffens down sum. Well, about a mile beyant, you come to a place whar thar's no roads. You kin take the right hand ef you want to; you'll foller it a mile or so, and you'll find its run out; you'll then have to come back and try the left; when you git about two miles on that, you may know you're wrong, fur they ain't any road thar. You'll then think you're mity lucky ef you kin find the way back to my house, whar you kin cum and play on thara'r tune as long as you please.

The Faulkner version of "The Arkansas Traveler" appears to be not only the earliest of all, but the best. Unlike a number of later versions, it is coherent; and it does not descend to the level of silliness. It contains a greater number of witticisms than any other. It is the only form of the dialogue that is known to have originated in Arkansas, and hence its dialect may be accepted as genuine. In short, Colonel Faulkner's Arkansas Traveler has better claims than any other to be regarded as standard; and accordingly it has been more often reprinted.—Masterson

In Simpkinsville

At the turn of the century, a prolific spinner of yarns at Washington, Arkansas, caught the attention of the reading public. Ruth McEnery Stuart became a regular contributor to a series known as Little Books by Famous Writers. Among her contributions to this series were Carlotta's Intended and Other Tales, The Golden Wedding and Other Tales, The Story of Babette, *and* Solomon Crow's Christmas Pockets and Other Tales. *The following excerpt comes from still another contribution to the series. According to the frontispiece of this Little Book, Simpkinsville is a fictitious name for Washington, and all the characters are drawn from Hempstead County people.*

An Arkansas Prophet

If you would find the warmest spot in a little village on a cold day, watch the old codgers and see where they congregate. That's what the stray cats do, or perhaps the codgers follow the cats. However that may be, both can be depended upon to find the open door where comfort is. They will probably lead you to the rear end of the village store, the tobacco-stained drawing-room, where an old stove dispenses hospitality in an atmosphere like unto which, for genial disposition, there is none so unfailing.

From November to May the old stove in the back of Chris Rowton's store was, to its devotees at least, the most popular hostess in Simpkinsville. And, be it understood her circle was composed of people of good repute. Even the cats sleeping at her feet, if personally tramps, were well connected, being lineal descendants of known cats belonging to families in regular standing. Many, indeed, were natives of the shop, and had come into this kingdom of comfort in a certain feline lying-in hospital behind the rows of barrels that flanked the stove on either side.

It was the last day of December. The wind was raw and cold, and of a fitful mind, blowing in contrary gusts, and throwing into the faces of people going in all directions various samples from the winter storehouse of the sky,

Ruth McEnery Stuart. *In Simpkinsville* (New York: Harper & Bros., 1897.

now a threat, a promise, or a dare as to how the new year should come in.

"Blest if Doc ain't got snow on his coat! Rainin' when I come in," said one of two old men who drew their seats back a little while the speaker pushed a chair forward with his boot.

"Reckon I got both froze and wet drops on me twix' this an' Meredith's," drawled the newcomer, depositing his saddle-bags beside his chair, wiping the drops from his sleeves over the stove, and spreading his thin palms for its grateful return of warm steam.

"Sleetin' out our way," remarked his neighbor, between pipe puffs. And then he added:

"How's Meredith's wife coming on, doctor? Reckon she's purty bad off, ain't she?"

The doctor was filling his pipe now and he did not answer immediately; but presently he said, as he deliberately reached forward and, seizing the tongs, lifted a live coal to his pipe:

"Meredith's wife don't rightfully belong in a doctor's care. She ain't to say sick; she's heartbroke, that's what she is; but of co'se that ain't a thing I can tell her—or him, either."

"This has been a mighty slow and tiresome year in Simpkinsville," he added in a moment, "an' I'm glad to see it drawin' to a close. It come in with snow an' sleet an' troubles, an' seems like it's goin' out the same way—jest like the years have done three year past."

"Jest look at that cat—what a dusty color she's got between spots! Th' ain't a cat in Simpkinsville, hardly, thet don't show a trace o' Jim Meredith's Maltee—an' I jest nachelly despise it, 'cause that's one of the presents *he* brought out there—that Maltee is."

"Maltee is a good enough color for a cat ef it's kep' true," remarked old Pete Taylor—"plenty good enough ef it's kep' true; but it's like gray paint—it'll mark up most anything it's mixed with, and cloud it."

"I reckon Jim Meredith's Maltee ain't the only thing thet's cast a shade over Simpkinsville," said old Mr. McMonigle, who sat opposite.

"That's so," grunted the circle.

"That's so, shore ez you're born," echoed Pete. "Simpkinsville has turned out some toler'ble fair days since little May Meredith dropped out of it, but the sun ain't never shone on it quite the same—to my notion."

"Wonder where she is?" said McMonigle. "My opinion is she's dead, an' thet her mother knows it. I wouldn't be surprised ef the devil that enticed her away has killed her. Once-t a feller like that gits a girl into a crowded city and gits tired of her, there's a dozen ways of gittin' shet of her.''

"Yas, a hundred of 'em. It's done every day, I don't doubt."

"See that stove how she spits smoke. East wind'll make her spit any day —seems to gag her."

"Yas," McMonigle chuckled softly, as he leaned forward and began poking the fire, "she hates a east wind, but she like me—don't you, old girl? See her grow red in the face while I chuck her under the chin."

"Look out you don't chuck out a coal of fire on kitty with your foolin'," said old man Taylor. "She does blush in the face, don't she? An' see her wink under her isinglass spectacles when she's flirted with."

"That stove is a well-behaved old lady," interrupted the doctor; "reg'larly gits religion, an' shouts whenever the wind's from the right quarter—an' I won't have her spoke of with disrespect.

"If she could tell all she's heard, settin' there summer and winter, I reckon it'd make a book—an' a interestin' one, too. There's been cats and mice born in her all summer, an' birds hatched; an' Rowton tells me he's got a dominicker hen thet's reg'larly watched for her fires to go out last two seasons, so she can lay in her. An' didn't you never hear about Phil Toland hidin' a whiskey bottle in her one day last summer and smashin' a whole settin' o' eggs? The hen, she squawked out at him, an' all but skeered him to death. He thought he had a 'tackt o' the tremens, shore—an' of a adult variety."

"Pity it hadn't a-skeert him into temperance," remarked the man opposite

"Did sober him up for purty nigh two weeks. Rowton he saw it all, an' he gave the fellers the wink, an' when Pete hollered, he ast him what was the matter, an' of co'se Pete he pointed to the hen that was kitin' through the sto'e that minute, squawkin' for dear life, an' all be-daubled over with egg, an' sez he: 'What sort o' dash blanketed hens hev you got round here, settin' in stoves?' And Rowton he looks round and winks at the boys. 'Hen,' says he —'what hen? Any o' you fellers saw a hen anywhere round here?'

"Of co'se every feller swo'e he hadn't saw no hen, an' Rowton he went up to Pete and he says, says he: 'Pete,' says he, 'you better go home an' lay down. You ain't well.'

"Well, sir, Pete wasn't seen on the streets for up'ards o' three weeks after that.

"Yas, that stove has seen sights and heard secrets, too, I don't doubt.

"They say old nigger Prophet used to set down an' talk to her same ez ef she was a person, some nights, when he'd have her all to hisself. Rowton ast him one day what made him do it, and he 'lowed thet he could converse with anything that had the breath o' life in it. There is no accountin' for what notions a nigger'll take.

"No, an' there's no telling' how much or how little they know, neither. Old Proph', half blind and foolish, limpin' round in the woods, getherin' queer roots, and talkin' to hisself, didn't seem to have no intelligence, rightly speakin', an' yet he has called out prophecies that have come true—even befo' he prophesied about May Meredith goin' wrong.

"Here come Brother Squires, chawin' tobacco like a sinner. I do love a preacher that'll chaw tobacco.

"Hello, Brother Squires!" he called out now to a tall, clerical old man who approached the group. "Hello! what you doin' in a sto'e like this, I like to know? Th' ain't no Bibles, nor trac's for sale here, an' your folks don't eat molasses and bacon, same ez us sinners, do you?"

"Well, my friends," the parson smiled broadly as he advanced, "since you good people don't supply us with locusts and wild honey, we are reduced to the necessity of eatin' plain bread an' meat—but you see I live up to the Baptist standard as far as I can. I wear the leathern girdle about my loins."

He laid his hand upon the long leather whip which, for safekeeping, he had tied loosely around his waist.

"Room for one more?" he added, as, declining the only vacant chair, he seated himself upon a soap-box, extended his long legs, and raised his boots upon the ledge of the stove.

"I declare, Brother Squires, the patches on them boots are better'n a contribution-box," said McMonigle, laughin, as he thrust his hand down into his pocket. "Reckon it'll take a half-dollar to cover this one." He playfully balanced a bright coin over the topmost patch on the pastor's toe.

"Stop your laughin', now, parson. Don't shake it off! Come up, boys! Who'll cover the next patch? Ef my 'rithmetic is right, there's jest about a patch apiece for us to cover—not includin' the half-soles. I know parson wouldn't have money set above his soul."

"No, certainly not, an' if anybody'd place it there, of co'se I'd remove it immediately." the parson answered, with ready wit, And then he added, more seriously:

"I have passed my hat around to collect my salary once in a while, but I never expected to hand around my old shoes—and really, my friends, I don't know as I can allow it."

Still he did not draw them in, and the three old men grew so hilarious over the fun of covering the patches with the ever-slipping coins that a crowd was soon collected, the result being the pocketing of the entire handful of money by Rowton, with the generous assurance that it should be good for the best pair of boots in his store, to be fitted at the pastor's convenience.

It was after this mirth had all subsided and the codgers had settled down into their accustomed quiet that the parson remarked, with some show of hesitation:

"My brothers, when I was coming towards you a while ago I heard two names. They are names that I hear now and then among my people—names of two persons whom I have never met—persons who passed out of your community some time before I was stationed among you. One of them, I know, has a sad history. The details of the story I have never heard, but it is in the air. Scarcely a village in all our dear world but has, no matter how blue its skies, a little cloud above its horizon—a cloud which to its people seems always to reflect the pitiful face of one of its fair daughters. I don't know the story of May Meredith—or is it May Day Meredith?"

"She was born May Day, and christened that-a-way," answered McMonigle. "But she was jest ez often called Daisy or May—any name thet'd fit a spring day or a flower would fit her."

"Well, I don't know her story," the parson resumed, "but I do know her fate. And perhaps that is enough to know. The other name you called was 'Old Proph,' or 'Prophet.' Tell me about him. Who was he? How was he connected with May Day Meredith?"

He paused and looked from one face to another for the answer, which was slow in coming.

"Go on an' tell it, Dan'l" said the doctor, finally, with an inclination of the head towards McMonigle.

Old man McMonigle shook the tobacco from his pipe, and refilled it slowly, without a word. Then he as deliberately lit it, puffed its fires to the glowing point, and took it from his lips as he began:

"Well, parson, ef I hadn't o' seen you standin' in the front o' the sto'e clean to the minute you come back here, I'd think you'd heerd more than names.

"Of co'se we couldn't put it quite ez eloquent ez as you did, but we had jest every one of us 'lowed that sence the day May Meredith dropped out o' Simpkinsville the sky ain't never shone the same.

"But for a story? Well, I don't see thet there's much story to it, and to them thet didn't know her I reckon it's common enough.

"But ez to the old nigger, Proph', being mixed up in it, I can't eggsac'ly say that's so, though I don't think about the old nigger without seemin' to see little May Day's long yaller curls, an' ef I think about her, I seem to see the old man, somehow. Don't they come to you all that-a-way?"

He paused, took a few puffs from this pipe, and looked from one face to another.

"Yas," said the doctor, "jest exactly that-a-way, Dan'l. Go on, ol' man. You're a-tellin' it straight."

"Well, that's what I'm aimin' to do." He laid his pipe down on the stove's fender as he resumed his recital.

"Old Proph'—which his name wasn't Prophet, of co'se, which ain't to say a name nohow, but his name was Jeremy, an' he used to go by name o' Jerry; then somebody called him Jeremy the Prophet, an' from that it got down to Prophet, and then Proph'—and so it stayed.

"Well, ez I started to say, Proph' he was jest one o' Meredith's ol' slave niggers—a sort o' queer, half-luney, no-'count darky—never done nothin' sence freedom but what he had a mind to, jest livin' on Meredith right along.

"He wasn't to say crazy, but—well, he'd stand and talk to anything—a dog, a cat, a tree, a toad-frog—anything. Many a time I've seen him limpin' up the road, an' he'd turn round sudden an' seemed to be talkin' to somethin' thet was follerin' him, an' when he'd git tired he'd start on an' maybe every minute look back over his shoulder an' laugh. They was only one thing Proph' was, to say, good for. Proph' was a capital A-1 hunter—shorest shot in the State, in my opinion, and when he'd take a notion he could go out where nobody wouldn't sight a bird or a squir'l all day long, an' he'd fill his game-bag.

"Well, sir, the children round town, they was all afeerd of 'im, and the niggers—the' ain't a nigger in the county thet don't b'lieve to this day thet Proph' would cunjer 'em ef he'd git mad.

"An' time he takin' to fortune-tellin', the school child'en thet'd be feered to go up to him by theirselves, they'd go in a crowd, an' he'd call out fortunes to 'em, an' they'd give him biscuits out o' their lunch-cans.

"From that time he come to tellin' anybody's fortune, an' so the young men, they got him to come to the old-year party one year, jest for the fun of it, an' time the clock was most on the twelve strike, Proph' he stood up an' called out e-vents of the comin' year. An', sir, for a crack-brained fool nigger, he'd call out the smartest things you ever hear. Every year for five year, Proph' called out comin' e-vents at the old-year party; an' matches thet nobody suspicioned, why, he'd call 'em out, an' shore enough, 'fore the year was out, the weddin's would come off. An' babies! He'd predic' babies a year ahead—not always callin' out full names, but jest insinuatin', so thet anybody thet wasn't deef in both ears would understand.

"But to come back to the story of May Meredith—he ain't in it, noways in partic'lar. It's only thet sence she could walk an' hold the ol' man's hand he doted on her, an' she was jest ez wropped up in him. Many's the time when she was a toddler he's rode into town, mule-back, with her settin' up in front of 'im. An' then when she got bigger it was jest as ef she was the queen to him—that's all. He saved her from drowndin' once-t, jumped in the branch after her an couldn't swim a stroke, an' mos' drownded hisself—an' time she had the dip'theria, he never shet his eyes ez long ez she was sick enough to be set up with—set on the flo' by her bed all night.

"That's all the way Proph' is mixed up in her story. An' now, sence they're both gone, ef you 'magine you see one, you seem to see the other.

"But May Day's story? Well, I hardly like to disturb it. Don't rightly know how to tell it, nohow.

"I don't doubt folks has told you she went wrong, but that's a mighty hard way to tell it to them thet knew her.

"We can't none of us deny, I reckon, thet she went wrong. A red-cheeked peach thet don't know nothin' but the dew and the sun, and to grow sweet and purty—it goes wrong when it's wrenched off the stem and et by a hog. That's one way o' goin' wrong.

"Little Daisy Meredith didn't have no mo' idee o' harm than that mockin'-bird o' Rowton's in its cage there, thet sings week-day songs all

Sunday nights.

"She wasn't but jest barely turned seventeen year—ez sweet a little girl ez ever taught a Baptist Sunday-school class—when *he* come down from St. Louis—though some says he come from Chicago, an' some says Canada—lookin' after some land mortgages. An', givin' the devil his due, he was the handsomest man thet ever trod Simpkinsville streets—that is, of co'se, but a outsider. Seen May Day first time on her way to church, an' looked after her—then squared back direct, an' follered her. Walked into church delib'rate, an' behaved like a gentleman religiously inclined, ef ever a well-dressed, city person behaved that way.

"Well, sir, from that day on, he froze to her, and, strange to say, every mother of a marriageable daughter in town was jealous exceptin' one, an' that one was May's own mother. An' she not only wasn't jealous—which she couldn't 'a' been, of co'se—but she wasn't pleased.

"She seemed to feel a dread of him from the start, and she treated him mighty shabby, but of co'se the little girl, she made it up to him in politeness, good ez she could, an' he didn't take no notice of it. Kep' on showin' the old lady every attention, an', when he'd be in town, most any evenin' you'd go past the Meredith gate you could see his horse hitched there—everything open and above boa'd, so it seemed.

"Well, sir, he happened to be here the time o' the old-year party, three year ago. You've been here a year and over, 'ain't you, parson?"

"Yes, I was stationed here at fall conference a year ago this November, you recollect."

"Yas, so you was. Well, all this is about two year befo' you come.

"Well, sir, when it was known thet May Day's city beau was goin' to be here for the party, everybody looked to see some fun, 'cause they knowed how free ol' Proph' made with comin' e-vents, an' they wondered ef he'd have gall enough to call out May Day's name with the city feller's. Well, ez luck would have it, the party was at my house that year, an' I tell you, sir, folks thet hadn't set up to see the old year out for ten year come that night, jest for fear they'd miss somethin'. But of co'se we saw through it. We knowed what fetched 'em.

"Well, sir, that was the purtiest party I ever see in my life. Our Simpkinsville pattern for young girls is a toler'ble neat one, ef I do say it ez shouldn't, bein' kin to forty-'leven of 'em. We ain't got no, to say, ugly girls in town—never had many, though some has plained down some when they got settled in years; but the girls there that night was ez perfec' a bunch of girls ez you ever see—just ez purty a show o' beauty ez any rose arbor could turn out on a spring day.

"Have you ever went to gether roses, parson, each one seemin' to be the purtiest tell you'd got a handful, an' you'd be startin' to come away, when 'way up on top o' the vine you'd see one thet was enough pinker an' sweeter 'n the rest to make you climb for it, an' when you'd git it, you'd stick it in the top of yore bo'quet a little higher 'n the others?

"I see you know what I mean. Well, that was the way May Day looked that night. She was that top bud.

"I had three nieces, and wife she had sev'al cousins, there—all purty enough to draw hummin'-birds; but I say little Daisy Meredith, she jest topped 'em all for beauty and sweetness an' modesty that night.

"An' the stranger—well, I don't hardly know jest what to liken him to, less'n it is to one of them princes thet stalk around the stage an' give orders when they have play-actin' in a show-tent.

"They wasn't no flies in his shape, nor his rig, nor his manners neither. Talked to the old ladies—ricollect my wife she had a finger wropped up an' he ast her about it and advised her to look after it an' give her a recipe for bone-felon. She thought they wasn't nobody like him. An' he jest simply danced the wall-flowers dizzy, give the fiddlers money, an'—well, he done everything thet a person o' the royal family of city gentry might be expected to do. An' everybody wondered what mo' Mis' Meredith wanted for her daughter. Tell the truth, some mistrusted, an' 'lowed that she jest took on indifferent, the way she done, to hide how tickled she was over it.

"Well, ez I say, the party passed off lovely, an' after a while it come near twelve o'clock, an' the folks commenced to look round for ol' Proph' to come in an' call out events same as he always done.

"So d'rectly the boys they stepped out an' fetched him in—drawin' him 'long by the sleeve, an' he holdin' back like ez ef he dreaded to come in.

"I tell you, parson, I'll never forgit the way that old nigger looked, longest day I live. Seemed like he couldn't sca'cely walk, an' he stumbled, an' when he taken his station front o' the mantel-shelf, look like he never would open his mouth to begin.

"An' when at last he started to talk, stid o' runnin' on an' laughin' an' pleggin' everybody like he always done, he lifted up his face an' raised up his hands, same ez you'd do ef you was startin' to lead in public prayer. An' then he commenced:

"Says he—an' when he started he spoke so low down in his th'oat you couldn't sca'cely hear him—says he:

"'Every year, my friends, I stands befo' you an' look throo de open gate into the new year. An','says he,'seem like I see a long percession o' people pass befo' me—some two-by-two, some one-by-one; some horseback, some muleback, some afoot; some cryin', some laughin'; some stumblin' ez they'd walk, an' gittin' up agin, some fallin' to rise no mo'; some faces I know, some strangers.'

"An' right here, parson, he left off for a minute, an' then when he commenced again, he dropped his voice clair down into his th'oat, an' he squinted his eyes an' seemed to be trying to see somethin' way off like, an' he says, says he:

"'But to-night,' says he, 'I don't know whar the trouble is,' says he, 'but look hard ez I can, I don't seem to see clair, 'cause the sky is darkened,' says he, 'an' while I see people comin' an' goin' an' I see the doctor's buggy on the road, an' hear the church bell, an' the organ, I can't make out nothin' clair, 'cause the sky is overshaddered by a big dark cloud. An' now,' says he, 'seem like the cloud is takin' the shape of a great big bird. Now I see him spread his wings an' fly into Simpkinsville, an' while he hangs over it befo' the sun seem to me I can see everybody stop an' gaze up an' hold their breath to see where he'll light—everybody hopin' to see him light in their tree. An' now—Oh! now I see him comin' down, down, down—an' now he's done lit,' says he. I ricollect that expression o' his—'he's done lit,' says he, 'in the limb of a tall maginolia-tree a little piece out o' town.'

"Well, sir, when he come to the bird lightin' in a maginolia tree, a little piece out o' town, I tell you, parson, you could 'a'heerd a pin drop. You see, maginolias is purty sca'ce in Simpkinsville. Plenty o' them growin' round the edge o' the woods, but 'ceptin' them thet Sonny Simkins set out in his yard years ago, I don't know of any nearer than Meredith's place. An' right at his gate, ef you ever taken notice, there's a maginolia-tree purty nigh ez tall ez a post oak.

"An' so when the ol' nigger got to where the fine bird lit in the maginolia-tree, all them thet had the best manners, they set still, but sech ez didn't keer—an' I was one of that las' sort—Why, we jest glanced at the city feller di-rec' to see how he was takin' it.

"But, sir, it didn't ruffle one of his feathers, not a one.

"An' then the nigger he went on: Says he, squintin' his eyes ag'in, an' seemin' to strain his sight, says he:

"'Now he's lit,' says he—I wish I could give it to you in his language, but I never could talk nigger talk—'now he's lit,' says he, 'an' I got a good chance to study him,' says he. 'I see he ain't the same bird he looked to be, befo' he lit.

"'His wing feathers is mighty fine, an' they rise in mighty biggoty plumes, but they can't hide his claws,' says he, 'an' when I look closeter,' says he, 'I see he's got owl eyes an' a sharp beak, but seem like nobody can't see 'em. They all so dazzled with his wing-feathers they can't see his claws.

"'An' now whiles I'm a-lookin' I see him rise up an' fly three times round the tree, an' now I see him swoop down right befo' the people's eyes, an' befo' they know it he's riz up in the air ag'in, an' spread his wings, an' the sky seems so darkened thet I can't see nothin' clair only a long stream o' yaller hair floatin' behind him.

"'Now I see everybody's heads drop, an' I hear 'em cryin'; 'but,' says he, 'they ain't cryin' about the thief bird, but they cryin' about the yaller hair —the yaller hair—the yaller hair.'"

McMonigle choked a little in his recital, and then he added: "Ain't that about yore riccollection o' how he expressed it?"

"Yas," said old man Taylor, "he said it three times—I riccollect that ez long ez I live; an' the third time he said 'the yaller hair' he let his arms drop down at his side, an' he sort o' staggered back'ards, an' turned round to Johnnie Burk an' says he: 'Help me out, please, sir, I feels dizzy.' Do you riccollect how he said that, Dan'l?

"But you're tellin' the story. Don't lemme interrupt you."

"No interruption, Pete. You go on an' tell it the way you call it up. I see my pipe has done gone out while I've been talkin'. Tell the truth, I'm most sorry thet you all started me on this story to-night. I gives me a spell o' the blues—talkin' it over.

"Pass me them tongs back here, doctor, an lemme git another coal for my pipe. An' while I've got 'em I'll shake up this fire a little. This stove's ez dull-eyed and pouty ez any other woman ef she's neglected.

"Hungry, too, ain't you, old lady? Don't like wet wood, neither. Sets her teeth on edge. Jest listen at her quar'l while I lay it in her mouth.

"Go on, now, Pete, an' tell the parson the rest o' the story. 'Tain't no more'n right thet a shepherd should know all the ins and outs of his flock ef he's goin' to take care o' their needs."

"You better finish it, Dan'l," said Taylor. "You've brought it all back a heap better n' I could 'a' done it."

"Tell the truth, boys, I've got it down to where I hate to go on," replied McMonigle, with feeling. "I've talked about the child now till I can seem to see her little slim figur' comin' down the plank-walk the way I've see her a thousand times, when all the fellers settin' out in front o' the sto'es would slip in an' get their coats on, an' come back—I've done it myself, an' me a grandfather.

"Go on, Pete, an' finish it up. I've got the taste o' tobacco smoke now, an' my pipe is like the stove. Ef I neglect her she pouts.

"I left off where ol' Proph' finished prophesyin' at the old-year party at my house three year ago. I forgot to tell you, parson, thet Mis' Meredith, she never come to the party—an' Meredith hisself he only come and stayed a few minutes, an' went home 'count o' the ol' lady bein' by herself—so they wasn't neither one there when the nigger spoke. An' ef they've ever been told what he said I don't know—though we've got a half dozen smarties in town thet would 'a' busted long ago ef they hadn't 'a' told it I don't doubt.

"Go on, now, Pete, an' finish. After Proph' had got done talkin' of co'se hand-shakin' commenced, an' everybody was supposed to shake hands with everybody else. I reckon parson there knows about that—but you might tell it anyhow."

"Of co'se, parson he knows about the hand-shakin'," Taylor took up the story now, "because you was here last year, parson. You know thet it's the custom in Simpkinsville, at the old-year party, for everybody to shake hands at twelve o'clock at the comin' in of the new year. It's been our custom time out o' mind. Folks thet'll have some fallin' out, an' maybe not be speakin', 'll come forward an' shake hands an' make up—start the new year with a clean slate.

"Why, ef 'twasn't for that, I don't know what we'd do. Some of our folks is so techy an' high strung—an' so many of 'em kin, which makes it that much worse—thet ef 'twasn't for the new-year handshakin', why, in a few years we'd be ez bad ez a deef and dumb asylum.

"But to tell the story. I declare, Dan'l, I ain't no hand to tell a thing so ez to bring it befo' yo' eyes like you can. I'm feerd you'll have to carry it on."

And so old man McMonigle, after affectionately drawing a few puffs from his pipe, laid it on the fender before him, and reluctantly took up the tale.

"Well," he began, "I reckon thet rightly speakin' this is about the end of the first chapter.

"The hand-shakin' passed off friendly enough, everybody j'inin' in, though there was women thet 'lowed thet they had the cold shivers when they shuck the city feller's hand, half expectin' to tackle a birdclaw. An' I know thet wife an' me—although, understand, parson, we none o' us suspicioned no harm—we was glad when the party broke up an' everybody was gone— the nigger's words seemed to ring in our ears so.

"Well, sir, the second chapter o' the story I reckon it could be told in half a dozen words, though I s'pose it holds misery enough to make a book.

"I never would read a book thet didn't end right; in fact, I don't think the law ought to allow sech to be printed. We get enough wrong endin's in life, an' the only good book-makin' is, in my opinion, to ketch up all sech stories an' work 'em over.

"Ef I could set down an' tell May Day Meredith's story to some book-writer thet'd take it up where I leave off, an' bring her back to us—she could even be raised from the dead in a book ef need be—my Lord! how I'd love to read it, an' try to b'lieve it was true! I'd like him to work the ol' nigger in at the end, too, ef he didn't think hissef above it. A ol', harmless, half-crazy nigger, thet's been movin' round amongst us all for years, is ez much missed ez anybody else when he drops out, nobody knows how. I miss Proph' jest the same ez I miss that ol' struck-by-lightin' sycamo'-tree thet Jedge Towns has had cut out of the co't-house yard. My mother had my gran'pa's picture framed out o' sycamo' balls, gethered out of that tree forty years ago.

"But you see I'm makin' every excuse to keep from goin' on with the story, an' ef it's got to be told, well—

"Whether somebody told the Merediths about the nigger's prophecy, an' they got excited over it, an' forbid the city feller the house, I don't know, but he never was seen goin' there after that night, though he stayed in town right along for two weeks, at the end of which time he disappeared from the face o' the earth—an' she along with him.

"An' that's all the story, parson. That's three year ago lackin' two weeks, an' nobody ain't seen or heard o' May Day Meredith from that day to this.

"Of co'se girls have run away with men, an' it turned out all right—but they wasn't married men. Nobody s'picioned he was married tell it was all over an' Harry Conway he heard it in St. Louis, an' it's been found to be true. An' there's a man living in Texarkana thet testified thet he was called in to witness what he b'lieved to be a genuine weddin', where the preacher claimed to come from Little Rock, an' he married May Day to that man, standin' in the blue cashmere dress she run away in. She was married by the 'Piscopal prayer-book, too, which is the only thing I felt real hard against May Day for consentin' to—she being well raised, a hard-shell Baptist.

"But o' co'se the man thet could git a girl to run away with him could easy get her to change her religion."

"Hold up there, Dan'l!" interrupted old man Taylor. "Hold on, there! Not always! It's a good many years sence my ol' woman run away to marry me, but she was a Methodist, an' Methodist she's turned me, though I've been dipped, thank God!"

"Well, of co'se, there's exceptions. An' I didn't compare you to the man I'm a-talkin' about, nohow. Besides, Methodist an' 'Piscopal are two different things," returned McMonigle.

"But, tellin' my story—or at least sence I've done told the story, I'll tell parson all I know about the old nigger, Proph', which is mighty little.

"It was jest three days after May Meredith run away thet I was ridin' through the woods twixt here an' Clay Bank, an' who did I run against but old Proph'—walkin' along in the brush talkin' to hisself ez usual.

"Well, sir, I stopped my horse, an' called him up an' talked to him, an' tried to draw him out—ast him how come he to prophesy the way he done, an' how he knowed what was comin', but, sir, I couldn't get no satisfaction out of him—not a bit. He 'lowed thet he only spoke ez it was given him to speak, an' the only thing he seemed interested in was the stranger's name, an' he ast me to say it for him over and over—he repeatin' it after me. An' then he ast me to write it for him, an' he put the paper I wrote it on in his hat. He didn't know B from a bull's foot, but I s'pose he thought maybe if he put it in his hat it might strike in."

"Like ez not he 'lowed he could git somebody to read it out to him," suggested the doctor.

"Like ez not. Well, sir, after I had give him the paper he commenced to talk about huntin'—had a bunch o' birds in his hands then, an' give 'em to me, 'lowin' all the time he hadn't had much luck lately, 'count o' his pistol bein' sort o' out o' order. 'Lowed thet he took sech a notion to hunt with his pistol thet 'twasn't no fun shootin' at long range, but somehow he couldn't depend on his pistol shootin' straight.

"Took it out o' his pocket while he was standin' there, an' commenced showin' it to me. An', sir, would you believe it, while we was talkin' he give a quick turn, fired all on a sudden up into a tree, an' befo' I could git my breath, down dropped a squir'l right at his feet. Never see sech shootin' in my life. An' he wasn't no mo' excited over it than nothin'; jest picked up the squir'l ez unconcerned ez you please, an', sez he, 'Yas, she done it that time—but she don't always do it. Can't depend on her.'

"Then, somehow, he brought it round to ask me ef I wouldn't loand him my revolver—jest to try it an' see if he wouldn't have better luck. 'Lowed that he'd fetch it back quick ez he got done with it.

"Well, sir, o' co'se I loaned it to the ol' nigger—an' took his pistol—then an' there. I give it to him loaded, all six barrels, an', sir, would you believe it, no livin' soul has ever laid eyes on ol' Prophet from that day to this.

"I'm mighty feered he's wandered way off som'ers an' shot hisself accidental'—an' never was found. Them revolvers is mighty resky weepons ef a person ain't got experience with 'em.

"So that's all the story, parson. Three days after May Day went he disappeared, an' of co'se he a-livin' along at Meredith's all these years, an' being so 'tached to May Day, and prophesying about her like he done, you can see how one name brings up another. So when I think about her I seem to see him."

"Didn't Harry Conway say he see the ol' man in St. Louis once-t, an' thet he let on he didn't know him—wouldn't answer when he called him Proph'?" said old man Conway.

"One o' Harry's cock-an'-bull stories," answered McMonigle. "He might o' saw some ol' nigger o' Proph's build, but how would he git to St. Louis? Anybody's common-sense would tell him better'n that. No, he's dead—no doubt about it."

"I suppose no one has ever looked for the old man?" the parson asked.

"Oh yas, he's been searched for. We've got up two parties an' rode out clair into the swamp lands twice-t—but there wasn't no sign of him.

"But May Day—nobody has ever went after her, of co'se. She left purty well escorted, an' ef her own folks never follered her, 'twasn't nobody else's business. Her mother 'ain't never mentioned her name sence she left—to nobody."

"Yas," interrupted the doctor, "an' some has accused her o' hard-heartedness; but when I see a woman's head turn from black to white in three months' time, like hers done, I don't say her heart's hard, I say it's broke.

"They keep a-sendin' for me to come to see her, but I can't do her no good. She's failed tur'ble last six months.

"Ef somethin' could jest come upon her sudden, to rouse her up—ef the house would burn down, an' she have to go out 'mongst other folks—or ef they was some way to git folks there, whether she wanted 'em or not—

"Tell the truth, I've been a-thinkin' about somethin'. It's been on my mind all day. I don't know ez it would do, but I been a-thinkin' ef I could get Meredith's consent for the Simpkinsville folks to come out in a body—

"Ef he'd allow it, an' the folks would be willin' to go out there tonight for the old-year party—take their fiddle an' cakes an' things along, an' surprise her—she'd be obliged to be polite to 'em; she couldn't refuse to meet all her ol' friends for the midnight hand-shakin', an' it might be the savin' of her. Three years has passed. There's no reason why one trouble should bring another. We've all had our share o' trials this year, an' I reckon every one o' us here has paid for a tombstone in three years, an' I believe ef we'd all meet together an' go in a body out there—

"Ef you say so, I'll ride out an' talk it over with Meredith. What's your opinion, parson?"

"My folks will join you heartily, I'm sure," replied the parson, warmly. "They did expect to have the crowd over at Bradfield's tonight, but I know they'll be ready to give in to the Merediths."

And this is how it came about that the Meredith's house, closed for three years, opened its doors again.

If innocent curiosity and love of fun had carried many to the new-year hand-shaking three years before, a more serious interest, not unmixed with curiosity, swelled the party tonight.

It was a mile out of town. The night was stormy, the roads were heavy, and most of the wagons without cover; but the festive spirit is impervious to weather the world over, and there were umbrellas in Simpkinsville, and overcoats and "tarpaulins."

Everybody went. Even certain good people who had not previously been able to master their personal animosities sufficiently to resolve to present themselves for the midnight hand-shaking, and had decided to nurse their grievances for another year, now promptly agreed to bury their little hatchets and join the party.

To storm a citadel of sorrow, whether the issue should prove a victory for besiegers or besieged, was no slight lure to a people whose excitements were few, and whose interests were limited to the personal happenings of their small community.

It is a crime in the provincial code-social to excuse one's self from a guest. To deny a full and cordial reception to all the town would be to ostracise one's self forever, not only from its society, but from all its sympathies.

The weak-hearted hostess rallied all her failing energies for the emergency. And there was no lack of friendliness in her pale old face as she greeted her most unwelcome guests with extended timorous hands.

If her thin cheeks flushed faintly as her neighbors' happy daughters passed before her in game or dance, her solicitous observers, not suspecting the pain at her heart, whispered: "Mis' Meredith is chirpin' up a'ready. She looks a heap better'n when we come in." So little did they understand.

If mirth and numbers be a test, the old-year party at the Merediths' was assuredly a success.

Human emotions swing as pendulums from tears to laughter. Those of the guests to-night who had declared that they knew they would burst out crying as soon as they entered that house were the ones who laughed the loudest.

"Spinning the plate," "dumb-crambo," "pillow," "how, when and where," such were the innocent games that composed the simple diversions of the evening, varied by music by the village string-band and occasional songs from the girls, all to end with a "Virginia break-down" just before twelve o'clock, when the handshaking should begin.

It seemed a very merry party, and yet, in speaking of it afterwards, there were many who declared that it was the saddest evening they had ever spent in their lives, some even affirming that they had been "obliged to set up an' giggle the live-long time to keep from cryin' every time they looked at Mis' Meredith.''

Whether this was true, or only seemed to be true in the light of subsequent events, it would be hard to say. Certain it was, however, that the note that rose above the storm and floated out into the night was one of joyous merrymaking. Such was the note that greeted a certain slowly moving wagon, whose heavily clogged wheels turned into the Meredith's gate near midnight. The belated guest was evidently one entirely familiar with the premises, for notwithstanding the darkness of the night, the ponderous wheels turned accurately into the curbe beyond the magnolia-tree, moved slowly but surely along the drive up to the door, and stopped without hesitation exactly opposite the "landing at the front stoop," wellnigh invisible in the darkness.

After the ending of the final dance, during the very last moments of the closing year, there was always at the old-year party an interval of silence.

The old men held their watches in their hands, and the young people spoke in whispers.

It was this last waiting interval that in years past the old man Prophet had filled with portent, even though, until his last prophecy, his words had been lightly spoken.

As the crowd sat waiting to-night, watching the slow hands of the old clock, listening to the never-hurrying tick-tack of the long pendulum against the wall, it is probable that memory, quickened by circumstances and environment, supplied to every mind present a picture of the old man, as he had often stood before them.

A careful turn of the front-door latch, so slight a click as to be scarcely discernible, came at this moment as the clank of a sledge-hammer, turning all heads with a common impulse towards the slowly opening door, into which limped a tall, muffled figure. To the startled eyes of the company it seemed to reach quite to the ceiling. Those sitting near the door started back in terror at the apparition, and all were on their feet in a moment.

But having entered, the figure halted just within the door, and before there was time for action, or question even, a bundle of old wraps had fallen and the old man Proph, bearing in his arms a golden-haired cherub of about two years, stood in the presence of the company.

The revulsion of feeling, indescribable by words, was quickly told in the fast-flowing tears. Looking upon the old negro and the child, everyone present read a new chapter in the home tragedy, and wept in its presence.

Coming from the dark night into the light, the old man could not for a moment discern the faces he knew, and when the little one, shrinking from the glare, hid her face in his hair, it was as if time had turned back, so perfect a restoration with the picture of a familiar one of the old days. No word had yet been spoken, and the ticking of the great clock, and the crackling of the fire mingled with sobs, were the only sounds that broke the stillness when the old man, having gotten his bearings, walked directly up to Mrs. Meredith and laid the child in her arms. Then, losing no time, but pointing to the clock that was slowly nearing the hour, he said, in a voice tremulous with emotion: "De time is most here. Is you all ready to shek hands? Ef you is—everybody—turn round and come wid me."

As he spoke he turned back to the still open door, and before those who followed had taken in his full meaning, he had drawn into the room a slim, shrinking figure, and little May Day Meredith, pale, frightened and weather-beaten, stood before them.

If it was her own father who was first to grasp her hand, and if he carried her in his arms to her mother, it was that the rest deferred to his first claim, and that their hearty and affectionate greetings came later in their proper order. As the striking of the great clock mingled with the sound of joy and of weeping—the congratulations and words of praise fervently uttered—it made a scene ever to be held dear in the annals of Simpkinsville. It was a scene beyond words of description—a family meeting which even lifetime friends recognized as too sacred for their eyes, and hurried weeping away.

It was when the memorable, sad, joyous party was over, and all the guests were departing, that Prophet, following old man McMonigle out, called him aside for a moment. Then putting into his hands a small object, he said, in a tremulous voice:

"Much obleeged for de loand o' de pistol, Marse Dan'l. Hold her keerful, caze she's loaded des de way you loaded her—all 'cept one barrel. I ain't nuver fired her but once-t."

The central characteristic of the "Big Windy" is hyperbole. Gross exaggeration, which inflates the teller's own abilities, lends itself well to stories of hunting and fighting, because the teller emerges as a virtual superman, the proverbial "half-man, half-alligator." A superb example of the "Big Windy" is Thorpe's "Big Bear" which follows. "A Fight" also illustrates the hyperbole of the "Big Windy."

Thomas Bangs Thorpe was one of the most popular Southern writers of his time. He made his home in Vidalia, Louisiana, a small village opposite the river from Natchez, where he edited the Concordia Intelligencer. *Besides his newspaper work, he enjoyed quite a reputation as a portrait painter. His paintings include portraits of such notables as General Zachary Taylor. The versatility of T. B. Thorpe is further exemplified by the fact that he was an accomplished writer. Today his reputation rests almost entirely on his story "The Big Bear of Arkansas."*

"The Big Bear of Arkansas" first appeared in March, 1841, in William T. Porter's Spirit of the Times, *a New York sporting magazine which compiled stories from Western contributors when the west was young. Thorpe began contributing to the* Spirit *in 1839 and soon became one of its most famous and prolific contributors. Porter considered him a man of decided genius and in 1843 he published* The Big Bear, *a volume of Thorpe's sketches. The "Big Bear" story is an epic of conflict. The awesome feeling of the hunter towards the bear is considered one of the fine points of the epic. Adding to this quality of excellence is the vital personality of the narrator. These elements, plus the colorful dialect of the hunter, contribute a piece of enjoyable reading in the regional literature of the South.*

The Big Bear of Arkansas

A steamboat on the Mississippi frequently, in making her regular trips, carries between places varying from one to two thousand miles apart; and as these boats advertise to land passengers and freight at "all intermediate landings," the heterogeneous character of the passengers of one of these up-country boats can scarcely be imagined by one who has never seen it with his own eyes. Starting from New Orleans in one of these boats, you will find yourself associated with men from every state in the Union, and from every portion of the globe; and a man of observation need not lack for amusement or instruction in such a crowd, if he will take the trouble to read the great book of character so favorably opened before him. Here may be seen jostling together the wealthy Southern planter, and peddler of tin-ware from New England—the Northern merchant, and Southern jockey—a venerable bishop, and a desperate gambler—the land speculator, and the honest farmer—professional men of all creeds and characters—Wolvereens, Suckers, Buckeyes, and Corn-crackers, beside a "plentiful sprinkling" of the half-horse and half-alligator species of men, who are peculiar to "old Mississippi," and who appear to gain a livelihood simply by going up and down the river. In the pursuit of pleasure or business, I have frequently found myself in such a crowd.

On one occasion, when in New Orleans, I had occasion to take a trip of a few miles up the Mississippi, and I hurried on board the well-known "high-pressure-and-beat-every-thing" steamboat *Invincible,* just as the last note of the last bell was sounding; and when the confusion and hustle that is natural to a boat's getting under way had subsided, I discovered that I was associated in as heterogeneous a crowd as was ever got together. As my trip was to be of a few hours' duration only, I made no endeavor to become acquainted with my fellow passengers, most of whom would be together many days. Instead of this, I took out of my pocket the "latest paper," and more critically than usual examined its contents; my fellow passengers at the same time disposed themselves in little groups. While I was thus busily employed in reading, and my companions were more busily employed in discussing such subjects as suited their humors best, we were startled most unexpectedly by a loud Indian whoop, uttered in the "social hall," that part of the cabin fitted off for a bar; then was to be heard a loud crowing, which would not have

Thomas Bangs Thorpe. The Big Bear of Arkansas and Other Sketches, T. B. Porter, ed. (Philadelphia: Carey and Hart, 1845).

continued to have interested us—such sounds being quite common in that place of spirits—had not the hero of these windy accomplishments stuck his head into the cabin and hallooed out, "Hurra for the Big Bar of Arkansas!" and then might be heard a confused hum of voices, unintelligible, save in such broken sentences as "horse," "screamer," "lightning is slow," etc. As might have been expected, this continued interruption attracted the attention of every one in the cabin; all conversation dropped, and in the midst of this surprise the "Big Bar" walked into the cabin, took a chair, put his feet on the stove, and looking back over his shoulder, passed the general and familiar salute of "Strangers, how are you?" He then expressed himself as much at home as if he had been at "the Forks of Cypress," and "perhaps a little more so." Some of the company at this familiarity looked a little angry, and some astonished; but in a moment every face was wreathed in a smile. There was something about the intruder that won the heart on sight. He appeared to be a man enjoying perfect health and contentment: his eyes were as sparkling as diamonds, and good-natured to simplicity. Then his perfect confidence in himself was irrestibly droll. "Perhaps," said he, "gentlemen," running on without a person speaking, "perhaps you have been to New Orleans often; I never made the first visit before, and I don't intend to make another in a crow's life. I am thrown away in that ar place, and useless, that ar a fact. Some of the gentlemen ther called me green—well, perhaps I am, said I, but I arn't so at home; and if I ain't off my trail much the heads of them perlite chaps themselves wern't much the hardest; for according to my notion, they were real know-nothings, green as a pumpkin-vine—couldn't, in farming, I'll bet, raise a crop of turnips: and as for shooting, they'd miss a barn if the door was swinging, and that too, with the best rifle in the country. And then they talked to me 'bout hunting, and laughed at my calling the principal game in Arkansas poker, and high-low-jack. 'Perhaps,' said I 'you prefer chickens and rolette'; at this they laughed harder than ever, and asked me if I lived in the woods, and didn't know what game was? At this I rather think I laughed. 'Yes,' I roared, and says, 'Strangers, if you'd asked me how we got our meat in Arkansaw, I'd a told you at once, and given you a list of varmints that would make a caravan, beginning with the bar, and ending with the cat; that's meat though, not game.' Game, indeed, that's what city folks call it; and with them it means chippen-birds and shite-pokes; maybe such trash live in my diggens, but I arn't noticed them yet; a bird any way is too trifling. I never did shoot at but one, and I'd never forgiven myself for that, had it weighed less than forty pounds. I wouldn't draw rifle on any thing less than that; and when I meet with another wild turkey of the same weight I will drap him.''

"A wild turkey weighing forty pounds!" exclaimed twenty voices in the cabin at once.

"Yes, strangers, and wasn't it a whopper? You see, the thing was so fat that it couldn't fly far; and when he fell out of the tree, after I shot him, on striking the ground he bust open behind, and the way the round gobs of tallow rolled out of the opening was perfectly beautiful.''

"Where did all that happen?" asked a cynical-looking Hoosier.

"Happen! happened in Arkansaw: where else could it have happened but in the creation state, the finishing-up country—a state where the sile runs down to the centre of the 'arth, and government gives you a title to ever inch of it? Then its airs—just breathe them, and they will make you snort like a horse. It's a state without a fault, it is.''

"Excepting mosquitoes," cried the Hoosier.

"Well, stranger, except them; for it ar a fact that they are rather enormous, and do push themselves in somewhat troublesome. But, stranger, they never stick twice in the same place; and give them a fair chance for a few months, and you will get as much above noticing them as an alligator. They can't hurt my feelings, for they lay under the skin; and I never knew but one case of injury resulting from them, and that was to a Yankee; and they take no set to foreigners, any how, than they do to natives. But the way they used that fellow up! first they punched him until he swelled up and busted; then he su-per-a-ted, as the doctor called it, until he was as raw as beef; then he took the ager, owing to the warm weather, and finally he took a steamboat and left the country. He was the only man that ever took mosquitoes to heart that I know of. But mosquitoes is natur, and I never find fault with her. If they ar large, Arkansaw is large, her varmints ar large, her trees ar large, her rivers ar large, and a small mosquito would be of no more use in Arkansaw than preaching in a cane-break.''

This knock-down argument in favour of big mosquitoes used the Hoosier up, and the logician started on a new track, to explain how numerous bear were in his "diggings," where he represented them to be "about as plenty as blackberries, and a little plentifuler.''

Upon the utterance of this assertion, a timid little man near me inquired if the bear in Arkansaw ever attacked the settlers in numbers.

"No," said our hero, warming with the subject, "no, stranger, for you see it ain't the natur of a bar to go in droves; but the way they squander about in pairs and single ones is edifying. And then the way I hunt them the old black rascals know the crake of my gun as well as they know a pig's squealing. They grow thin in our parts, it frightens them so, and they do take the noise dreadfully, poor things. That gun of mine is perfect epidemic among bar; if not watched closely, it will go off as quick on a warm scent as my dog Bowie-knife will: and then that dog—whew! why the fellow thinks that the world is full of bar, he finds them so easy. It's lucky he don't talk as well as think; for with his natural modesty, if he should suddenly learn how much he is acknowledged to be ahead of all other dogs in the universe, he would be astonished to death in two minutes. Strangers, the dog knows a bar's way as well as a horse-jockey knows a woman's: he always barks at the right time, bites at the exact place, and whips without getting a scratch. I never could tell whether he was made expressly to hunt bar, or whether bar was made expressly for him to hunt: any way, I believe they were ordained to go together as naturally as Squire Jones says a man and women is, when he moralizes in marrying a couple. In fact, Jones once said, said he, 'Marriage according to law is a civil contract of divine origin; it's common to all countries as well as Arkansaw, and people take to it as naturally as Jim Doggett's Bowie-knife takes to bar.'"

"What season of the year do your hunts take place?" inquired a gentlemanly foreigner, who, from some peculiarities of his baggage, I suspected to be an Englishman, on some hunting expedition, probably at the foot of the Rocky Mountain.

"The season for bar hunting, stranger," said the man of Arkansaw, "is generally all the year round, and the hunts take place about as regular. I read in history that varmints have their fat season, and their lean season. That is not the case in Arkansaw, feeding as they do upon the spontenacious productions of the sile, they have one continued fat season the year round: though in winter things in this way is rather more greasy than in summer, I must admit. For that reason bar with us run in warm weather, but in winter, they only waddle. Fat, fat! it's an enemy to speed; it tames everything that has plenty of it. I have seen wild turkeys, from its influence, as gentle as chickens. Run a bar in this fat condition, and the way it improves the critter for eating is amazing; it sort of mixes the ile up with the meat, until you can't tell t'other from which. I've done this often. I recollect one perty morning in particular, of putting an old fellow on the stretch, and considering the weight he carried, he run well. But the dogs soon tired him down, and when I came up with him wasn't he in a beautiful sweat—I might say fever; and then to see his tongue sticking out of his mouth a foot, and his sides sinking and opening like a bellows, and his cheeks so fat he couldn't look cross. In this fix I blazed at him, and pitch me naked into a briar patch if the steam didn't come out of the bullet-hole ten foot in a straight line. The fellow, I reckon, was made on the high-pressure system, and the lead sort of bust his biler."

"That column of steam was rather curious, or else the bear must have been warm," observed the foreigner, with a laugh.

"Stranger, as you observe, that bar was WARM, and the blowing off of the steam show'd it, and also how hard the varmint had been run. I have no doubt if he had kept on two miles farther his insides would have been stewed; and I expect to meet with a varmint yet of extra bottom, who will run himself into a skinfull of bar's grease: it is possible, much onlikelier things have happened."

"Whereabouts are these bears so abundant?" inquired the foreigner, with increasing interest.

"Why, stranger, they inhabit the neighbourhood of my settlement, one of the prettiest places on old Mississippi—a perfect location, and no mistake; a place that had some defects until the river made the 'cutoff' at 'Shirt-tail bend,' and that remedied the evil, as it brought my cabin on the edge of the river—a great advantage in wet weather, I assure you, as you can now roll a barrel of whiskey into my yard in high water from a boat, as easy as falling off a log. It's a great improvement, as toting it by hand in a jug, as I used to do, evaporated it too fast, and it became expensive. Just stop with me, stranger, a month or two, or a year if you like, and you will appreciate my place. I can give you plenty to eat; for beside hog and hominy, you can have bar-ham, and bar-sausages, and a mattress of bar-skins to sleep on, and a wildcat-skin, pulled off hull, stuffed with corn-shucks, for a pillow. That bed would put you to sleep if you had the rheumatics in every joint in your body. I call that ar bed a quietus. Then look at my land—the government ain't got another such a piece to dispose of. Such timber, and such bottom land, why you can't preserve any thing natural you plant in it unless you pick it young, things thar will grow out of shape so quick. I once planted in those diggins a few potatoes and beets: they took a fine start, and after that an ox team couldn't have kept them from growing. About that time I went off to old Kentucky on business, and did not hear from them things in three months, then I accidentally stumbled on a fellow who had stopped at my place with an idea of buying me out. 'How did you like things?' said I. 'Pretty well,' said he; 'the cabin is convenient, and the timber land is good; but that bottom land ain't worth the first red cent.' 'Why?' said I. 'Cause,' said he. 'Cause what?' said I, 'Cause it's full of cedar stumps and Indian mounds,' said he, 'and it can't be cleared.' 'Lord,' said I, 'them ar ''cedar stumps'' is beets, and them ar ''Indian mounds'' ar tater hills.' As I expected, the crop was overgrown and useless: the sile is too rich, and planting in Arkansaw is dangerous. I had a good-sized sow killed in that bottom land. The old thief stole an ear of corn, and took it down where she slept at night to eat. Well, she left a grain or two on the ground, and lay down on them: Before morning the corn shot up, and the percussion killed her dead. I don't plant any more: natur intended Arkansas for a hunting ground, and I go according to natur.''

The questioner who thus elicted the description of our hero's settlement, seemed to be perfectly satisfied, and said no more; but the ''Big Bar of Arkansaw'' rambled on from one thing to another with a volubility perfectly astonishing, occasionally disputing with those around him, particularly with a ''live Sucker'' from Illinois, who had the daring to say that our Arkansaw friend's stories ''Smelt rather tall.''

In this manner the evening was spent; but conscious that my own association with so singular a personage would probably end before morning, I asked him if he would not give me a description of some particular bear hunt; adding that I took great interest in such things, though I was no sportsman. The desire seemed to please him, and he squared himself round towards me, saying, that he could give me an idea of a bar hunt that was never beat in this world, or in any other. His manner was so singular, that half of his story consisted in his excellent way of telling it, the great peculiarity of which was, the happy manner he had of emphasizing the prominent parts of his conversation.

''Stranger,'' said he, ''in barhunts I am numerous, and which particular one, as you say, I shall tell, puzzles me. There was the old she devil I shot at the Hurricane last fall—then there was the old hog thief I popped over at the Bloody Crossing, and then—Yes, I have it! I will give you an idea of a hunt, in which the greatest bar was killed that ever lived, none excepted: about an old fellow that I hunted, more or less, for two or three years; and if that ain't a particular bar hunt, I ain't got one to tell. But in the first place, stranger, let me say, I am pleased with you, because you ain't ashamed to gain information by asking and listening, and that's what I say to Countess's pups, because they are continually nosing about; and though they stick it sometimes in the wrong place, they gain experience any how, and may learn something useful to boot. Well, as I was saying about this big bar, you see when I and some more first settled in our region, we were driven to hunting naturally; we soon liked it, and after that we found it an easy matter to make the thing our business. One old chap who had pioneered 'afore us, gave us to understand that we had settled in the right place. He dwelt upon its merits until it was affecting, and showed us, to prove his assertions, more marks on the sassafras trees than I ever saw on a tavern door 'lection time. 'Who keeps that ar reckoning?' said I. 'The bar,' said he. 'What for?' said I. 'Can't tell,' said he; 'but so it is: the bar bite the bark and wood too, at the highest point from the ground they can reach, and you can tell, by the marks!' said he, 'the length of the bar to an inch.' 'Enough,' said I; 'I've learned something here a'ready, and I'll put it in practice.'

''Well stranger, just one month from that time I killed a bar, and told its exact length before I measured it, by those very marks; and when I did that, I swelled up considerable—I've been a prouder man ever since. So I went on, larning something every day, until I was reckoned a buster, and allowed to be decidedly the best bar hunter in my district; and that is a reputation as much harder to earn than to be reckoned first man in Congress, as an iron ramrod is harder than a toadstool. Did the varmints grow over-cunning by being fooled with by green-horn hunters, and by this means get troublesome, they send for me as a matter of course; and thus I do my own hunting, and most of my neighbours'. I walk into the varmints though, and it has become about as much the same to me as drinking. It is told in two sentences—a bar is started, and he is killed. The thing is somewhat monotonous now—I know just how much they will run, where they will tire, how much they will growl, and what thundering time I will have in getting them home. I could give you this history of the chase with all particulars at the commencement, I know the signs so well—Stranger, I'm certain. Once I met with a match though, and

I will tell you about it; for a common hunt would not be worth relating.

"On a fine fall day, long time ago, I was trailing about for bar, and what should I see but fresh marks on the sassafras trees, about eight inches above any in the forests that I know of. Says I, 'them marks is a hoax, or it indicates the d—t bar that was ever grown.' In fact, stranger, I couldn't believe it was real, and I went on. Again I saw the same marks at the same height, and I knew the thing lived. The conviction came home to my soul like an earthquake. Says I, 'here is something a-purpose for me: that bar is mine, or I give up the hunting business.' The very next morning what should I see but a number of buzzards hovering over my cornfield. 'The rascal has been there!' said I, 'for that sign is certain'; and, sure enough, on examing, I found the bones of what had been as beautiful a hog the day before, as was ever raised by a Buckeye. Then I tracked the critter out of the field to the woods, and all the marks he left behind, showed me that he was the bar.

"Well, stranger, the first fair chance I ever had with that big critter I saw him no less than three distinct times at a distance: the dogs run him over eighteen miles and broke down, my horse gave out, and I was as nearly used up as a man can be, made on my principle, which is patent. Before this adventure, such things were unknown to me as possible; but, strange as it was, that bar got me used to it before I was done with him; for he got so at last, that he would leave me on a long chase quite easy. How he did it, I never could understand. That bar runs at all, is puzzling; but how this one could tire down and bust up a pack of hounds and a horse, that were used to overhauling everything they started after in no time, was past my understanding. Well, stranger, that bar finally got so sassy, that he used to help himself to a hog off my premises whenever he wanted one; the buzzards followed after what he left, and so between bar and buzzard, I rather think I was out of pork.

"Well, missing that bar so often took hold of my vitals, and I wasted away. The thing had been carried too far, and it reduced me in flesh faster than an ager. I would see that bar in every thing I did: he hunted me, and that, too, like a devil, which I began to think he was. While in this fix, I made preparations to give him a last brush, and be done with it. Having completed every thing to my satisfaction, I started at sunrise, and to my great joy, I discovered from the way the dogs run, that they were near him; finding his trail was nothing, for that had become as plain to the pack as a turnpike road. On we went, and coming to an open country, what should I see but the bar very leisurely ascending a hill, and the dogs close at his heels, either a match for him in speed, or else he did not care to get out of their way—I don't know which. But wasn't he a beauty, though? I loved him like a brother.

"On he went, until he came to a tree, the limbs of which formed a crotch about six feet from the ground. Into this crotch he go and seated himself, the dogs yelling all around it; and there he sat eyeing them as quiet as a pond in low water. A green-horn friend of mind, in company, reached shooting distance before me, and blazed away, hitting the critter in the centre of his forehead. The bar shook his head as the ball struck it, and then walked down from that tree as gently as a lady would from a carriage. 'Twas a beautiful sight to see him do that—he was in such a rage that he seemed to be as little afraid of the dogs as if they had been sucking pigs; and the dogs warn't slow in making a ring around him at a respectful distance, I tell you; even Bowie-knife, himself, stood off. Then the way his eyes flashed—why the fire of them would have singed a cat's hair; in fact that bar was in a wrath all over. Only one pup came near him, and he was brushed out so totally with the bar's left paw, that he entirely disappeared; and that made the old dogs more cautious still. In the mean time, I came up, and taking deliberate aim as a man should do, at his side, just back of his foreleg, if my gun did not snap, call me a

coward, and I won't take it personal. Yes, stranger, it snapped, and I could not find a cap about my person. While in this predicament, I turned round to my fool friend—says I, 'Bill, you're an ass—you're a fool—you might as well have tried to kill that bar by barking the tree under his belly, as to have done it by hitting him in the head. Your shot has made a tiger of him, and blast me, if a dog gets killed or wounded when they come to blows, I will stick my knife into your liver, I will—'my wrath was up. I had lost my caps, my gun had snapped, the fellow with me had fired at the bar's head, and I expected every moment to see him close in with the dogs, and kill a dozen of them at least. In this thing I was mistaken, for the bar leaped over the ring formed by the dogs, and giving a fierce growl, was off—the pack, of course, in full cry after him. The run this time was short, for coming to the edge of a lake the varmint jumped in, and swam to a little island in the lake, which it reached just a moment before the dogs. 'I'll have him now,' said I, for I had found my caps in the lining of my coat—so rolling a log into the lake, I paddled myself across to the island, just as the dogs had cornered the bar in a thicket. I rushed up and fired—at the same time the critter leaped over the dogs and came within three feet of me, running like mad; he jumped into the lake, and tried to mount the log I had just deserted, but every time he got half his body on it, it would roll over and send him under; the dogs, too, got around him, and pulled him about, and finally Bowie-knife, clenched with him, and they sunk into the lake together. Stranger, about this time, I was excited, and I stripped off my coat, drew my knife, and intended to have taken a part with Bowie-knife myself, when the bar rose to the surface. But the varmint staid under—Bowie-knife came up alone, more dead than alive, and with the pack came ashore. 'Thank God,' said I, 'the old villain has got his deserts at last.' Determined to have the body, I cut a grape-vine for a rope, and dove down where I could see the bar in the water, fastened my queer rope to his leg, and fished him, with great difficulty, ashore. Stranger, may I be chawed to death by young alligators, if the thing I looked at wasn't a she bar, and not the old critter after all. The way matters got mixed on that island was onaccountably curious, and thinking of it made me more than ever convinced that I was hunting the devil himself. I went home that night and took to my bed—the thing was killing me. The entire team of Arkansaw in bearhunting, acknowledged himself used up, and the fact sunk into my feelings like a snagged boat will in the Mississippi. I grew as cross as a bar with two cubs and a sore tail.

The thing got out 'mong my neighbours, and I was asked how come on that individual that never lost a bar when once started? and if that same individu-al didn't wear telescopes when he turned a she bar, of ordinary size, into an old he one, a little larger than a horse? 'perhaps,' said I, 'friends'—getting wrathy—'perhaps you want to call somebody a liar,' 'Oh, no,' said they, 'we only heard such things as being rather common of late, but we don't believe one word of it; oh, no,' and then they would ride off and laugh like so many hyenas. It was too much, and I determined to catch that bar, go to Texas, or die,—and I made my preparations accordingly. I had the pack shut up and rested. I took my rifle to pieces and iled it. I put caps in every packet about my person, for fear of the lining. I then told my neighbours, that on Monday morning—naming the day—I would start THAT BAR, and bring him home with me, or they might divide my settlement among them, the owner having disappeared. Well, stranger, on the morning previous to the great day of my hunting expedition, I went into the woods near my house, taking my gun and Bowie-knife along, just from habit, and there sitting down also from habit, what should I see, getting over my fence, but the bar! Yes, the old varmint was within a hundred yards of me, and the way he walked over that fence—stranger, he loomed up like a black mist, he seemed so large, and he walked right towards me. I raised myself, took deliberate aim, and fired. Instantly the varmint wheeled, gave a yell, and walked through the fence like a falling tree would through a cobweb. I started after, but was tripped up by inexpressibles, which either from habit, or the excitement of moment, were about my heels, and before I had gathered myself up, I heard the old varmint groaning in a thicket near by, like a thousand sinners, and by the time I reached him he was a corpse. Stranger, it took five men and myself to put that carcass on a mule's back, and old long-ears waddled under the load, as if he was foundered in every leg of his body and with a common whopper of a bar, he would have trotted off, and enjoyed himself. 'Twould astonish you to know how big the spread of his skin, and the way it used to cover my bar mattress, and leave several feet on each side to tuck up, would have delighted you. It was in fact a creation bar, and if it had lived in Samson's time, and had met him, in a fair fight, it would have licked him in the twinkling of a dicy-box. But, strangers, I never like the way I hunted, and missed him. There is something curious about it, I could never understand,—and I never was satisfied at this giving in so easy at last. Perhaps, he had heard of my preparations to hunt him the next day, so he jist come in, like Capt. Scott's coon, to save his wind to grunt with in dying; but that ain't likely. My private opinion is that bar was an unhuntable bar and died when his time come."

When the story was ended, our hero set some minutes with his auditors in a grave silence; I say there was a mystery to him connected with the bear whose death he had just related, that had evidently made a strong impression on his mind. It was also evident that there was some superstitious awe connected with the affair,—a feeling common with all "children of the wood," when they meet with any thing out of their everyday experience. He was the first one, however, to break the silence, and jumping up, he asked all present to "liquor" before going to bed,—a thing which he did, with a number of companions, evidently to his heart's content.

Long before day, I was put ashore at my place of destination, and I can only follow with the reader, in imagination, our Arkansas friend, in his adventures at the "Forks of Cypress" on the Mississippi.

A Fight

James R. Masterson earned his Doctor of Philosophy degree at Harvard University and later became an associate professor of English at Hillsdale College, Michigan. His book contributes abundantly to the regional literature of Arkansas.

James R. Masterson. *Arkansas Folklore* (Little Rock, Rose, 1974).

At a landing on the Arkansas shore of the Mississippi the wharf consisted of two moored flatboats, constantly butting their heads together as the water rose or fell. The teller of the tale was a passenger on a steam boat which made a stop at this improvised wharf. As soon as the steamboat was moored along side this floating wharf, the rush to board her was tremendous. One man, dressed in a hunting shirt of coarse homespun, and coonskin cap, with a knife, something like that which sailors wear, sticking in his girdle, was the first to get on the plank that led from the flatboat to the steamer, and in his hurry to get on board, he was pushed into the water by a gigantic fellow in a bear skin coat, a coarse wool hat, and a pair of green baize leggings. The immersion of the gentleman in the hunting shirt was altogether accidental, but it was sufficient foundation, in the estimation of the cavaliers of Arkansas, for the tournament ground to be marked off, and the trumpets to blow "largesse" to the knights of the coonskin cap and the green baize leggings.

As soon as the dunked man arose from the top of the mulatto colored river, he clenched one hand above his head, and hallowed, "Hold on there—you thin milk-livered skunk! Hold on till I get on shore, and may I be cut up for shoe pegs if I don't make your skillet-faced phizcymahogany look like a cabbage made into sour kraut!"

"See here stranger," replied the offender, "your dunkin' was axesidental; but if you want a tussel I am har—just like a fish on a cat-fish's back!"

"The plank was mine by seniority, as the doctors say, old cat skinner, and may I be ground into gunpowder, if I don't light on to you like a bull bat on a gallinipper," remarked the dripping man, as he shook himself like a Newfoundland dog, and stepped on shore.

"Stranger," said the causer of the accident, while his eye gleamed like that of an enraged panther, and his fists clenched so forcibly that his nails were driven into the palms of his hands, "perhaps you don't know that I'm the man that fought with Wash. Coffee, and dirked wild Jule Lynch?"

"May I be run on a sawyer, and may my brains fall down into my boot heels as I am walking up a stony hill, if I care if you had a rough and tumble with the devil. You pushed me off the plank and you must fight," was the peaceable reply of the wet gentleman.

"See here man," said the opponent of Wash. Coffee, as he bared his breast and pointed to a large scar that ran across three or four of his ribs, "Wild Jule done this, but I laid him up for a time—these big scratches on my face was got through my trying to hug a young bar—and this has been broke twice. I'm a cripple, but if you will fight, why strip and let's be at it."

In an instant a ring was made, and the two combatants, when doffed of their clothing, looked like middle aged Titans, preparing for battle. The youngest, who had fallen into the water, was about twenty-eight years of age, and his opponent was thirty-four or five. With eyes made fiery by anger, and lips quivering with intense passion, the youngest dealt his adversary a tremendous blow in the breast. Until this affront the elder man had maintained a strange coolness, and manifested a disposition rather in favor of an apology than anything else; but the instant he felt the blow, his nostrils became white, and twitched like a steed's scenting battle. Closing his teeth hard together, he planted himself for the attack, and as his adversary approached him, he dealt him a fierce lick on the side of the face with his iron-bound knuckles, that laid his cheek bone as bare as though the flesh had been chopped off by an axe. Smarting with rage the other returned the compliment, and as the blood gushed in a torrent from his mouth, he turned around and spit out one or two of his teeth that were hanging by the gums, and with a "rounder" as it is technically termed, he hit a dead, heavy sound, like that of a falling tree.

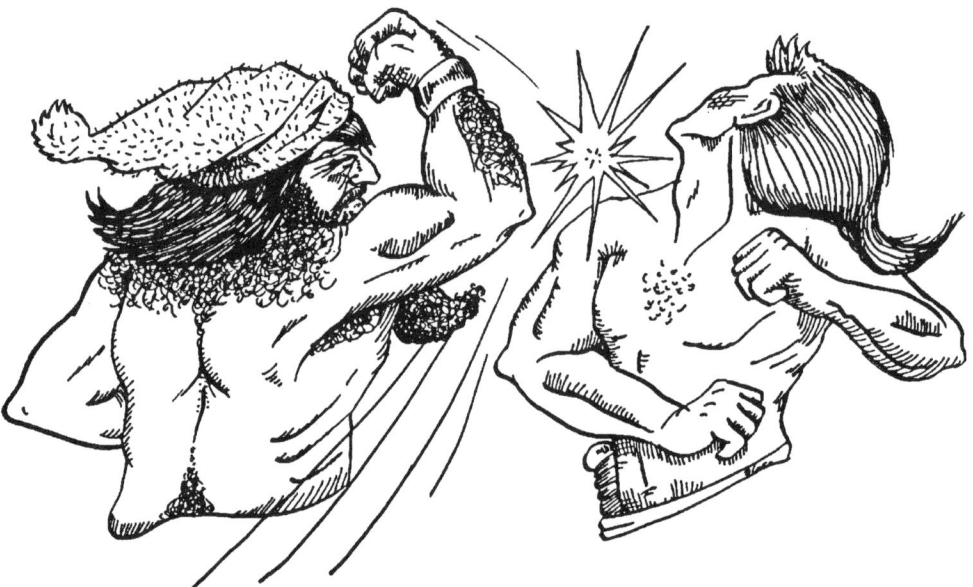

"Thar, I hope he is got enough," said the elder of the two, at almost every word stopping to spit out some fragment of his broken jaw. One of his companions handed him a flask of brandy, and with a long deep drawn swallow, like that of a camel at a spring on an oasis, he gulped down enough of the fiery liquor to have made a common man mad.

"Enough," cried the other party, who had been in a like manner attended to by his friends, "yes, when I drink your heart's blood I'll cry enough, and not till then. Come on you white wired—

"See here, stranger, stop thar. Don't talk of my mother. She's dead—God bless her! I'm a man from A to izzard—and you—you thin gutted wasp, I'll whip you now if I die for it!"

With a shout from the by-standers, and passion made furious by hate and deep draughts of liquor, with a howl, the combatants again went to work. Disengaging his right hand from the boa constrictor grip of his opponent, the younger brute buried his long talonlike nails directly under the eye-lid of his victim, and the orb clotted with blood hung by a few tendons on his cheek! As soon as the elder man felt the torture, his face for an instant was as white as snow, and then a deep purple hue overspread his countenance.

Lifting his adversary in the air as though he had been a child, he threw him to the earth, and clutching his throat with both hands, he squeezed it until his enemy's face became almost black. Suddenly he uttered a quick sharp cry, and put his hand to his side, and when he drew it away it was covered with blood! The younger villain while on his back, had drawn his knife, and stabbed him. As the elder of the combatants staggered up, he was caught by some of his friends, and holding him in their arms, with clenched fists they muttered curses towards his inhuman opponent, who being shielded by his own particular clique, made for the river and plunged in. When about half way across, he gained a small island, and rising to his full height, he clapped his hands against his sides and crow'd like a cock.

"Ruoo-ru-oo-o! I can lick a steamboat! My finger-nails is related to a saw-mill on my mother's side, and my daddy was a double breasted catamount! I wear a hoop snake for a neck-handkerchief, the brass buttons on my coat have all been boiled in poison! Who'll Ru-oo-ru-oo-o!!"

Another field which is well suited to the "Big Windy" is the field of politics. Arkansas has produced her share of political "exaggerations," while molding some distinguished statesmen.

These political tales are characterized by superlatives of the most elaborate, though not always complimentary, nature.

Newt Shafer, Candidate

This colorful example of electioneering comes form a native Ozarker. Wayman Hogue grew up in the Ozark mountain area of northern Arkansas. His home was typical of the mountaineer home—a log house, chinked and daubed, complete with spinning wheel and loom. His education in his boyhood was also typical. A term of two or three months in a one room school was available to the mountain children. Hogue taught in such a school for several "terms" before attending Little Rock University. His book Back Yonder *gives its readers some interesting pictures of life in the Ozark mountains, an area which is just now feeling the effects of civilized, sophisticated society.*

Wayman Hogue. *Back Yonder—An Ozark Chronicle* (New York: Minton, Balch & Co., 1932).

The best is usually saved for the last. The last speaker was Newt Shafer, who was a candidate for the Legislature. Newt was about forty years old, six feet tall, clean shaven and he had coarse black hair and wore a long linen duster. He could not read or write, but his natural abilities were creditable to say the least.

He opened by saying, "Feller citizens, an' gentlemen, as youens all know, I'm running for repzentive, an' these two frien's that youens has jist hyeard is runnin' fer sheriff an' assessor, an' you'll be makin' no mistake when you vote fer 'em.

"Before goin' any furder, I want to say about the Fourth uv July. I've jist been listenin' to Dr. Creasy's speech on this great and glorious day, an' the Doc is right. Hit is a great day. An' when I wuz listenin' at the Doc, I wuz thankin'—Thar is three reasons why we orter preserve this great day. Firs' hit's about the turnin' pint from sprang to summer; secon' hit's gin'ly a clear day an' a warm day, an' the best day in the year to give our barbecues; and last, but not least, hit's the day that orter fin' all uv us with our crops laid by an' a hook an' line in our han's tellin' the fish to look out.''

Mr. Shafer paused here to take a drink of water. My father and Sam looked as if they were highly pleased at this learned way of explaining why we should observe the Fourth. I heard my father tell Sam that he could stand and listen to that man talk all day.

After drinking a gourdful of water, Newt drew a red bandana handkerchief from his ulster pocket, and wiping the perspiration from his face and hands, proceeded:

"Now, feller citizens an' gentlemun, as I have done told you, I am a candidate fer the legislater, an' as most uv youens know, Cal Johnson, the man that's got the job now, is runnin' agin me. Now, who is this man Johnson? Why he's a upstart uv a lawyer that lives in town an never done a honest day's work in his life.

"He wuz sent to the legislater the last term, an' what did he do? Why nothin' cep drank whiskey an' play kyards an' galavant aroun' with furriners.

"Now, gentlemun, here is a few things he wants to do. He wants to build a new court house. Thatar ole court house is a better house than I'm livin' in. Hit's better'n you air livin' in, an' hit's good enough fer many a year yit.

"He wants to build a ar'n bridge acrost Devil's Fork. Now listen here, men. I've swum that ar creek on my hoss a many a time. My father swum it before I was born; my grandfather swum it; an' my boys can swim it arter I'm gone. Nex', he wants to enlargen the free schools. Listen here, fellers, the Devil has never quit laffin' yit at gittin' the free schools in Arkansas. Now, feller citisens an' gentlemun, all these thangs that Johnson wants to do means spendin' money. Hit means more taxes an' bigger taxes fer you to pay. If you send this man back to the legislater, hit won't be long till this country will be dreened uv ever' loose dime in it.''

Here the speaker paused for more water.

Shafer's reputation as an orator had preceded him, and he was not in the least disappointing. My father and Sam, both of whom had been standing with their mouths open, drinking in every word that the speaker said, looked at each other and nodded approvingly. It was noticeable that Shafer's speech was making a favorable impression on the audience. Here and there, out through the crowd could be heard, "'Raw fer Shafer! 'Raw fer Shafer!'"

The speaker continued: "Now, gentlemun an' fellers, if I'm elected, an' I'm shore to be elected—there ain't nothin' that can keep me frum it—here is a few thangs I'm goin' to do. I'm goin' to do away with all the free schools in Arkansas."

There was not much demonstration at this, but the audience stood at attention. "Nex," went on the speaker, "I'm goin' to lessen all the taxes in this county."

A few more shouted "Raw fer Shafer!" and the speaker went on, "Men, lis'en to me. The corn that you work an' raise in your own field is yourn, hain't it? It you take that corn an' grind it into meal an' make bread outen the meal an' eat it, hit's yourn, hain't it? If you feed that corn to yore hawg, an' kill an' eat the hawg, hit's yourn, hain't it? If you make lye hominy outen that corn an' eat the lye hominy, hit's yourn, hain't it? Now, fellers, here's what I got to say. If you take that corn an' make a gallon uv whiskey outen it an' drank the whiskey, why in the name uv God hain't it yourn?"

At this, there was a great demonstration. Whoops, yells, cries, of "Raw fer Shafer!" could be heard from many of the bystanders. It was some time before order was restored.

Shafer continued: "I'm goin' to have a act passed makin' it agin the law fer any revenuer to set foot anywhar in Arkansas. Now, men, I hope ever'body here is my frien'. If you vote fer me, I know you air my frien', if you don't vote fer me, I still want you to be my frien'. I hain't got no grudge agin nobody.

"I hain't got no book larnin'. I don't know how to cipher. I don't know how to spell. I don't know how to read an' write. But I do know what is right an' what is wrong: an' youens can be shore to know that, when I am elected, I'm goin' to do what is right."

By this time the other two candidates had placed three gallon-sized brown jugs on the platform, and the speaker said, "Now, men, me an' these other two candidates have got a little mountain dew here, an' we want all uv youens to come up an' taste it. Hit don't make no difference whether you 'ten to vote fer us or not. We want ever' one uv youens to come right up here an' drank an' be merry."

Tall tales and stories of exaggeration are not confined to the area of politics. Fights, weddings, and just people are often used as principal subjects of exaggerations. Whatever the subject, the language is always colorful and picturesque.

Change The Name of Arkansas

The following speech is one of several versions supposedly delivered on the floor of the House of Representatives in the State Legislature during a dispute as to the spelling of the name of the state. The move was purported to have been the changing of "Arkansas" to "Arkansaw." The speaker of this particular version is supposed to have been Cassius M. Johnson of Pope County.

"Mr. Speaker: The man who would CHANGE THE NAME OF ARKANSAS is the original iron-jawed, brass-mounted, copper-bellied corpse-maker from the wilds of the Ozarks! Sired by a hurricane, damed by an earthquake, half-brother to the cholera, nearly related to the smallpox on his mother's side, he is the man they call Sudden Death and General Desolation! Look at him! He takes nineteen alligators and a barrel of whiskey for breakfast, when he is in robust health; and a bushel of rattlesnakes and a dead body when he is ailing. He splits the everlasting rocks with his glance, and quenches the thunder when he speaks!

"Change the name of Arkansas! Hell, no! stand back and give him room according to his strength. Blood's his natural drink! and the wails of the dying is music to his ears! Cast your eyes on the gentleman, and lay low and hold your breath, for he's 'bout to turn himself loose! He's the bloodiest son of a wild-cat that lives, who would change the name of Arkansas! Don't attempt to look at him with your naked eye, gentlemen use smoked glass. The man who would change the name of Arkansas, by gosh, would use the meridians of longitude and the parallels of latitude for a seine, and drag the Atlantic Ocean for whales! He would scratch himself awake with the lightning, and

James R. Masterson. *Arkansas Folklore* (Little Rock: Rose, 1974).

Although rearranged somewhat, the ritual boasting here is borrowed directly from Chapter XVI of Mark Twain's *The Adventures of Huckleberry Finn,* with minor additions to fit the situation.

purr himself asleep with the thunder! When he's cold, he would "bile" the Gulf of Mexico and bathe in it! When he's hot, he would fan himself with an equinoctial storm! When he's hungry, famine follows in his wake! You may put your hand on the sun's face, and make it night on the earth; bite a piece out of the moon, and hurry the seasons yourself and crumble the mountains; but, sir, you will never change the name of Arkansas!

"The man who would change the name of Arkansas, would massacre isolated communities as a pastime. He would destroy nationalities as a serious business! He would use the boundless vastness of the Great American Desert for his private grave-yard! He would attempt to extract sunshine from cucumbers! Hide the stars in a nail-keg, put the sky to soak in a gourd, hang the Arkansas River on a clothesline; unbuckle the belly band of Time, and turn the sun and moon out to pasture; but you will never change the name of Arkansas! The world will again pause and wonder at the audacity of the lop-eared, lantern-jawed, half-breed, half-born, whiskey-soaked hyena who has proposed to change the name of Arkansas! He's just starting to climb the political banister, and wants to knock the hayseed out of his hair, pull the splinters out of his feet, and push on and up to the governorship. But change the name of Arkansas! hell, no!"

The Spirit of the Times *was a sporting journal, published weekly in New York by William T. Porter for a number of years during the nineteenth century. While its life was rather short, its content was, and still is, a delight to read. Not only is much humor found there, but a big slice of American life and thought is contained in its pages. These excerpts from* The Spirit of the Times *are in the form of Letters to the Editor and are related as actual experiences. Their tenor, however, is most assuredly of the "Big Windy" tradition.*

An Arkansas Storm
Or the Screecher's fight with a painter

The recent storm in Arkansas, where the hail fell in such big lumps as to kill wild geese, brant, and ducks, while flying to their summer quarter in Nova Zembla reminds us of the story of a real Arkansas storm related by one of the "screechers." It was told on board of a Mississippi boat, on her way up the river. A young midshipman, who had made his first cruise, dressed out in complete toggery, and full of the vanity of "one who has travelled," was relating to quite a knot of listeners the terrible gales in the tropics, where a ship's rudder was sometimes blown into the maintop, and anchors twisted into corkscrews before the "first luff" could give orders to pipe down the binnacle.

Spirit of the Times, XVIII, 293 (12 Aug. 1848).

A long-legged, pancake-shaped fellow, like a wire drawn out and then flattened, who wore a yellow blanket coat, alligator-skin cap and leggings, had listened until he felt he should bust unless the bung of his mouth-piece was loosened.

"I say, you young swamp sprout in the unicorned coat and turkey buzzard buttings, talk about gales on the topics—hoo! as the owl says, go to Arkansas if you want to see a gale. Thar it blows, accordin' to the thermometer, forty-five degrees below horizonticklar. As to barometers, compasses, and other instruments, they ain't of no use in Arkansas. I've seed some you see, gentlemen. I didn't go out a week with Squire Hawk, surveyin' and liftin' chains, for nothing—not I. If I'd been edercated, I'd—but no matter, Mister Polk mightn't ben where he is!

This reference is undoubtedly to President Polk

"But about that gale. Joe Gibbs ('Whiskey Gibbs' we use to call him) and I had been out six days on dog river trapp'n' minks; but the luck was bad, and, what was worse, the whiskey barrel was gettin' as low as the Ohio after a dry spell.

"We'd built a small cabin on the side-hill, and one mornin' it come on to rain, so I and Joe thought we'd play a little bluff. By'me by there come such a clap of thunder I thought all h___ and a little more was around them diggins. Trees, big rocks, stumps, all tumbled down in a heap, some flyin' in the air jest as if they'd been feathers.

"Out I jumped, when the roots of a big old oak caught me by the slack of my t'other extremities, and in a minute I was a mile up in the clouds. I managed to crawl round the trunk of the tree and get a seat. Away we went as if fifty thousand high pressure engines and locomotives were givin' us a boost. In this way we travelled two days and two nights. The skin of my bread basket began to wrinkle somewhat gentlemen, and my whiskey tub sounded like a cracked drum.

"Something stirred in the boughs of the tree, and I looked ahead and thar was a bar and a painter grinnin' at each other so lovely! Go at it, my angels, says I, I'll see to the one that is left. And they did go at it. In the mornin' I looked around and could only see the painter—the bar was gone. He'd stepped out, or down!

"But I had to look out for myself. The painter had his eye on me, and down he crawled. I dodged round the lower side of the tree, and round he trotted after me. Only think! five miles up in the air and going at the rate of a whirlwind, and fightin' with a painter! I began to grow dizzy and was about dropping, when the painter caught my right arm in his claws and held on. I got my left thumb in his right eye, and give him a double-shuffle gouge.

"Didn't he yell, gentlemen? Well, some how or other my head got twisted. I looked round, and instead of being on a tree, I was in the cabin by Dog river, and there was Joe Gibbs with his mouth to the bung of the whiskey barrel, holdin' on to my right arm, and I was gougin' him with my left hand."

'Let me up,' says Joe, 'and you shall have half the whiskey.'

"Don't you think the rascal tried to make me believe I'd been dreamin'? I know better. Come, gentlemen, let's liquor after that Arkansas gale—it makes a fellow dry."

A Day's Sport in Arkansas

Willoway, Ark., May 10, 1848.

To the Editors of the Louisville Journal.

Gentlemen: Spring, with all its beauties, has come again. And the world, clothed in the laughing charms of the new-born year, with its birds and flowers, its green leaves and changeful winds, is as joyous, as fresh, and as beautiful, as if it had known but the eighth day of its existence. Its pleasures, like its beauties, never grow old. I have often amused myself in imagining that the nine hundred and ninety-ninth spring which gladdened old Methuseleh's declining years must have appeared as welcome and as charming as the first that smiled upon his infancy.

My pursuits during this delicious season have been as changeful as "the uncertain glory of an April day"—hunting and fishing in all their varieties, my books, and the more serious duties of planting, have each in turn chained my mind in their delights.

It was one of those clear, bright, spring mornings, when not a drifting cloud was seen to break the deep blue of the heavens, or to veil the fiery brilliancy of the sun, that we resolved upon an expedition on the lake to harpoon fish. Three of us composed the party; and armed with our harpoons we quickly proceeded to the lake bank, where my long canoe or "dugout" awaited our movements. We took our positions, Col. R standing in the bow, armed with a harpoon for the first throw at the game, Dr. F. seated in the stern, as being more skillful with the paddle, whilst I occupied a half-way position to assist in paddling, or to relieve guard, as the case might be. We had pushed off from the shore, when a fourth individual gave some decided and unmistakable demonstrations of either being one of the party, or keeping in striking distance of it by swimming; this was no less a personage than "Damon," who was frisking and barking about the shore, in his distress at being left behind. As he had several times before followed the canoe when I was in it, it was resolved to take the gentleman aboard as a cabin passenger without any particular employment, rather than have him swallowed by a hungry alligator, or our sport interrupted by his following after us. Damon required no very urgent invitation, but quickly jumping in, he seated himself by my side, where he remained quiet all day, a silent but highly interested spectator of the sport.

It was a dead calm—all nature was hushed—not a breath of wind stirred the leaves along the shore—the birds were silent, and the tall delicate grass that grew upon the old logs near the bank alone trembled to the whisperings of some zephry, too gentle to break even the polished surface of the lake. The lake itself lay stretched before us in all the magnificence of repose, and like some huge shield of highly burnished brass, it threw back into our face the sun's fiery beams, as they flashed dazzlingly bright upon its unbroken surface. It was indeed piping hot. Not a word was spoken as we silently and slowly glided along; the paddles noiselessly dipped into the water, and the long line of rippling eddies alone told that we had passed.

There stood the Colonel, harpoon in hand, ready to make the deadly throw upon the slightest movement of a fish; not a leaf that silently kissed the glittering surface of the lake, not a minnow that skipped from its bosom, but caused an involuntary movement of his muscles, strung to their highest tension by the breathless anxiety with which he watched for the game. We had been out some twenty minutes, when slowly he raised his arm—one instant of intense excitement as he steadied his aim, and the harpoon is launched with fatal quickness—a plunge through the water, and a harsh grating sound, as of iron against the scales of a fish, told us that his weapon had been true. With lightning speed the handle of the harpoon disappears beneath the water; in an instant our line that is attached by a ring to the bow of the canoe is all out, and for an instant more we are swiftly dragged along by the dying efforts of the fish—but a few more tremendous lunges, that break the glossy stillness of the lake into a thousand wide-spreading circles, and the fish has yielded himself to his fate, rarely offering any farther resistance. The line is again hauled in, and some huge finny monster of the vasty deep is thrown flapping and floundering into the bottom of the canoe. It would be difficult, without actual observation, to form an idea of the number, size, and variety of fish that lurk beneath the still waters of most of the Southern lakes. Some of them from their strength and appearance are really terrible.

The harpoon was with some difficulty withdrawn from our first fish and with it the Doctor then took his stand at the bow. I came after him, and we each succeeded in capturing a fine fish before the breeze, so long hushed, came rustling through the trees, and curling the lake into myriads of mimic waves, and effectually interrupted our sport for the time. We were not at all disappointed at this temporary cessation of hostile movements towards the fish, as we had gradually neared the hospitable home of the Colonel, where additional zest was given to a particularly good dinner by a hearty welcome and fine appetites.

Again we are gliding through the slightly agitated surface of the lake, I being "on watch" in the bow. Picture to yourself the pleasurable emotions of the position—the smallest nerve of my body seemed wrought upon by the intense anxiety with which I peered into the clear depths of the lake for the doomed fish that were to become my prey; my heart was agitated by a thousand alternate hopes and fears as I watched the movements of the fish around me; some were floating lazily upon the surface of the water, with their broad silvery sides glistening in the sunbeams; others would remain perfectly still till almost in reach of them, when, with a noisy plunge, they would, as if suddenly aroused, disappear from sight. But sometimes we do glide within throwing distance of them; then the almost painful impatience as we slowly near our game—the thrilling excitement of the instant when with uplifted weapon we stand calling to our aid all our energy to give force and steadiness to the blow—the hope that animates us and wings the harpoon to its prey —the grating sound of its entering the fish, which announces success, and the violent struggles of the fish, itself—altogether afford emotions of the most thrilling pleasure and the highest excitement.

I had succeeded in striking an uncommonly large buffalo, and the Colonel had by an extraordinary throw pierced a gar through the head, when we entered a small cove protected entirely from the wind by a projecting point of woodland. The water here was perfectly calm, and as we stole noiselessly along through it, I saw a long dark object, which at first sight appeared to be a log, floating a little beneath the surface; but as we slowly approached it, we saw it was an immense alligator, perfectly motionless as if in sleep. I could hear my heart beat as we neared him, and my flesh seemed to crawl as if animated by a distinct and separate life. There he lay in all his huge proportions and his ugliness. I could not resist the temptation, deaf to Col. R's commands not to throw, and, ignorant, or rather heedless for the moment of the danger. I resolved at all hazards to strike. It was a moment of intense and varied excitement; pleasure and apprehension, hope and anxiety, were strangely mingled into a most fascinating compound of feeling. I called up all my strength, and hurled with true aim my harpoon, which instantly rebounded from the back of the monster. He made a desperate lunge, and with one blow of his massive tail washed the surrounding waters into foam, with a noise and effect very similar to a small tree falling into the lake. The water was thrown like a

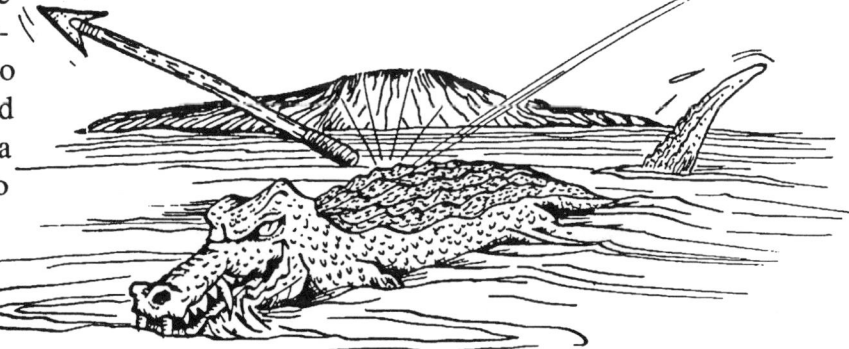

small shower of rain upon us, and after my blow I was fain to follow the example of the others in crouching down into the bottom of the dugout, to steady her amidst the commotion of foam and waves which threatened to upset us. Had I succeeded in sending the harpoon through his almost impenetrable hide, we must inevitably have been turned over, as the line was attached to the canoe.

Many, I fear, will regard the latter portion of my letter as being rather too highly colored with the marvelous; but could any of your readers be fortunate enough to strike an alligator with a harpoon, I feel confident of his vouching for the unvarnished truth of what I here affirm. They formerly abounded in our lake, but civilization is gradually driving them off, though a good many are seen and a few shot almost every season.   M.

P. S.—For the benefit of the uninitiated, I inform you that every spring it is usual for the larger fish to float during certain portions of the day near the surface of the water, when great numbers of them are killed as I have attempted to describe.

"Bar" Hunting in Arkansas

Laconia, Arkansas, Dec. 15th, 1851

Spirit of the Times, XXI, 603 (7 Feb. 1852)

Dear ——, —It was a matter of deep regret to me that you declined coming down with L., and if you only knew the capital sport we have since had, in hunting, I am sure you would regret it too.

We have not failed to catch a bear every day we hunted. The last hunt was a regular encampment; we remained out two days, and complained of hard luck at killing only two bears. I am still of the opinion they were the hardest bears to take I ever got after; they, at first, took to their heels, until they failed, but then they relied on fighting their way through—the last particularly. We started him about half an hour by sun; he ran us until twelve before we could get up to him. A more exciting chase you cannot imagine. He passed within forty yards of me three times during the race; the first time about a quarter ahead of the dogs, the last time about fifty yards only. Several of the pack had fallen from exhaustion, whilst others were just in hearing. About a quarter from me I heard the front dogs come up, and a murderous fight commence—it lasted some thirty minutes. I had ample time to have got up and ended the fight, but trusted to Charles, whom I knew to be in that part of the cane-brake, and who, I thought, would certainly fire every moment. It turned out that the fight was so brisk a one that it had frightened him, until he came to Falstaff's conclusions, "that discretion was the better part of valor," and he took himself the other way.

The dogs, unsupported, had a length to give back, and Bruin again betook himself to flight, with but little over half the pack able to pursue, and that half so crippled and disabled as to leave but little hopes that anything could be done. It was then the Horatii and Cuiratii over again. We could barely hear the chase growing fainter and fainter, as it went directly out of hearing. The huntsmen, all dispirited, had gathered up the crippled dogs, and were assembled on the banks of the Bayou, mourning our loss in killed and wounded, and talking over the soreness of the defeat, when "hark!" 'tis the voice of "Old Thunder," though faint as a whisper! In a moment all is silent as the grave, in anxious listening. That silence was broken by the joyous exclamation—"'Tis he! 'tis he! He comes unaided and alone, sustaining the contest. All his comrades have fallen on the way, unable to continue the fight." It grows nearer! The crippled dogs first prick their ears, then with an effort, rise, and with limping, staggering gait, press on to meet the coming war. Then, like two charging armies, eager for the shock, they meet vindictive. The fight is then renewed, with such determined fury as indicates that each felt the tide of war turned upon himself alone. With hurried, panting strides, up came the huntsmen. Then quick as thought, the rifles' bang! announce the dirge of Bruin, near the precise spot where the chase had opened that very morning, and which must have lasted for thirty miles, at never more than two or three from the starting point.

"Old Thunder" is the same Spartan hound that you were so kind as to give me four years ago. He is in these diggings what Boston was in yours. We want some more of his stock. Can you not be so kind as to give me another? George, your nephew, says you must let him have one of the breed.

Sir, you must yet come down this winter, and let us have a glorious hunt. I do insist upon it! Bears never were thicker in the "Bar State," and it would greatly improve your health. L. joins me in love to you all.

Your devoted,   T. B. F.

P.S. If you come, bring the General. Give him our love.

The Old Bear of Tironga Bayou, Arkansas
Tarney's Hunt

Spirit of the Times,
XVI, 603 (13 Feb. 1847)

Not a hundred years since, Arkansas was a Territory, and in that section of it which is washed by the Mississippi, there lived scarcely a dozen men who professed honesty, the inhabitants generally consisting of outlaws, and lazy rascals who practiced innumerable artifices to avoid working. Travelling about in gangs, each individual carried a hat full of counterfeit bank notes, which he passed off on ignorant persons trading in boats, and on illiterate immigrants on the look-out for land speculations; and it was not a matter of pleasure to those with whom they traded whether they would receive such or such a note, because the holders (I should say the makers) of those particular bills declared them to be current, upon their honor, and if any man, on the authority of "Bicknell" should doubt the same, they were ready to make fish bait of him in the setting of a hair-trigger.

"Bicknell's" counterfeit detector

Among, but not of, this gentry was a "friend of our family," whom I shall call Tarney, an old settler, a friend of the far-famed Mike Fink, and one of whom the money-passers stood in respectful awe, by virtue of his ready aim and quick trigger, which never failed to compensate, in an unpleasant manner, any gentleman who selected his fields or property for his depredations. Old Tarney, conceiving himself under obligations to my father, owing to the successful termination of a certain law suit, extended an invitation to him particularly, and to his heirs—male generally—to spend any length of time at his farm, on the banks of the Big-muddy, where dining on bear meat had ceased to be a luxury. I have often since, wondered why I accepted his invitation, but accept it I did.

'Twas on a beautiful day in the spring of 183-, that I first put foot in Arkansas, whither a lazy, rotten remnant of a steamboat called the "Tuscarora," carried me, in search of adventure. There was quite a congregation on the banks when I landed; there stood Tarney, surrounded by a score of the above-mentioned financiers, who made a point of being "thar," when any hunting was talked of: as clever fellows as need be (honest and honorable, too, for even in the heat and excitement of the moment, they scornfully avoided interfering, in any personal reencounter between a friend and a bear) while a score of fierce, service-worn dogs of the wolf hound species, kept up a deafening hubbub with their glad howls, which were redoubled, whenever Tarney sounded his horn, until the woods re-echoed again. I was received by the "friend of the family" with much cordiality, and by the natives as some curiosity from "furrin parts." After many pros and cons, it was decided that I should go along, under the immediate protection of Tarney, who had taken up bets to a considerable amount, that he himself would on that day, kill the famous old bear of Tironga Bayou, who had foiled all previous attempts.

My arrival had created some delay, and the sun would have braved the sky awhile, if the clouds had not intervened; it was after ten o'clock when we were all mounted and started for Tironga. This stream flows directly westward from one of the thousand lakes which lie in the vicinity of the Mississippi, until it empties into the St. Francis River; on each side of it the cane stood to a height perfectly amazing to one who had before only seen fishing poles. My connection with the caravan was a matter rather of honor than of pleasure to me; I was then a mere shaver of fifteen years, unused to hardships of any kind, mounted on a hard-mouthed mule, who went the way that pleased him best, and carrying, to the great peril of all concerned, a huge rifle, which waxed heavier and heavier each moment. Tarney, with his head bound up in a bandanna, mounted on a huge black horse, rode steadily forward, scarcely seeming to escape the stout boughs which came athwart him, looking a fit match for the most terrible bear that ever decimated the denizens of a pig sty.

We reached the bayou, and the dogs soon opened on a trail. Tarney shouted to his followers to hasten to the stands, and turning to me, he bid me follow him. I kicked my beast, who, taking the hint, made some very tall walking in the direction that Tarney was going, when he disappeared. The horrible din which the dogs made in concert with the yells of the hunters somewhat deprived my mule of his appetite, which before was so keen that he fed upon the cane leaves as we went along, despite the incessant blows which I dealt him between his ears with the barrel of my gun. He wished to go one way, I was resolved on another, and between us, matters grew alarming, as I had my doubts but the Bruin might be upon us at any moment. The brake was so thick that the bear would have been invisible at ten paces, and the howling of the dogs and the yelling of the sportsmen were so reechoed that I could not know in what direction they were. Perfectly bewildered, I dismounted and groped my way on foot, in the direction, as I thought, of the river.

The noise grew louder and louder, and now and then a yelp of agony from some wounded dog convinced me that the "fur was flying" somewhere in the neighborhood, but whether to the right or left, I knew not. About this time an extra crackling of the brush and cane was heard, as I thought, directly behind me, which caused me to rush forward in 1:52 time. After struggling for about ten seconds with my eyes fast shut, I plunged headlong into an open space where there was no cane growing. I stood in an open area about thirty feet in diameter, surrounded by tall cane, which closed up again on my entrance, so perfectly compact that it seemed as though a pair of wings alone could free me.

I was no longer alone! Directly before me, but looking the other way, stood the largest bear I had ever seen, in menageries or elsewhere! In his paw he held a dog, gasping in the throes of death; another was crushed to death beneath his foot, and scattered around, dead and dying, lay a number of our gallant pack. I was deprived by fear of all sensation for a while, when I heard a sharp click and a "D— the gun, to miss fire just at this moment!" I looked up and saw directly in a line with me and Bruin, Tarney standing with his rifle directed at the beast. I fell flat to avoid a glancing ball, no little relieved by the presence of my friend, in whom I had such confidence, albeit his gun did snap; that confidence was fast fleeting, however, when time after time his gun harmlessly snapped. I was convincing myself of the necessity of getting up "a fire in the rear," when old Tironga (for it was he) dropped the dog, and with a snort which set the dry leaves to flying in every direction, he walked composedly up to Tarney and hugging him affectionately, he proceeded, as I was convinced, in the abruptest manner possible, to devour him without salt.

Old Tarney was perfectly cool; as the bear advanced he dropped his rifle, and drawing his "Bar-dissector," as he called his enormous butcher-knife, he received him with due attention. The bear seized upon his enemy's thigh, and with a low, greedy growl, was gnawing it horribly, and his head was soon covered over with the warm blood which spouted from the dissevered veins. Over and over they rolled and plunged; afraid to shoot lest I should hurt my friend, I stood by, and when bruin came uppermost, I regaled him with a furious blow, which he apparently regarded as equivalent to a musquitoe bite. The bar dissector glittered in the sun, which now shone brightly into the arena;

again and again it ascended and descended, carving great gashes in the side of the ferocious beast. At length, too much weakened by loss of blood to continue the battle much longer, Tarney collected all his strength, and driving the knife up to the haft, he bored and twisted it around in the wound, when reaching a vital part, Old Tironga gave a hideous growl and yielded up the ghost.

I knelt by Tarney's side; he had fainted. How long we remained in that little amphitheatre, I know not (for to keep Tarney company, I dropped over myself, to my shame be it said, for I had never a wound, save what the briars made,) but I was suddenly aroused by a loud shout from a number of our party, who had dashed in upon us. Our old friend was conveyed home by some of them, while others remained to attend to the game; as for myself, as I walked along behind the men who carried poor Tarney, I made up my mind that bears would have to grow very troublesome indeed, before I would turn out to help kill, (kill or be killed by) another.

On that day week Tarney was on his legs, or rather on his horse again, ready to rally out with his friends in chase of another fearless depredator well known in those parts as second only to "Old Tironga." It is not to my present purpose to say whether or not I accepted Old Tarney's invitation, but I do agree with my old friend that "bar hunting is mighty attracting!" De Grachia.

Cambridge, Mass., Jan., 1847.

A Bear Hunt

An Arkansas friend of the editor of the Louisville Journal give a glowing description of the pleasures of his lonely life in the backwoods, concluding his enumeration with the following account of a bear hunt:

In the catalogue of my enjoyments I have reserved for the last the greatest. Let me remind you that I am in the State where "the Big Bar of Arkansaw" flourished, and that I have acquired the right to apply for my citizenship by having slain several of the black denizens of the forest. I have known the high excitement of the race course when I had fortunately staked "my pile" on the winning horse; I have felt the deep, absorbing interest in games of chance; I have been carried away by the intoxicating influence of music

Spirit of the Times, XVI, 530 (2 Jan. 1847)

and beauty in a ball-room; and having run the gauntlet of all these, like the man in the play, I had despaired of finding a new sensation,—but I had never then tried a bear hunt. Believe me, in comparison to the thrilling interest and almost painful excitement of this noble exercise, this manly chase, all former pleasures seem "as tedious as a twice told tale, vexing the dull ear of a drowsy man."

Many Englishmen have pronounced the fox hunt to be the noblest exercise that a man can enjoy; and I must confess that few excitements can surpass it—with the music of the dogs in full cry, the exhilarating exercise of riding at top speed a spirited horse, the halloos of the hunters and the merry notes of the horn; but in the bear hunt we have all this, and in the end, instead of the contemptible death of an unresisting little fox, we enjoy a noble struggle, in which the combined energies of men and dogs are necessary to subdue one of the fiercest and most powerful inhabitants of the forest.

It was on a bright November morning that the unusual number of horses tied to my neighbor's fence, and the bustling activity of all around, announced the preparations for an approaching hunt. Old Sol was shining with the more than usual brilliancy of a November sun, the blackbirds chirped gaily as they fluttered across the road, the little wren poured forth his joyful notes as if the spring were come again, and such was the animation and brightness of all around, it seemed as if Nature had clothed herself in her sweetest smiles to resist the chilly thraldom of coming winter. The pearly dew drops that gemmed the grass, threw back the sun's blithsome rays in a thousand sparkling reflections. There was an exhilarating purity, a bracing elasticity in the frosty morning air which sent the blood coursing more rapidly through our veins, with an animation which seemed to impart itself to the horses, impatiently champing the bit as their feet gaily clattered over the half frozen ground. Frequent was the loud halloo, and many the merry jests often interrupted by the deep loud bark of some dog as we rapidly galloped to the hunting ground.

Scarcely had we emerged from "the deadening," which extends some half mile back of the plantations, and long before the dogs had been sent out to commence the hunt, we all three, J., Y., and myself saw at the same moment a bear very leisurely watching our approach. In an instant every horse was spurred into a run, but J., who was better mounted, and is one of the best riders I ever saw in the woods, instantly shot like an arrow by us, and, taking a near cut, succeeded in heading the scampering bear, pursued, by this time, by the whole "team" of dogs, whose long, loud cries made the welkin ring with many a merry echo. At length the leader of the dogs "nipped" the old gentleman, and caused him to think the earth too hot to hold him, so he, for refuge, took a tree. Y. and myself were rather behind, but, as we rushed our way through the tall cane, never can I forget my sensation when first hove in sight. A coon was then the largest animal I had ever seen "treed," but this seemed as if a huge black cow had been suddenly gifted with claws, and had ascended a tree to avoid her yelping pursuers below.

Old Bruin, alarmed by the additional number of men, commenced "backing down" the tree when J. fired, but did so too quickly to take any effect. Then did truly commence the tug of war. The black king of the Southern forest was instantly seized by a dozen fine dogs, and never did I witness a contest so deadly, so terrible. The dogs bravely attacked him on every side, and the infuriated beast dealt at every turn his deadly blows to his assailants. My whole system was wrought up by excitement, every nerve seemed gifted with a separate existence, and each hair stood on end like the quills of the fretful porcupine.

Amidst the roaring of the dogs, mingled with an occasional cry of pain, the growls of the bear, as he tore up the ground in his efforts to shake off his pursuers by his bites, hugs and slaps, Y. fired, but instantly exclaimed, "I have missed him, shoot quick or we are ruined." My gun was now the only one in the party not discharged, but I was laboring too much with the "bar ager" to find my cap-box. Y. kindly offered to cap my gun, and in the excitement of the moment, I foolishly let him have it, but instead of returning it to me, he wheeled and fired, this time wounding the bear, but not dangerously. The pain redoubled the indomitable fierceness of the bear, who now dealt destruction at every blow; Y. again cried, "Reload quick for God's sake, he's killing all the dogs." Whilst they fell to work, I thought of my rifled-barrelled belt pistol, and rushing up close I fired, striking the bear in the "sticking place" as he had one dog in his deadly hug, and another locked in his jaws, whilst many a bleeding victim that still clung to him was there to prove his strength and ferocity. His death struggles were awful, and, after the shot which entered his heart from the pistol, Y. coming up with his knife plunged it into him, and after a few death throes his grasp upon the dogs around gradually relaxed, and he died. As I stood gazing upon his bloody black carcass, I could not but regret that I had so foolishly given up my gun, when I might have had not only the honor of giving the death wound; but also drawing the first blood. But I was consoled by the skin's being awarded to me in the "council of war" held over the dead body, as a proof of my having most largely contributed to his death. Never was a hero of old so proud of the skin of a captured dragon, the guardian of some enchanted castle, as I of this first trophy of my success in sylvan sports. My knife and hatchet were withdrawn from my belt, and soon were they dyed in the blood of my first bear as I assisted in butchering him.

Fishing in Arkansas

Spirit of the Times, XV, 327 (6 Sept. 1845).

Mr. Editor: —I have been a fishing; and as there has not been a fishing frolic similar to mine since the days of Izaak Walton, I beg to report it in your columns.

On the 21st day of June, the longest and hottest of the year '45, Ned Scott and Ned Scott's little son, Ned,—Waller Wright, and Waller Wright's father-in-law, "Old man Gibbons," and myself, arrived at the bank of the "slue" that runs from McLaughlin's Lake into Mrs. May's stream. Here we embarked in an old canoe and paddled up the "slue" to a landing place where the waters of the lake empty into it. At this point we struck camp, and immediately commenced preparations for our night's trout fishing.

Now the trout of this country is not the trout of Long Island, nor the trout of Vermont. Much less is it the Mountain trout of Virginia. But the Western people call it by this name because it approaches nearer that unrivalled fish than any other. Maj. Dillard, a celebrated fish epicure, formerly of Virginia, but for the last twenty years a citizen of this wild country, has pronounced it unequivocally to be the common bass. We are willing to abide his decision, and shall call it by that name.

We were well equipped in every respect, excepting bait. This necessary article had been neglected from the supposition that we could find grasshoppers and worm in abundance. But when we went in search of them, the grasshoppers had all hopped off, and after turning over every old log and chunk within half a mile, we returned wormless to camp. We have no gilded flies out here—no artificial bait of any kind; but just as we were about despairing of finding anything that would serve, someone of the company remembered to have taken bass with young bull frogs. We all started a bull frog catching, but they out hopped the grasshoppers, and we returned again to try our luck with fat meat as a last resource.

It did not fail us. Success perched upon our rods, and we took twenty or thirty of the largest sized perch. They were fried and eaten for our supper. We now could see our way clear, for bass bite more readily at perch than any other bait. But not a bite could we get. Cat, after cat, was, however taken, and although it was against our wishes, we had gone a catting. What made it worse, they were all mud-cats. These fish are far from being dainty; they are slimy to the touch, and disagreeable to the nose. The tongue does not love them, and in short they are the connecting link between the grindle and bull frog;— indeed they greatly resemble a full formed tad pole.

Philosophers have traced the chain of mental existence from man to the humblest plant,—the baboon and the zoophyte being the brightest links. The world doubts. But in the present case it would be folly to disbelieve our senses. There is a regular gradation from the gar fish down to the mud in which the bull-frog croaks. If any one doubts, I will go with him to McLaughlin's Lake, and there prove it. The gar is a mean fish in every sense;—the grindle is meaner still,—no honest man will eat of it twice; the mud-cat is one degree below; and as for the frog,—(no one but a Frenchman would take his part,) every body knows the frog.

The "slue," on which we were encamped, abounded with gars, grindles, mud-cats, and frogs, and another species of the "sportive finny tribe" that I had forgotten, mud turtles. Such was the place to which we had come a bass fishing.

Having fished from supper 'till ten, catching with great success, we took our blankets and laid down, agreeing as we did so, to rise at break of day and commence our sport. But as we retired, the mosquitoes waked up. It seemed as if they had been watching us like a parcel of buzzards over a poor horse. Squadron upon squadron came 'till a countless army collected, every creature of which was his own trumpeter. Five hundred loaves and two hundred fishes would scarcely have performed a miracle amongst them. In vain we fought them off. Forbearance was not a virtue for a moment. Mackinaw blankets were but flimsy shields. We rose and put on a fresh cup of coffee, for sleep was driven out of the woods.

The Goddess Luck had put a sperm candle in Ned Scott's wallet, and a pack of cards in mine. We used them. Fish were staked, won and lost. At two, we ceased playing and resumed fishing. Not one of us dreamed of sleep. But Waller Wright resigned himself with rod and line, to the old canoe, like Shelly's Alastor to the little boat. We asked him where he was going, and he poetically replied—"he didn't care a d—n." It was a solemn hour. Waller had floated to the other side of the "slue" and landed in silence among the flags, and among those who remained, not a word was spoken, except it was an imprecation on the musquitoes. Ten thousand bull frogs were croaking in the neighboring marshes; some were big, and some were little; some shrill and others hoarse; lots were lively and lots lazy; some sputtered out their songs, whilst others gurgled them in their throats. One of those monster concerts in Germany, where fifteen or twenty thousand musicians join in at once, might give a faint idea of the sounds that poured forth from every quarter. Never was such a tumultuous jargon heard upon earth; never will such another be heard, till every tree of the forest bears cow-bells, and the limbs are rocked by a hurricane.

Grave men have pointed out the ant and the bee as worthy examples of industry and content. I'm a grave man now; but I would point you to the frog in preference. Nature affords not another example as bright. There are frogs far in the depths of the flags of McLaughlin's Lake that have never been beheld by the eye of man, reptile, or vermin. Yet they care not. With their noses and eyes above the mud, and their back and bellies below, they croak all summer long. The bee and ant are seen only in fair weather, while the frog cares not a fig for the bright blue sky above, but gladdens and bellows a more boisterous song when clouds and thunder betokens a storm. Go, ye restless of mankind—roll up your breeches—wade through mud and water—part the interlapping flags, and when you come across the lowest frog of the marsh, learn from him a lesson of humility.

All things earthly terminate. Such was the case with our fishing; a red bird's song opened upon us, and we opened our ears with joy to hear it; there is no surer harbinger of day. Just to us I heard its first note. I looked around towards camp and heard Ned Scott exclaim "thank God!" Ned had been keeping the musquitoes off little Ned with a big brush. Poor Ned! he had not been in so bad a streak since the old bull ate up all his peaches and cotton.

There he had been sitting for two hours, keeping little Ned from getting bites—the reverse of the object of his coming.

Morn came, and we made a breakfast of cat-fish. Hardly had we finished when Old Roan and Dr. Dibrell came whooping down the "slue." Old Roan wished to know "whether or not they bit." Old man Gibbons was perched up on a log, and answered that "they didn't bite much then, but they bit like h—l last night." We fished for a few hours longer, but gave it up, catching during our stay, only two bass, which were of the smallest size.

Since then one mortal month has passed. It is now 21st of July. But the croaking of the frogs and the song of the musquitoes are still ringing in my ears. As well might the old soldier try to forget his battle wounds as I the musquitoe bites of the 21st of June. Henceforth I have done with McLaughlin's Lake; and never will I advance "on rod, perch or pole" towards fishing there. But when another party shall be allured by the hearsay of glorious sport—provided I can be free from the fangs of the musquitoes—as the simple Cowper said of Gilpin's race,

"May I be there to see!"

I have the honor, Mr. Editor, to be   W. QUESENBURY.
Prairie, July 21st, 1845.

William Minor Quesenbury, known to his friends as "Cush," was born near Fort Smith in 1822. He earned quite a reputation as a newspaper man and poet in the early days of Arkansas.

Marion Hughes was a native Arkansan, born in Pike County. His Three Years in Arkansas, *however, was written in 1905 from Muskogee, Indian Territory. The flysheet of this entertaining little book announces that "This book sent postpaid to any address on Receipt of 25 cents."*

Hughes, Marion. *Three Years in Arkansaw.* (Chicago: M. A. Donohue & Co., c.1904), pp.32-34.

Fishing was great sport in Arkansaw. They organized fishing parties; sometimes thirty or forty in a drove, and go fishing and camp out for two or three days. They have a great time getting their hooks, lines and baits all in good shape. They take frying pans and grease along to cook them while there, but generally they put a few sticks of dinamite in a box and take that along, and kill their fish with dinamite, and never catch scarcely any with a hook. There was one fishing party went from town, and there was an old fat hotel man along. He had a very fine large dog, that he thought a great deal of, as they always do in Arkansaw. The dog was well trained, and very smart and industrious. If you would shoot a duck he would go and get it, or if you would throw a stick in the water the dog would swim in and bring it out to his master. So they threw a stick of dinamite in the water with a fuse to it. The fuse was on fire. The dinamite struck a brush and did not sink, so the dog started to swim to get it. They all commenced to holler at the dog to make him come back, but all in vain. He swam to the dinamite; got it in his mouth, and started to shore, and the fuse burning all the while. When he got near the shore, they all ran for their lives; as they knew it would explode very soon. They all ran up the river, but the old fat hotel man. He started out through the green briars and brush, running with all his might, and hollering: "Go home, Tige," every jump, and old Tige at his heels, and the fuse a burning. Finally the dinamite exploded, and did not hurt the old man, but poor old Tige all they found of him was about half an inch of his tail, hanging on a green briar, forty yards away. The old man took the piece home that they found, and had it kiln-dried and sugar-cured, and was wearing it for a watch-charm when I left Arkansaw.

But when it comes to catching large fish Arkansaw has all the states beat.

The largest fish I ever saw, read or heard tell of, was caught out of the Arkansaw river below Little Rock. It kept getting their bait and breaking their lines. Finally they had a blacksmith to make a fishhook out of a crowbar; they tied it to a steamboat cable and baited it with a muly cow that had died with the holler horn, tied the cable to a tree and the next morning they had him; they was afraid he would pull a team in the river, so they got all the negroes for miles around and pulled him out on the bank, and hauled him to town in sections. When they cut him open they found inside of him another fish that weighed 200 lbs. (by guess), three fat hogs, one yoke of oxen and an acre of burnt woods.

There was an old gentleman that lived near Hatan Gap that they called Deafy Smith. One Saturday night Deafy's cow got out and run off and Deafy started out on Sunday morning to hunt her. He met Brother Boanurges the Baptist preacher, and told him his troubles, well, said the preacher, you go right along with me to church and when I get through preaching before I dismiss the congregation, I will describe the cow and see if any one has seen her, all right says Deafy, that will save me of walking all over the country to look for her.

Deafy went to church took a seat in the back of the house and waited patiently until the sermon was over, but there was a wedding in the neighborhood that afternoon and the preacher proceeded to announce the wedding; but Deafy thought he was telling his troubles about the cow, and sat holding his hand behind his ear and catching a word once and a-casianly; the preacher advised the congregation to go, as the young man was a gentleman in every respect, but Deafy thought he was talking about the cow all the while, then he began to describe the young lady, but Deafy thought he was describing the cow, he said she was the finest young lady in all the land, was well educated, inteligent, good looking, kindharted, industrious and a good cook, then he stoped and Deafy thinking he had bin describing the cow, he yelled out at the top of his voice and said, she is Bob-tailed and got one spoilt tit.

Hughes, Marion. *Three Years in Arkansaw*. (Chicago: M. A. Donohue & Co., c.1904), pp. 39 - 40.

CHAPTER 3

THE FOLKLORE TRADITION

Storytelling provided the first form of literature for mankind, and folklore has one of the longest histories in literary annals. Long before printed material was made available to man, he was engaging in literary pursuits. The oral tradition of passing stories from one generation to the next is ageless.

The tradition of the folktale enjoys a unique position in Arkansas literature. In the Ozark mountains, folktales have been handed down from father to son for many years. Only since the the early twentieth century have these tales been placed on the printed page. They have long been circulated, however, in the mountainous regions of Arkansas.

The storytellers of the Ozarks constitute a rare quality in the native character of the region. Their art represents a form of recreation unknown to urban people, and storytelling is considered a social accomplishment among the "hill folk." Innumerable hours are spent on porches of rural homes, beside campfires in wooded areas, and on banks of streams telling and retelling the folktales. Vance Randolph, Arkansas' gatherer of these tales, says of them and their tellers, "Their songs and stories and wisecracks are heirlooms, rather than recent acquisitions."

The dialect which is peculiar to the "Ozarker" has quite a background. It carries the name of Piedmont, one of two southern dialects which is exclusively the property of "hill people" —Kentucky, Tennessee, Missouri, and Arkansas "hill" people. With the gradual conversion of Arkansas from rural to urban areas with tourist attraction for the Ozarks increasing, these "hillbilly" tales and their dialect provide the last vestige of an early heritage left to Arkansas.

A presentation of Arkansas folklore would be incomplete without the rich supply of tales provided by the Black people. Like the Ozark tales, these stories come from the oral tradition and have illustrious analogues. And just as the Ozark tales reveal the unique storytelling art of the of hill people, the tales of the Black people contain their own artistic strain of storytelling.

As will be seen, Black storytellers, like their Ozark counterparts, follow a pattern set by tradition. The comical figures and situations reveal a rare ability to laugh at themselves. The matching of wits and emerging as the superior trickster is a conventional theme in Black folklore. The exaggerated Black dialect is also a traditional mannerism found in Black tales. The Negro art of storytelling was developed, like the Ozark art, while sitting on porches, lying beside campfires, and working in fields.

An analysis of many of these tales reveals that they have a long and illustrious history. Some can be traced directly to the ages of Chaucer and Shakespeare. Still others are of the art type of stories—animal stories with moral purposes—which come from Aesop. These ancient backgrounds, interestingly enough, do not emerge as the stories are told. Instead they are told as recent and factual events.

In our sophisticated society of today, one may have some difficulty relating to the themes and particularly to the dialect of both the hill tales and the Black tales. To fully appreciate the cultural value of folklore, one must recognize that it represents a part of the heritage left from the past. That our society has left much of the tradition behind is a sign of progress, but progress does not erase the past. Therefore it is hoped that the voices heard in this chapter will be accepted as echoes of a distant time. No longer can we find among the hill people or the Black people of Arkansas the types or the dialects portrayed in these tales, but they are a part of our cultural fabric.

In searching for new materials for this chapter, I soon discovered that I could do no better than to go back to the original sources and simply add more tales. Every source I consulted had also turned to Vance Randolph for material. It is safe to say that Randolph covered the Ozark Mountains of Arkansas and Missouri to such an extent that he effectively exhausted the available sources. Although some of the tales cite as their sources a Missouri location, the same tale, or some variant of it was also circulated in Arkansas. While Richard Dorson may not have exhausted the available sources of Black Tales, his collection is still the most comprehensive and serves as the best source.

Lore and Legend

Otto Rayburn, in Ozark Country, *added to the store of folklore in a chapter labeled "Lore and Legend." He recounts one typical Ozark tale and provides a discussion of legends which enjoyed some popularity among the hills. From these accounts one catches the flavor of superstition which has been traditionally associated with hill people.*

The Fighting Parson

Otto E. Rayburn, *Ozark Country.* New York: Duell, Sloan & Pearce, 1941 by Otto Ernest Rayburn

The fighting parson is a legendary figure who still stalks the hills after two generations have been laid under the sod. His courageous spirit continues to chill the wayward and warm the righteous. A record of the hill country would be incomplete without a glimpse of Brother Smithers and his hard-shell philosophy. Lorna Ball told me the story of his arrival in the hills, which I repeat here with her special permission.

Ed Sinkler was the bully of the neighborhood. He was tall and muscular, with deep-set black eyes and dark curly hair which, because of infrequent combings, was bushy and unruly. He was known throughout the community as a good and willing fighter. Nobody had ever seen him fight, nor had anybody ever known anybody who had seen him in action, but the idea persisted that he could, and would, whip any man who happened to incur his displeasure.

Ed was a garrulous fellow, given to boasting, and he advertised the fact that he could hold a kicking mule with his bare hands, that he had once twisted the barrel off a rifle-gun, and that he could draw nails out of a board with his teeth. Despite lack of proof of these claims, belief in them grew. Ed Sinkler's prodigious strength became a byword in the community. A man was "as strong as Ed Sinkler" or could "lift as much as Ed Sinkler."

Old Squire Greenup and the new preacher sat on the squire's porch talking. The preacher was a shrewd-looking fellow in his middle thirties who wore his long-tailed black coat with self-concious dignity. Ed Sinkler ambled up the road and stopped before the gate.

"Howdy, Squar," he said.

"Evenin', Ed. Won't you come up an' take a char." Ed came up and the squire introduced him to the new preacher.

"Reckon I ain't got time t' set, Squar," said Ed, assuming a businesslike tone. "I jist come down t' see Brother Smithers hyar. I hearn as how he had driv up t' see you'ens."

"Anything private?" asked the squire. "If'n 'tis, I'll go in th' house an' let you fellers talk by yerselves."

"Jist keep yer chur," Ed assured him. "Tain't nothin' private atall. Th' chances air that hit'll be knowed from hyar t' yander 'fore nightfall anyhow. Hit's come t' my yurs, Brother Smithers, that you've been a-makin' some slurrin' remarks 'bout me, an' I've come down t' ast you 'bout it."

Slowly the preacher rose to his feet. His face indicated no emotion. He was fully five inches taller than Ed, and when he straightened up his head rustled the strings of beans and dried apples that the squire's wife had festooned from rafter to rafter. "I ain't sayin' nothin' one way er 'nuther," the preacher replied quietly. "Until I know whut I've been quoted as sayin', I ain't admittin' nothin' ner denyin' nothin'."

Ed struck an antagonistic pose. "I hearn that you said that ef I'd come into th' meetin' house while meetin' was goin' on 'stead o' settin' outside with my arm 'round some gal, I'd be a more useful citizen t' th' community. Did you say that?"

"Do you do that, Brother Sinkler?" The preacher's eyes twinkled.

"That ain't the pint," Ed insisted. "I ast you, did you say it?"

"You answer my question fust."

"All right, I'll answer you. 'Tain't none o' yer business. Preachin's yer business, not mindin' my courtin' transactions. Take off yer coat an' come out hyar in th' road. We'll settle this thing right now. Yer guilty, an' I don't want to mess up Mis Greenup's flower beds a-thrashin' you hyar in the yard."

"Ed, Ed." Squire Greenup pleaded for peace. "You ain't goin' t' do nuthin' rash, air ye? Ca'm yerselves, fellers, ca'm yerselves." Neither of the men appeared to hear him, and the little squire, his dignity insulted, drew himself up pompously. "Gentlemen," he said in his best magisterial voice, "ef ye fight I'll have t' deal with you accordin' t' th' law."

By this time the preacher had removed his coat, loosened his collar, and rolled up his sleeves. His arms were sinewy, and his shirt, clinging damply to his body, disclosed ridges of fine, pliant muscles upon his shoulders and back.

"May I pray?" he asked quietly of his adversary.

"Pray ef ye want to. In fack, I'd advise it."

The preacher knelt at the edge of the porch. "O Lord," he prayed in a loud voice, "thou knowest that when I kilt Bill Thompson an' Clate Jennings that I done it in self-defense. Thou knowest, too, Lord, that when I splattered th' brains uv Kemp Staples all over his co'n patch that hit wus forced upon me. An' now, O Lord, when I am jist on th' verge o' puttin' this hyar poor wretch in his grave, I'm askin' ye t' have mercy on his soul. Amen."

The preacher arose, took a long-bladed knife from his pocket and began whetting it on the sole of his shoe. Dismally, plaintively, his voice rose in song.

> Hark from the tomb the doleful sound,
> Mine ears attend th' cry.

Now Ed Sinkler was nothing if not resourceful. Living in comparative comfort for thirty years without having engaged in any gainful occupation had sharpened his wits to a remarkable degree. He burst out laughing loudly. The preacher, surprised, stopped whetting his knife. Ed laughed because he had his reputation at stake. To run would be ruinous to that reputation. To fight would be equally ruinous. He had to stand his ground and craftily he chose his course of action. Striding up to the porch, he held out his hand. "Yer all right, parson," he said. "I wus jist a-testin' out yer metal. When I hearn that you'd ariv 'mongst us I says t' myself, "I'm goin' down t' see what kind o' goods that feller's made of fer no feller that ain't got no backbone has got any business in these hyar parts.'"

By this time the preacher had recovered from his surprise. Wrath overcame him. "I want ye t' know I made that thar remark you mentioned. What air ye goin' t' do 'bout it?"

"Nuthin' atall, Brother Smithers. Surposin' you did say it. I reckon th' only way you could feel that way 'bout it is because you ain't ever done no sparkin' settin' outside a meetin' house. Ef you had ever tried it onct, you' never say nary word agin it. Hit's th' most satisfactory courtin'...."

Abruptly the preacher donned his coat. Casually he pulled his chair up beside the one on which the squire had collapsed. "As I wus a-sayin', Brother

Greenup," he said, as if no interruption had occurred, "thar's baptizin' by sprinklin' an' by pourin', an' thar's baptizin' by dippin', but thar's only one uv 'em that's right."

Ozark Folktales

Vance Randolph first visited the Ozark region in 1899. His mission was the compiling of ballads sung by the "hill" people. Randolph recognized immediately the luxury of living in these remote areas where life was simple, relaxing, and comfortable. He son returned and established his residence in Eureka Springs. From his first encounter with the natives, Randolph was interested in their favorite pastime of storytelling. He began seriously collecting the Ozark tales in 1920. In the beginning he recorded the tales in longhand as the storyteller spoke. Later he resorted to stenographers and tape recorders, though the longhand method was always the most successful. Many of the oldtimers were reluctant to tell their stories before strangers or into those "new-fangled" machines. Randolph won the confidence of his neighbors and friends by hunting with them, fishing with them, attending their frolics, and sitting on their porches. The result was rewarding, not only for the collector, but for the Arkansas tradition as well.

Sticks in the Knapsack

Source: Berryville, Arkansas

One time there was a man had three boys, and he sent them out to pasture the goat. Pretty soon the goat says, "I couldn't hold another blade of grass, and it all round me for the pulling." But that night the old man come out to the barn, and the goat says, "I am staving to death." So the old man runs the boys off the place, and they went down three new-cut roads to seek

Vance Randolph, *Sticks in the Knapsack*. New York: Columbia UP, 1958

their fortune.

When the boys finally come home, the oldest one was carrying a magic tablecloth. He'd put it on the table and holler, "Set out victuals!" Quick as a wink there was big piles of good things to eat. Any kind of victuals a body could think of, and the best of everything whether it was in season or not.

The second boy come in leading a magic mule. All he had to do was holler, "Brither bit!" and the mule would spit out a shower of gold money.

The least boy didn't have nothing but an old knapsack full of sticks. So he just kind of hung back, and didn't have much to say.

When the old man seen how the magic tablecloth would set out victuals and the magic mule would spit out gold money, him and the two biggest boys made up their minds not to give the least boy nothing. They was fixing to run him off the place, as they figured it would be good riddance.

The least boy told 'em the old knapsack was magic too, but they just laughed at him. Finally he seen they was going to gang up on him, so he hollered, "Sticks out of sack." Well sir, them sticks just jumped out of the knapsack and beat the old man and the boys pretty near to death, so all three of 'em run off through the woods a-hollering, with blood running down their legs. They never did come back, neither.

So then the least boy got the old place, with the magic tablecloth to keep him in victuals, and the magic mule to spit out gold money whenever he wanted it. He just hung the old knapsack full of sticks up over the fireboard and lived happy ever after.

Source: Originally from Boone County, Arkansas.

Vance Randolph, *The Devil's Pretty Daughter*. New York: Columbia UP, 1955

What Candy Ashcraft Done

One time there was a man and woman come a-traveling through the country with a good team and a brand-new Springfield wagon. They was Yankees, and both of them loved money. So they got a fine coffin with silver handles and put it in the wagon. Whenever they come to a big house the woman would rub whitening on her face and lay in the coffin like she was dead.

The man would go to the door and ask the people if he could sleep in the barn, and then he wanted to put the corpse in the house till morning. He is used to sleeping in barns himself, but he didn't want it said that his poor sister has laid a corpse in no barn, because they come of a good family back home and it would break his mother's heart. So the folks would help carry the coffin into the house, and everybody says it is a handsome corpse. Away in the night the woman would get up out of the coffin and unbar the door, so the man could come in. And then they would rob the house and maybe kill the people besides.

When they come to the old Ashcraft place it was a fine big house but there wasn't nobody living there, only Lige Ashcraft and his wife Candy. They didn't like Yankees much, but no Ashcraft could turn down travelers, and it was coming on to rain anyway. So they helped carry the coffin into the big hall. They give the fellow a good supper and offered to let him sleep in the spare room. But he says no, as he is all dirty from traveling. And his poor sister's jewelry and keepsakes are packed in the wagon, so he will sleep out there in the wagonshed, he says.

Lige and Candy give him the lantern, and then they barred the door and went to bed. After they laid there awhile Candy says, "Listen, Lige, there's something funny about them people." Lige he just grunted. Pretty soon Candy says, "Lige, I could swear I seen that corpse's eye-winker move, right after we set the coffin on them chairs." Lige says it is all foolishness, because he has seen thousands of dead Yankees in the War, and their eye-winkers never moved a bit. "You better go to sleep," says he, "because we got to get up early. That poor fellow wants to get a soon start in the mornin', and we must give him a good breakfast." And then Lige he rolled over and begun to snore.

Candy laid there and thought about it awhile, and then she got up easy and went downstairs barefooted. She picked up a hatchet by the kitchen stove, and she slipped into the hall and hunkered down close to the coffin. After while there come a little noise, and the woman in the coffin set up. She had a gun in her hand, so Candy just swung the hatchet. The Yankee woman fell back in the coffin, and Candy set down on the floor because she was kind of dizzy. Candy hadn't never killed anybody before, and she felt like maybe she was going to faint.

Pretty soon she went back and woke up Lige. When she told him what happened he says she must have dreamed it. But he slipped down to the hall and seen how things was. Then he picked up the hatchet and motioned for Candy to unbar the door. Soon as it swung open the other Yankee come asneaking in. Lige just split his head like it was a pumpkin. The fellow never knowed what hit him.

After Lige lit the lamp, him and Candy just set there awhile, looking at them corpses. Both of the Yankees had pistols and knives under their clothes. The man was wearing a money-belt full of gold, and the woman had three diamond rings in a little sack around her neck. There was a big bundle of greenbacks and silver in the coffin, too. Soon as it got light enough, Lige dug a hole out in the cornfield and buried the corpses and the coffin with the silver handles. Then he drove off down the road, and after while he come back afoot. Lige never did say what he done with them fine horses and the Springfield wagon and Candy had sense enough not to ask no questions. She just scrubbed the hall right good and washed the hatchet. Lige wrapped the money and the rings up in a piece of rawhide and put it in a safe place. He showed Candy where the stuff was hid, so she could find it if anything happened to him. And then him and her set down and eat their dinner, just like they always done.

Lige and Candy talked some about going out West, but they never done it. They raised a big family right there on the old farm. The kids all went to school, and one of the boys made a big lawyer, and finally he got to be prosecuting attorney. After Lige died Aunt Candy just visited around amongst the children. Whenever they give a party the old lady would dress up just as fine as anybody. She had three gold rings, too, with big diamonds in them.

Source: A small hamlet on the Missouri and Arkansas border.

The Devil's Pretty Daughter

Big Knives in Arkansas

One time a traveler from up North somewhere went down the other side of Blue Eye, and he stayed all night at a settlement way out in the woods. Along in the night he heard a lot of fiddling and hollering and stomping, because some of the neighbors was having a dance. The Yankee went over there. He hadn't never been to a square dance before, and he wanted to see how they do things in Arkansas.

The dance was in a long cabin with a puncheon floor. The folks was all good people, but they looked kind of tough to a city fellow. The young men wore their hair pretty long, and they danced Arkansas style with their hats on. Some of 'em hollered a little now and then, just to show they was having a good time. All them boys had big bowie knives in their belts, and the stranger was worried because he had never been around people like that before. The folks up in Missouri told him a lot of windy stories about how it was dangerous to travel in Arkansas, because the Arkansawyers are always a-feuding, and would kill each other any minute and think nothing of it.

When the set was over the boys led the girls over where they could set down on a bench, and they all bowed very polite. But a minute later every man stepped back and pulled out his big long bowie knife. The city fellow thought there was going to be a terrible fight, so he broke right through the crowd. Everybody stared at him kind of surprised, but nobody said anything. The poor Yankee run into a corner far as he could and shut him eyes.

But he didn't hear nothing out of the ordinary, and when he looked around the young men was all down on their knees, in front of the bench where the girls was a-setting. They didn't do no fighting at all, and there wasn't nothing to be afraid of. The Arkansas boys was all very quiet and peaceable. They just used them big knives to pick splinters out of the girls' feet.

Tobe Killed a Bear

Source: Benton County, Arkansas.

Sticks in the Knapsack

One time there was a fellow named Toby that lived up on the Cowskin, and he was the stoutest man ever come to this country. He was near seven feet tall, and weighed three hundred pounds. Tobe was a good worker and a terrible fighter, but not very smart. He would do whatever you told him, so long as he didn't get mad, and then he was liable to do most anything. One Sunday he throwed a fiddler pretty near halfway across the river. The fiddler would have drowned sure, only some of the boys swum out and got him.

The country was full of bears in them days, and a great big bear got to using around the Widow Tarkey's smokehouse. It would bust in the door, and gobble up everything in sight. The widow lived all by herself, and she was scared pretty bad, so she asked Tobe to come over and kill the varmint. He come over all right, but he didn't bring no gun. "The bear ain't got no gun, has he?" says Tobe. "That makes us even, and I aim to fight him fair."

Tobe was one of them fellows that goes to sleep whenever he sets down, and that's what happened on the widow's porch. But when the bear busted down the smokehouse door it woke him up, and he run out there. Him and the bear fought something terrible, and the Widow Tarkey figured Tobe would get killed sure. But after while he come back up the path. "Did you kill the critter?" says the widow. "I reckon not, ma'am," says Tobe, "but he won't bother your smokehouse no more," and with that he throwed about fifty pounds of bear-meat down on the porch. Tobe had tore one of the bear's legs right off, just pulled it out by the roots!

Next day the boys follered the trail down the river bank, and they found the bear in a cave, but he was dead. One on his front legs was gone, all right, tore off right at the shoulder. The varmint had spilled a barrel of blood, and that's what killed him.

One finds a distinct similarity to Beowulf here, even to the detail of nailing up the sritter's arm as a trophy

Mostly the folks figured it was a lie, because everybody knows there ain't no man stout enough to pull a bear's leg off like it was a June bug. They seen the leg, all right, nailed up over the smokehouse door, with claws a-sticking out four inches long. "That don't prove nothing," says Wes Galbraith, "they got elk horns nailed on the tavern at Pea Ridge, but nobody claims they tore 'em off a live elk bare-handed." There was considerable talk about it. Tobe says this is a free country, and folks can believe whatever they want. But if anybody calls him a liar he will pull their arms and legs off one at a time, right in front of the courthouse. Wes Galbraith and them Rutledge boys didn't have no more to say after that.

Nobody ever did find out just what happened, and Tobe's been dead for fifty years. But there's old settlers around here yet that believe Tobe did pull the bear's leg off, just like he told the Widow Tarkey.

Source: Farmington, Arkansas.

The Well Digger

Vance Randolp, *The Talking Turtle*. New York: Columbia UP, 1957

One time there was a fellow named Buck Price, that was digging a well out in the pasture. When he went to work one morning he seen where the bank had caved in, so the hole was half full of rocks and dirt. Buck hung his hat and coat on the fence same as always, but everything looked mighty discouraging, and he didn't feel like working anyhow. Pretty soon he throwed the pick and shovel under some bushes. Just then the Starbuck boys come along with a jug, and so they all went a-fishing over on Big Piney.

The sun was about two hours high when one of the neighbors come through the pasture, a-looking for a colt. There was Buck's hat and coat on the fence, and no tools in sight, so he figured Buck must be under the cave-in. Pretty soon guns was a-firing and horns blowing all over the neighborhood, just like somebody's house was afire. Buck's woman was hollering louder'n a steam whistle, because she thought poor Buck was dead, sure. Folks come a-running to see what was the matter, and they all began to throw rocks and dirt out of the well.

With everybody working together that way, it wasn't no time till they cleaned out the hole, but they didn't find no corpse. Pretty soon a boy stumbled onto the pick and shovel, where Buck had throwed them under the bushes. The folks didn't know what to think. Most of the neighbors went back home, soon as they found out for sure that Buck wasn't in the well. Some of them was pretty mad, but they didn't say much.

After while here come Buck a-walking up the land. Him and the Starbucks had drunk the big jug plumb dry, and he had a nice string of catfish. Buck was feeling pretty good, and when they told him about what happened he laughed like a fool. "It sure was neighborly of them boys to clean out my well," says he. "I reckon it would have took me a week to get all them rocks out by myself."

Most of the folks never opened their mouth, but they figured that Buck must have hid out a-purpose, just to fool the neighbors into doing all the work for him. Everybody knows a fellow like Buck Price don't go fishing without his hat on, unless there's some special reason for it.

Source: Farmington, Arkansas.

You Ain't Coming Back

One time there was a city fellow come through the country, pretending like he was just a tourist. He went wandering around kind of aimless, trying to get people to sing songs. Told them he was going to write a book about old-time music. He hung around square dances too, and got mighty friendly with fiddlers and guitar players and banjo pickers. Everybody knows that a fiddler would rather drink moonshine whiskey than eat. That city fellow thought he was mighty smart, but the home folks knowed what he was after, all right. They called him the singing revenuer.

Things just kind of drifted along all summer, till finally that singing revenuer come across one of Tom Christy's boys away up on Goober Mountain. Soon as the howdies was over the fellow sung one of them fool songs, and then he wanted to talk about moonshine. "They tell me your pappy's running off a batch today," says he, but the boy never returned no answer. "If I knowed where the boys have got the still," says the revenuer, "I'd go up there and visit with 'em awhile." But Tom Christy's boy didn't have nothing to say.

Pretty soon the fellow come right out and offered the youngster five dollars to tell him where the still was at. Tom Christy's boy looked at him contemptuous. "Just go up the path, and turn left at the first fork," says he. "The still's under the bluff, right by the second pouroff." The revenuer hitched up his belt. "Give me the five dollars," says Tom Christy's boy. The fellow just kind of grinned. "I'll give you the money when I come back," says he. The boy just sat there, a-looking out over the valley. "Mister," says he, "If you go up to that still, you ain't never coming back."

The revenuer didn't say nothing, but you could see that he was a-thinking mighty serious. Pretty soon he got up and walked down the trail towards the settlement. Tom Christy and his boys moved their contraption that night, but there wasn't no need of it. About a week after that, the singing revenuer found two or three stills down on Buffalo Creek. But nobody ever seen him fooling around Goober Mountain again.

Source: Branson, Missouri

The Devil's Pretty Daughter

Yellow Bread

One time there was a fellow named Job Eskin, and he come a-walking up to where the ladies was giving a dinner-on-the-ground at the Methodist Church. Job was a ragged old peckerwood and pretty dirty, but you can't turn people away from a church sociable, no matter if he puts any money in the hat or not. They had fried chicken and vegetables and pies and all the trimmings, but Job didn't touch nothing but Mary Weatherman's yellow poundcake. He just cut off slice after slice and put butter on it. You wouldn't believe that a skinny little old man could eat so much, unless you seen it with your own eyes.

Pretty soon it looked like Job was going to eat the cake plumb up, and the ladies was getting desperate. So they ask him won't he please sample the fried chicken and the nice beat biscuits. "Thank you, ma'am," says he, "but you just save them things for the high-toned folks. This here yaller bread is good enough for me." In the early days we lived on cornbread mostly, and biscuits made out of white flour was something extra fine. Country folks didn't have biscuits only on Sundays, or when company was a-coming. Job was a good soul, but he didn't know much.

Finally one of them Ledbetter girls whispered something in Job's ear. He looked considerable set back, and after that he didn't gobble no more poundcake, but just et chicken and biscuits like the rest of the boys. Poor Mary Weatherman was plumb sick. "I don't care about my cake bein' gone," she says, "and I don't mind men actin' like hogs, because that's their nature. It's what that old feller said that's a-killin' me!" And with that she begun to giggle, and acted like she was goin' to throw a fit, so she had to be took home in the buggy.

Mary Weatherman was kind of upset for about a week, and then she come out of it and bustled round same as ever. But she stayed away from the Methodist dinners after that. And so did poor old Job Eskin.

Stiff as a Poker

Source: Garland County, Arkansas

One time there was an old man, and some say his name was Benton. He was a heavy drinker, and one night he passed out, so his friends put him in the icehouse. Then they got to drinking, and forgot all about him. Two or three days later somebody happened to go in the icehouse, and there was the old man froze stiff as a poker. The boys felt awful bad about it, but they didn't know what to do. They jowered awhile, and then decided to thaw the body out and tell the folks he died of heart trouble or something. So they fetched the old man into the house and laid him on the bed.

Next day a woman went in to look at the corpse, and when she seen that old Benton was a-breathing she fainted plumb away. The folks sent for the doctor and put hot towels on him, and they poured some whiskey between his teeth. Pretty soon the old devil was setting up chipper as a jaybird. He says he feels better than he had in a long time. The old man didn't remember nothing about being froze in the icehouse, so the folks never told him. They figured he wouldn't believe it, anyhow.

They told the doctor what happened, though, and he just laughed at 'em. The doctor says he seen catfish froze solid for two or three months and then thawed out alive, but he never heard tell of it being tried on a man. Old hunters claim that bears and groundhogs and chipmunks lay up all winter; maybe a man could do the same, if he set his mind to it. But everybody knowed that Doc was a-joking.

It was about a year after that when old man Benton got to drinking and raising hell worse than ever. One night him and his friends all got drunk, and the old man passed out. The first thing anybody knowed them damn fools put him in the icehouse again, and this time they let him freeze solid for

more'n a month. Then they fetched him in the house, and he thawed out a-feelin' fine. One of the boys told him this time, but the old man just laughed, as he did not believe a word of it.

After that the folks used to freeze old man Benton every so often, and seemed like it agreed with him fine. A quick freeze and a slow thaw-out done the old devil good. Doc Holton come along one day, so the boys took him down to the icehouse and he seen old man Benton a-layin' there, froze hard as a rock. Doc says a joke is a joke, but this man's dead! You damn fools have killed him, and I will have to tell the sheriff about it. But the boys says just keep your shirt on, Doc, and watch us thaw him out. So they done just like always, and pretty soon old man Benton got to breathing again. He was pretty slow coming out of it this time, though. Doc set up with him all night, but the next morning old man Benton was dead sure enough.

"Well, boys," says Doc, "I never seen nothing like this before, and maybe I am going crazy. I don't know what this fellow died of, but there ain't no sign of frostbite. He was an old man anyhow, so I am going to put it down heart disease and try to forget the whole business. But from now on if you freeze anybody else I will see that you go to the penitentiary, and I ain't joking neither." So then Doc got in his buggy and went back to town.

Everybody is mighty close-mouthed about them things nowadays, on account of the tourists and all. But the folks up that way are still a-putting up ice, and lots of 'em have got padlocks on their icehouses.

Casting Out The Devil

Source: Caverna, Missouri

One time there was a preacher come a-riding up to a house. The man was away from home, but the woman had a young fellow in there, and the preacher seen him through the window. It was a little log cabin, and they didn't have but one door. The woman asked the preacher to come in, and he set down by the fire. Pretty soon he figured out that the young fellow must be hid in a barrel with some cotton rags on top, but he never let on.

The woman talked polite enough, and she says she's a Methodist, but her husband is a out-and-out infidel. She kind of hinted maybe the preacher better go away, because her man is kind of mean, particular if he's been a-drinking. But the preacher says he knows how to handle infidels, and he has brought hundreds of 'em to the repentance of their sinful ways. So he just set right where he was.

After while her man come home, and he was pretty drunk. He says right off that preachers don't do nothing nowadays only run after the womenfolks and eat yellow-leg chickens. Why don't they heal the sick and raise the dead and cast out devils, he says, like the saints done back in Bible times?

The preacher just looked at the man a little bit, and then he says, "Is anybody sick in this house, that you want me to heal 'em?'' The man says no. ''Is anybody dead here, that you want me to raise 'em up?'' So the man says no again. ''Well,'' says the preacher, ''there's a devil in the house, all right. Just watch me cast him out!'' And with that he throwed a shovelful of live coals into the barrel.

Well, sir, them cotton rags blazed up just like gunpowder, and filled the house full of smoke. The young fellow in the barrel roared like a bull, and out he come with his clothes afire. Right through the door he went, a-trailing smoke and yelling every jump. You could hear him a-hollering plumb to the creek, and then come a big splash. The infidel just set there with his mouth open. He was pretty drunk, and the room was full of smoke, so he thought maybe it was the devil sure enough. ''Let's pray!'' says the preacher, and there they was both down on their knees, with the unbeliever a-praying loud as anybody.

When the preacher says ''Amen'' they got up, and both of 'em was looking mighty solemn. After while the man says, ''Parson, how did you know the devil was in that barrel?'' The preacher just looked at him a minute. ''I never seen a infidel's house yet, but what there was a devil in it,'' says he. ''Sometimes there's two or three of 'em.'' And with that he told the folks goodbye and rode off down the trail.

The infidel stayed close to home for a long time after that, and he quit drinking, too. It looked for awhile like he was going to join the church, but he never done it. Him and his woman treated preachers mighty respectful though, and he didn't have nothing more to say about yellow-leg chickens.

Source: Eureka Springs, Arkansas

The Boy That Made Up Songs

One time there was a woman that only had one baby. It was a little boy, and he was pretty near two years old. She was setting beside him, wondering what he would do when he growed up. Just like every woman thinks maybe her boy will be a lawyer or a doctor or a preacher or something. She said a little prayer, and she prayed he would be a great man some day.

All of a sudden the woman heard a tap on the door, and there stood a little stranger. She was one of the good people all right, because she had a regular fairy wand in her hand. There was a little gold thing, like a pen with diamonds on it, hung round her neck. But her clothes was just plain brown, instead of green and other bright colors like the little people are supposed to wear.

The woman asked her to come in and set down. But the little stranger says she is terrible thirsty, as her throat is a-burning up, and could she have a glass of milk? When the milk was poured out she wanted to know is it from a red cow, because if it is from a red cow she can't drink a drop. The woman told her no, because their cow is yellow. So then the little stranger drunk the milk.

Pretty soon she says, "Is your baby a boy or a girl?" and the woman told her it is a boy. She waved her wand over him and says, "Your son will be a great man, and he will make up songs for people to sing all over the country." A minute later the little stranger was gone, and the woman thought maybe she dreamed the whole thing. But there was the glass setting on the stand-table, with a little milk in the bottom of it.

The boy grew up just like other children, only kind of quiet. He didn't have much to say around the house, but sometimes they would find him out in the woods a-talking to himself, and the other kids couldn't make out what he was talking about. By the time he was sixteen that boy didn't do nothing but read books, and his mother wouldn't see him at all for three or four days a-running. Finally he walked off down the road one day, and the folks didn't have no idea what become of him.

They found out after while how he wrote verses and made up songs that people was a-singing all over the country. Everybody thought he was a great man all right, but the folks never seen hide nor hair of him. His mother was pretty old by this time, and she got lonesome. She thought a lot about her boy that had run off to make up songs, and she wished he would come back home. Finally one day he walked right in the door. He told her he was sorry about running off that way, but he had to make up songs, so there wasn't no help for it. The songs was all done now, and he was sick, so he come home to die. Pretty soon he did die sure enough, and the old woman was all alone again.

After the burying was over, the woman thought about it for a long time. And then she says another little prayer. She prayed that the little stranger wouldn't come to anybody else's house and send their boy away to make up songs for people to sing all over the country.

Source: Benton Country, Arkansas

Who Blowed Up the Church House?,

The Big Old Giant
(An Ozark version of "Jack and the Beanstalk")

One time there was a boy found a dead crow, and the crow had a funny looking grain of corn in his mouth. It was big as a walnut, and blue instead of yellow. So the boy planted it down by the big bluff and poured a hatful of stump water on it. Next time he come that way, the corn had growed up big as a tree, with regular bark on it, and blade-fodder hanging down forty foot long. The boy couldn't see no tassel, on account of the trees on top of the bluff, and he couldn't see no ears on the stalk, neither. He went home and told the folks, but they just laughed and didn't pay no attention. So finally he says to himself, "I'll go back and climb that there cornstalk, if I never see the back of my neck!"

Well, he clumb and he clumb and he kept on a-climbing, right on up past the top of the bluff, but there wasn't no ears on the stalk yet. He got so high up he couldn't see nothing but clouds. After while he come to a big pasture, so he got off the cornstalk to look around and stretch his legs. The grass in that pasture was ten foot high, and there was buckbrush in it bigger than apple trees. Pretty soon he seen some monstrous big sheep. There was one old sheep had a fine brass bell on it, about the size of a molasses barrel.

"The folks won't never believe this," says he to himself, "without I take something back to show 'em." So he out with his knife and started to cut the bell off'n the big sheep's neck. It took a long time to saw through the leather strap, pretty near a foot thick, but he finally done it. The bell was too heavy for him to lift, so he rolled it along on the ground, and it kept a-ringing. Just as he got to the edge of the big pasture, the boy heard a terrible loud hollering, and here come the big old giant that owned them sheep. He was maybe thirty foot high, and he was a-waving a club big as a saw-log.

Well, when the boy seen this here giant a-coming, he just rolled the bell over the edge, and then he jumped onto the big cornstalk and slid down. The big old giant threw the club, but it missed him. The boy was pretty near to the bottom, when the old giant jumped on the cornstalk and started down after him. Just as the boy lit on the ground the cornstalk broke off, and the big old giant come a-roaring down the mountain and busted open like a rotten apple. By the time the boy's folks got there the big old giant was dead, and that was the end of him.

The folks got the neighbors to help, and they went out and buried the big old giant in the night, and never did tell no outsiders, so as to keep down scandal. But next winter every family for miles around showed up with quilts and laprobes and saddle blankets made out of some mighty funny looking wool. Nobody in the country ever seen cloth like that before, and the old-timers say them things was made out of the big old giant's pants.

Some berry pickers found the big sheep bell four miles up the creek. The boy's pappy wanted to put it in the new churchhouse, but the preacher says a bell like that was not made with human hands, and maybe it was the Devil's work. And he says good Christian people better not ring that bell, because who knows what might come a-running? So they just left the big sheep bell there in the brush where it fell. And it's still a-laying there to this day.

THREE LITTLE PIGS

Source: Joplin, Missouri

One time there was three little pigs. One pig built him a chip house, one built him a stick house, and one built him a rock house. When the old fox come to the chip house he says, "Let me in, Piggy-Wee. If you don't, I'll puff and I'll blow till I blow your house down." But the little pig was afraid, and he wouldn't open the door. So the old fox he puffed and he blowed till the house fell down, and then he et the little pig up.

Next day the old fox come to the stick house and he says, "Let me in, Piggy-Wee. If you don't I'll puff and I'll blow till I blow your house down." But the little pig was afraid, and he wouldn't open the door. So the old fox

(Of this story the interviewee said,"We didn't have any story-books. I was a grown woman, and married, before I ever saw this tale in print." The same could be said of the preceding story, I think. Editor's Note)

he puffed and he blowed till the house fell down, and then he et the little pig up.

Finally the old fox come to the rock house, and he says, "Let me in, Piggy-Wee. If you don't I'll puff and I'll blow till I blow your house down." But the little pig was afraid, and he wouldn't open the door. So the old fox he puffed and he blowed, but the rock house wouldn't fall down. Then the old fox says, "Let me get the end of my nose in," and the little pig opened the door a crack. Then the old fox says, "Let me get a little more of my nose in," and the little pig opened the door another crack. Then the old fox says, "Let me get my eyes in," and the little pig opened the door another crack. The the old fox says, "Let me get a little more of my eyes in," and the little pig opened the door another crack. Then the old fox says, "Let me get my ears in," and the little pig opened the door another crack. And so it went, with the old fox getting a little more of his ears in. Then his neck, and a little more of his neck. Then his front feet, and a little more of his front feet. Then his ribs, and little more of his ribs. Finally the old fox was all inside the house but his tail, and then he just busted on in without asking the little pig nothing.

Next the old fox set down by the fire, and he says, "Warm belly gut. Eat a pig pretty soon." Just then they heard the hounds a-coming round the mountain, and the old fox says, "Piggy-Wee, where can I hide?" And the little pig says, "Jump in that big trunk." So the old fox jumped in the big trunk, and Piggy-Wee slammed down the lid and locked it.

The little pig he set and thought awhile. Then he got some hot water out of the kettle and poured it through a little hole, and the old fox says, "Piggy-Wee, there's a flea biting me." Then the little pig poured in some more water, and the old fox says, "Piggy-Wee, there's a fire burning me." Then the little pig poured in the whole kettle of hot water, and the old fox hollered something terrible, but it didn't do him no good. Pretty soon the old fox was scalded plumb to death, and the little pig lived happy in his rock house till the butcher cut him down.

Uncle Johnny's Bear

Source: Carroll County, Arkansas

One time when this town was a-booming we had a fine big whorehouse up on the hill where Sam Leath's tourist camp is now, and they called it the White Elephant. There wasn't no waterworks in them days, and the girls had to carry water from Oil Spring. Two of them girls come running back up the hill one evening, and they kept hollering about a big bear down by the spring. Another woman went down to get the buckets, and she seen the bear too, so after that the girls that lived in the whorehouse would not go to the spring, because they was afraid of the big bear. The old lady that run the place says the girls must be crazy, because no bear is going to come right into town like that. But she knowed something had to be done, so she sent for Uncle Johnny Hickson.

So finally Uncle Johnny come over with his shotgun, but he says it is all damn foolishness. "There ain't no bears in this town," he says, "and if anybody is looking for bears they got to go way out in the hills with dogs, and even then they might not find any, because bears is getting scarce. Also," he says, "it don't look right for a man to be hanging around places like this at my time of life. And if anybody was to hear how Johnny Hickson is hunting bears at the White Elephant, people would laugh at me all over town," he says.

"I told them fool girls there wasn't no bear," says the old lady. "But they claim they seen it with their own eyes, and now we ain't got no drinking water." So Uncle Johnny says give me the goddam bucket, and he started down to the spring. He seen tracks in the path, and a big she bear jumped right out pretty near on top of him. Uncle Johnny was a man that always had hammers cocked, but he got tangled up with the waterbucket some way, and it slowed him down considerable. Next thing he knowed, the bear had the muzzle of the shotgun in her mouth, so Uncle Johnny pulled the triggers and fell over backwards into a mess of green brambles.

The bear was dead, all right, and Uncle Johnny was not hurt, except he was scratched up considerable in them briars. But when he picked up the shotgun he seen that the barrels was both busted at the end, and he figured the White Elephant people ought to give him twelve dollars to buy a new gun. But the old lady said, "You are a bear hunter, and you have got the bear, so you ought to be satisfied. And if anybody has fooled around and broke their gun it sure ain't my fault," she says.

Uncle Johnny wasn't satisfied by no means, and he says that is what a man gets for trying to be neighborly, specially if the neighbors ain't got nothing better to do except run whorehouses. And he says there is a lot of undesirable citizens in this town, and the fact is damn near all of them are undesirable. So then he went and skinned the bear and cut off the best meat to sell down at the hotel. After he left there was some foreigners come and got the rest of the meat, and that was the end of Uncle Johnny's bear.

Source: Joplin, Missouri

The Banjo-Picking Girl

One time there was a man named Joe Keene, and he was a carpenter, and after while he got to be kind of a jackleg preacher, too. He had a wife and four children, and they all belonged to the New Ground Church, which is something like the Holy Rollers. There was a pretty girl come along from down South somewheres, and she could play the banjo besides. The New Ground folks used to have big meetings out in the woods, and then they built a brush-arbor just about where the Playmore Tavern is now. Them people used to pray and holler and roll on the ground pretty near all night, with the pretty girl picking her banjo and the elders a-preaching fit to bust their guts. They preached mostly in the unknown tongue, and you couldn't tell what it was about.

But everybody could tell that the banjo-picking girl was going to have a baby, and one night old Joe Keene throwed a fit, and then he says the Lord God come to him in a vision. Joe says the Lord told him to leave his wife and kids, as they was living sinful anyhow. And then Joe says it is revealed to him that he must marry the banjo-picking girl, because she has never been with a man but she is going to have a child by the Holy Ghost. Joe says he would never have believed such a thing, only the Lord God told him about it with His own mouth.

Well sir, them New Ground folks had swallered a lot of mighty peculiar doctrine, but this here revelation kind of took their breath away. And Joe Keene's woman says she didn't have no idea who's been laying up with the banjo-picker, but she knowed it warn't no ghost. Most of the folks figured maybe Joe Keene did have some kind of a revelation, and he better do what God told him, because it's plumb dangerous to go against the will of the Lord God. And it is best not to take no chances in these latter days, when everybody knows the end of the world ain't far off, anyhow.

And so all the preachers and elders got together, and they voted to give Joe Keene a divorce. Him and his wife had been married in the church without no papers, so the law didn't have nothing to do with it. The New Ground folks done all their marrying that way. They says paper weddings is all right for rich infidels in town, but genuine Christian people must be joined in holy wedlock by God Almighty, and they don't need no papers from the courthouse. The New Ground saints don't believe in taxes, neither, and they never buy no dog-license because there ain't no Scripture for it.

Soon as they give Joe his divorce, he begun to holler "Praise God! Blessed be His holy name!" and he shook hands with everybody in the arbor. And him and the banjo-picking girl got married right then and there. After the service was over they started out afoot for Oklahoma, and you could hear them singing hymns all the way up Gander Mountain.

Along about New Year's there was a letter come from over in the Osage Nation, all about how the baby was borned in a barn somewheres; it was a fine boy, and they was expecting great things of him. There wasn't no more letters after that, but we heard that Joe Keene was arrested for selling whiskey to the Indians, and the girl run off with a trout-mouthed parson from Sallisaw. But it all happened a long time back, and nobody don't rightly know what ever did become of them people.

Folk Tales of Black Folks

The contribution of Arkansas' black population is well-known throughout the state. They have for centuries poured their energies and their desires into the fields, the factories, the schools and homes of the state they call "home." In addition to their physical efforts, they have also added their share to our literary heritage. In 1931, when Fred W. Allsopp compiled his Folklore of Romantic Arkansas, *he included the following selections which reflect the black culture of the past. Just as the culture of the Ozarks is rapidly disappearing, so is the colorful, rich culture of the Negro. And just as the hill folk heritage deserves preservation, so does the black heritage. The richness of dialect and the warmth of humor makes these selections particularly delightful.*

A "Dry-Clean" Baptizing

Fred W. Allsopp. *Folklore of Romantic Arkansas*, Vol. II (Grolier Society, 1931).

Two negro women were in their respective back yards engaged in hanging out the day's wash. One of them was singing and shouting, "Glory, halleleuia!" The other said to her, "Honey, yo' seems to be mighty happy dis mawnin'."

"I is happy; I'se powerful happy, and you'd be happy, too, if you'd been baptized like I wuz las' Sund'y."

"Whar wus yo' baptized?"

"I wus baptized down at Mount Vernon Baptist Church—wus buried wid Christ in baptism."

"Huh, yo' talk like I ain't been baptized," said the other; "I'se baptized in the Methodus church, but we sprinkle un, 'stead o' sousin' um under."

"Yo' sprinkle um, nuthin'; dat ain't no reg'lar baptizin'. Yo' ain't had no sins wahed away at tall; you jist bin *dry-cleaned;* dat's all yo' Methodus do wid yo' sprinklin' baptizin'."

A Darkey "Draps" A Talking Turtle

Arkansas is a fisherman's paradise, and the average country darkey of course would much prefer to fish than hoe cotton. At a saw mill camp on the banks of White River in Monroe County, Ark., a negro who worked at the mill and lived at the camp, kept trot lines set in the river to catch fish.

As more fish are caught after twelve o'clock at night, many fishermen run their lines just before the break of day.

For several mornings the negro in question who had run a particluar line found that the bait had been taken from his hooks. He was near exasperation, until one morning he caught a large turtle. He landed the reptile on the bank and placed it in his strong box while readjusting his hooks and line. He then took the turtle by the tail and started down the trail on the bank of the river toward the camp. As he trudged along, he was addressing the turtle somewhat in this fashion:

"Uh-huh; so, you is de genmun whuts bin stealin' the bait offen my hooks; I'se gwine to fix yo', sah. I'se gwine to take yo' home, git my butcher knife an' peel you outen dat ar hull o' youren, put yo' in a pot, wid sum water, cawn and 'taters and sum salt and pepper, and I'se gwine to make yo' inter turtle soup; yas, sah, I sho' is."

But the darkey was almost scared out of his wits by an unheard of thing. The turtle talked back to him. (It happened that an old oxdriver who was also something of a ventriloquist had heard the negro talking to the turtle, and, concealing himself behind a tree, he threw his voice to the turtle and had it seem to say:

"What dat yo' gwine to do wid me?"

The negro held the turtle at arm's length, and, looking around in astonishment, ejaculated, "What's dat I hear?"

Again the ventriloquist said, "Now, jist zackly whut is yo' gwine to do wid me?"

Quickly dropping the turtle, the negro said, "I'se gwine to drap yo' right here," and hastily repaired to the log camp. The turtle leisurely crawled back into the river, while the ox-driver leaned against the tree behind which he had hidden and laughed himself sick.

A folklorist from Michigan, Richard Dorson was introduced to Arkansas by a speaking engagement at the University of Arkansas. Following leads given him by a student at the University and gaining encouragement from Vance Randolph, Otto Rayburn, and Lawrence Davis, he spent eight days as the only white man on the campus of A M & N (now the University of Arkansas at Pine Bluff). During these eight days in 1953, he collected literally hundreds of Black folk tales from aged Negroes in Southeast Arkansas. This field trip provided material for the Folklore Monograph Series at Indiana University.

Mr. Dorson not only collected traditional tales from Arkansas' Black citizens, he also traced these tales to their original sources. Interestingly enough, he discovered that many of the tales possess the same ancestors that Vance Randolph discovered in tracing the Ozark tales. Dorson cites the various motifs which constitute typical folklore patterns. Included here are Dorson's notes, explaining origins and motifs.

Animal and Bird Stories

Stealing the Butter
(Maria Summers)

Richard M. Dorson, *Negro Tales from Pine Bluff, Arkansas, and Calvin, Michigan.* Bloomington: Indiana UP, 1958.

This Negro favorite, I found, is far more popular than "Tar Baby." The final incident in the present text resembles many in which the trickster kills the stupid ogre.

One time a man had his butter down in the spring where it could keep cool—people didn't have wells in them times—and the Rabbit he saw it. And the Bear and the Rabbit was hunting partners for things to eat, and the Bear found it first, and was calling it his'n. And the Rabbit was always the sharpest y'know, and he told the Bear he had some babies to christen (we call it baptize now). And the Bear asked him how many. And he said, "Four." So he would get up early that morning, would get down to the spring, ate one part of the butter.

When he went back the Bear said, "Where you been, Brother Rabbit?"

"Been christening the baby."

"What did you name him?"

"One Part Gone."

So next morning he went again.

"Where you been, Brother Rabbit?"

"I been christen another baby."

"What the baby name?"

"Two Part Gone."

He goes off again, and the same thing happen. He calls the next baby "Three Part Gone." The last one is "All Gone and Lick the Bottom."

And so the Bear went down there to the spring to get the butter. And when he come back he asked the Rabbit, had he been down to the spring to et the butter. The Rabbit said, "No, no, I tell you what to do. First one get up in the morning with the belly grease et the butter."

So they both went to bed, and both went to sleep. And the Rabbit got up that night and he greased Old Bear's belly right good. And he said to the Bear, "I told you I said the first one get up in the morning with the belly grease et the butter. So you et the butter." So the Bear commenced getting mad, and the Rabbit was scared. He knowed the Bear could whip him, so he said, "There's going to be a party tonight." He went to jumping around and dancing. And so he had a large box, said, "Brother Bear, you better get in the box and stay here tonight, while I run over and get the girls and bring them back." So Brother Bear jumped in the box, and the Rabbit locked him up.

He could see out, he said, "Brother Rabbit, what you doing with all the vessels on the fire?"

He said, "I'm going to scald you, that's what." He commenced hollering and going on, and at last the Rabbit scalded him and that was the end of that.

(Second version)

Brother Fox, Brother Bear and all of 'em was picking cotton. And they were all staying in the same house, and they'd buy their groceries together. So every evening they'd come in they'd go to the store. Brother Rabbit's money was kinda short, he wasn't making much that day 'cause he felt a little ill. So they was all going to book their money in and buy some butter. Brother Rabbit he didn't eat butter, and he was short. So they went on and bought them two pounds of butter. They all went to the field next morning. There they worked all the next day. They come in, Brother Rabbit was the first to go to bed. He'd catch them all sleeping; he'd get up and eat some butter. And next morning Brother Rabbit'd be up early smoking his cigar with his legs crossed.

And they were going on to the field and work that day. So when they come in they missed that butter. Say, "Who was eating that butter? We didn't eat all that butter!"

Brother Fox said, "We won't work tomorrow, we'll have a test on the butter. One eat that butter we'll find him out."

So they built a great big fire next morning. And then Brother Buzzard he was going to be the captain, the boss of it. Because practically everywhere he go he flew. So they got the fire built, a great big log heap fire. So Brother Buzzard says, "Okay, Brother Fox, you may be first." Brother Fox he backed up and he lit out—Woody, woody, woody. And he jumps, he jumps it clear. And he comes on back. Brother Buzzard says, "Okay, Brother Rabbit you're next." Brother Rabbit he backed up, pulled his derby off, and he hits it just as hard as he could go right toward the fire. And Brother Rabbit got close to the fire—Boody, boody, boody, boody—then whipped his belly agin the ground and run around the fire. And they thought they heard him the other side. Brother Buzzard say, "Okay, Brother Bear, you're next." So Brother Bear he backed up and he lit out. And he leaps right in the fire.

Brother Rabbit say, "Yeah, I told you Brother Bear eat that butter."

So Brother Bear walks on back close to Brother Rabbit, and he made a break at him, and it was a hollow log right down close to him. So Brother Rabbit run in that hollow log, wasn't but one way in. So Brother Bear fastened up the other end of that log with Brother Rabbit in. "I'll show you about tricking me." And they all went on and left Brother Rabbit in the log.

Next morning they went down to see about it.

"Brother Rabbit." (*High*)

"Hunh." (*Loud*)

"Oh let's go on back and forget about you." So they went on back and Brother Rabbit stayed in there. They went back to see him again. So they called him again, "Brother Rabbit."

"Hunh." (*Weak*)

He answered like he was nearly about gone. "O yes, nearly about got him." They went away and left him. So next morning would be the end of the week he'd been in there. "I know he'll be dead this morning." They went down to see about it.

"Brother Rabbit." (*High*)

Brother Rabbit wouldn't answer. He'd done study a trick on them.

"Brother Rabbit." Call him twice.

"Oh yeah, we got him." Brother Fox, Brother Bear they pulled that chunk out of the log. Brother Fox reached up in there to get Brother Rabbit. Out come Brother Rabbit, out by Brother Fox's hands.

"Oh yes, you son of bitches think you're smart, I can be your schoolteacher yet."

Bear and Buzzard
(Tobe Courtney)

I don't know just who it was tied the Bear, but I think it started like this. There was two mens in the woods hunting. Well they was a good little piece apart. So the Bear was coming out of the cornfield. So the man was sitting down on a log, and the bear slipped up on him, he was 'bout half asleep you know, had been hunting all night. And he commenced hollering for the other fellow was out there with him. And he run round a tree (now look at me). The bear tried to catch him, and this was a pretty good man, he jumped behind the tree. And the bear was reaching at him, and he caught the bear's foot, both of 'em. And he holding the bear and hollering for his friend in the woods, the other man. And when the other man come he say, "Now you hold him, and I'm going to tie him."

Well when that other fellow got hold of him, he so weak and tired he sat down and said, "Now when you've hold him as long as I have, then I'll tie him." Finally he decided he'd get up and tie him you know, and they left him out there. They wouldn't kill him, they left him tied.

So Mr. Buzzard he flew around, till the Bear got weak you know. He found out where his meal was at. And when he flew down on him, the bear hit him with his foot, and knocked that patch of hair outa his head. He knocked him kind of crazy and he flew backwards into a tree, and knocked off the rest of that patch. And he been bald-headed ever since.

(Editor's Note: A popular Negro folktale incident, telling how the buzzard became bald, has been neatly added to this version of an old tale.—Dorson)

Tar Baby
(Julia Courtney)

Was a long summer drouth among the animals. And Brother Rabbit played like he'd get up every morning and lick the dew off the grass. That's why he stayed so slick and fat. So Rabbit had found a spring, and he wouldn't tell none of the rest of the animals. Every morning he would get up real early and go down to the spring and get a drink of water. Next morning he got up just a little bit earlier and went down to the spring, and got him a drink of water. But Brother Fox beat him up and followed him down there. Brother Fox come back and told the rest of the animals how dirty Brother Rabbit was. All the animals got together and made them a tar baby, and put it in front of the spring.

And the spring was very small spring. Brother Rabbit couldn't go round the tar baby to get no water. So when he got there he stooped down, and he could see the tar baby standing there. He thought it was someone. Brother Rabbit walked up to it and told him to move out of the way. And he repeated again, "Move out the way. If you don't I'll slap you." So he hauled off and slapped him with one front paw. That one stuck. Brother Rabbit said, "Turn me loose. I have three more paws." So he slapped him with the other one. Brother Rabbit said, "All right, you better turn me loose. I have two more." Slapped him with one more. He said, "I have one more." And he slapped with the other one. Then he said, "If you don't turn me loose I'll butt you with my head." So all the animals caught Brother Rabbit stuck to the tar baby.

(By him pulling the tar would give, and he thought it was someone there.)

Mr. Rabbit and Mr. Frog Make Mr. Fox and Mr. Bear Their Riding-Horses
(John Courtney)

Mr. Rabbit and Mr. Frog were courting two girls, and Mr. Bear and Mr. Fox were liking them too. Mr. Fox and Mr. Bear they had the best going, the girls cared most for them. So Brother Rabbit went down to Brother Frog's house, and built up a scheme to play on Brother Bear and Brother Fox. So they set a night that they were going to the girls' house, an off night from what Brother Bear and Brother Fox were courting. And so they went on a Friday night, and they told the girls, "Brother Fox and Brother Bear's our riding-horses. You're crazy about them boys but there ain't nothing to them."

So the girls says, "Oh no, I can't believe that."

So Brother Rabbit told them, says, "I'll prove it if you'll be my girl friend." And Brother Frog said he would too. So they set a night that they was going to prove it, in the next following week. So that evening Brother Fox and Brother Bear come over to Brother Rabbit's house.

Brother Rabbit say, "You just the man I want to see." So Brother Rabbit say, "We ought to go to some extra girls' house tonight, we need some more girls." So they finally made it up and begin to get ready. They carried them a saddle apiece, Brother Rabbit and Brother Frog, and hid them by Brother Bear's girl friend's house. So they went on that night down to this extra girls' house. So they stayed there till nine o'clock. Brother Bear and Brother Fox they had to stay by their girl friend's house. So they all got ready and started out. Brother Rabbit took sick. Brother Rabbit was so sick, Brother Bear 'cided to try to tote him. So Brother Frog he had a bellyache. So that made him sick too.

So Brother Fox said, "Well we'll just tote them two guys up here and we'll stop over."

Brother Bear told them, says, "Crawl up on my back, Brother Rabbit, I'll tote ya." And Brother Fox told Brother Frog to crawl up. Both of them was so sick, he could get up there but he couldn't stay up there.

Brother Rabbit told him, says, "I just can't stay on your back. I gotta get something to hold to." Brother Rabbit told him, "I know what, I see the very thing I can hold to." [Excited] Brother Frog say the same thing. So Brother Rabbit say, "Here's some saddles here, here's the very things we can

---

Other variants were told me by Tobe Courtney and Mrs. L. J. Toler. The present text is unusual in having two riders and riding horses.... Martha W. Beckwith describes the story as "very common in Jamaica and presents no local variations from the form familiar in America.."

hold on to." So they put the saddles on, and Brother Rabbit and him climbed up in the saddle. Both of 'em was so sick they couldn't hardly stay in the saddle.

And when they got to the girls' house, Brother Bear say, "Now you've got to get down, Brother Rabbit, at the steps. That is far as I can carry you."

So Brother Rabbit told him, says, "You take me to the top steps, we can make it." He had done put him a pair of spurs on he and Brother Frog. So when they got up to the top step, Brother Rabbit popped them spurs to Brother Bear. Brother Bear ran right on in his girl friend's door. Brother Rabbit said, "I told you Brother Bear was my riding horse, I told you Brother Bear was my riding horse."

Brother Frog said, "I told you Brother Fox was my riding horse."

Old Marster and John Stories

Most persons associate American Negro Tales with animal characters, but Old Marster and John figure in at least as many stories as Mr. Rabbit and Mr. Fox. The plantation owner, Old Marster, and his roguish slave John, engage in a perpetual battle of wits, with now one and now the other emerging victorious. John resembles two other traditional American scapegraces, the Indian trickster and the New England Yankee, in his combination of low cunning and obtuse stupidity. The Old Marster cycle reflects the circumstances and relationships of plantation life with often surprising detail. In the variants that deal with a fight between two strong slaves on neighboring plantations, for example, the plots hinge about an institutional feature of slavery, the selection by the planter of a husky hand for breeding purposes and general strong-arm duty. Curiously, for all their localized references and apparent origin in actual historical situations, many Old Marster narratives issue from Europe, Africa, and the British Isles, and adapt themselves skillfully to the features of antebellum life. Emancipation and the creation of freedmen failed to alter the basic relationship between Old Marster, who now becomes Old Boss or the Boss-man, and his hired hand, who still attempts to shirk his work and fool the boss.—Dorson

John and the Horse
(John Courtney)

John went out for a dance one night. They'd let him out for enjoyment, and he was getting a little better treatment than some of 'em, he was out from under the belt, he was the handy boy. But he was always trying to he'p some of them and he'd get caught. Boss let him go to the dance and John stole the Captain's horse, to make a showdown. And riding to the dance, John had big time. He came out from the dance to go home, and found the horse, Mollie, stiff dead.

So John called two or three of the boys there, says, "Listen," says, "What am I going to do?"

And boys says, "I don't know what you going to do."

And John say, it come to him right away, "Just help to get the horse on my shoulder, down to the big gate anyhow." And after he got him to the big gate, that's as far as the other boys could go. They all got to beat it home so they could give an account of theirself, it getting close to daylight. Old John said, "Listen here, you can't leave him here, you-all got to help get him on my shoulder, so I can take him to the stable."

So they all got around him and helped get Molly on his shoulder, so John could carry him to the stable. And John get him into the stable, he thought about all the tracks he'd made from the gate to the stable, so he got a broom and dusted out all the tracks. Then he lie down.

Just about that time the Boss called him to get up. John generally feed in the morning. So John got up, went in the stable, come tearing back to tell the boss about it.

"You know Boss, old Mollie's deader'n hell out there."

So Boss says, "What seemed to be the matter with her."

"I don't know Boss, just stiff dead."

So Boss he got up and put his clothes on and went out there. He kind of searched over, and felt to see whether she was warm or sweating you know.

So Boss let it slide for two or three days. Then he called John in question about it. "John, wasn't Sam riding over to the dance the other night?"

And he said, "Nossir, Boss."

And Boss said, "Well I was told there was two seen riding together, Sam and another one."

"Nossir, Boss."

So he say, "Now John, don't tell me no damn lie."

And John owned up, "Yessir, Boss, I did ride him over."

"John, how did you get the horse back in the stable?"

John said, "Boss, I just picked him up on my shoulder and carried him over there."

"Well John, if you picked him up you'll have to pick him up again this morning."

John said, "Boss, I'm a little sick this morning, I can't pick him up this morning."

"Okay, John."

He went into the house and got that gin belt. (That's a big old thick belt they whip 'em with.) And he called John. John ran out and answered the Boss. The Boss was going towards the lot. John knowed it was going to be hell then.

Boss says, "John, I want you to pick up that horse this morning."

Then John say, "Boss, I-I can't pick that horse up."

"Didn't you tell me you brought that horse from that big gate?"

He says, "Yessir, Boss, but I had a hell of a lot of help with it."

Master Gone to Philly-Me-York
(Silas Altheimer)

Slave named John was in the confidence of his Master, a trusty. John did everything, meted out the rations to his slaves—Master didn't use a slave-driver—John kept his accounts, in his head. He couldn't read or write, but he had a wonderful memory. So his Master would often go away on a big trip, would stay sometimes as much as a month. And so his Master was finally warned by some of his neighbors that John didn't always behave as he ought, that he often had frolics with the neighboring Negroes when his Master was away. So his Master resolved to find out if John was betraying his trust. He and his wife and daughter feigned to go to New York on a visit. And so John as usual barbecued his pork, barbecued a lamb, or calf, or kid, whatever he could get his hands on, and sent a runner to tell his friends on neighboring plantations to come to a big dance, a big barbecue.

The slaves all dressed in their best, came in early that night to the frolic.

So the dance began in the danceroom in the big house. John always stayed in the big house to take care of things. And of course the dance would be carried on by his comrades while he would be out superintending the tables, having the food placed on. And so after John get things arranged so and eating could begin, he'd go in and observe the dance hisself.

In the meantime his Master had slipped in in disguise, his hands blackened, his face blackened, and a cap on his head. And so while his Master was observing all this he went in and began to shout:

> "Joy yourself, joy yourself,
> Master's gone to Philly-Me-York."

Then Master disappeared and took the soot off his hands and face. When he returned John was patting and stamping and hollering:

> "Joy yourself, joy yourself,
> Master's gone to Philly-Me-York."

And when he came out again he saw his Master, and recognized him fully. And as a matter of course his feathers fell, and the slaves fell out of the windows, and that broke up the party, and John was left on his knees begging his Master's forgiveness.

Talking Turtle
(Julia Courtney)

Everyday John had to tote water from the bayou, and every time he'd go to the bayou he would start fussin'. "I'm tired of toting water every day." The next day he went to the bayou and he repeated the same thing (you know just like you repeat the same thing). So last one day John went to the bayou, the turtle was sitting on a log.

Turtle raised up and looked at him, and told John, "Black man, you talk too much."

So John didn't want to think the turtle was talking. He went back to the bayou, got another bucketful of water. The turtle told him the same

(Editor's Note: There is among Randolph's Ozark tales a variant of this story.)

thing. John threw the buckets down, took and run to the house, and called Old Marster, and told him the turtle was down there talking. And so Old Marster didn't want to go because he didn't believe it. But John kept telling him the turtle was talking. So finally Old Boss 'cided he could go. But he told John if the turtle didn't talk he was going to give him a good beating.

So they all went on down to the bayou, and when they got down to the bayou the turtle was sitting on a log with his head back halfway in his shell.

And so John told the turtle, "Tell Old Marster what you told me." So John begged the turtle to talk. So the turtle still didn't say anything. So Old Marster taken him on back to the house, and give him a good beating, and made him git his buckets, and keep totin' water.

When John got back down to the bayou, the turtle had his head sticking up. John dipped up his water, and the turtle raised up and told him, says, "Black man, didn't I tell you you talked too much?"

John Praying
(Harrison Stanfill)

This old Boss-man said he was going to whip John within an inch of his life on Wednesday night. John started praying every day from Sunday to Wednesday. On Wednesday evening that was his last prayer. He told him, "Lord, I been praying every day since Sunday and you've never failed me. I want you to take me away this evening." The boys heard the prayer and they went down and climbed the tree with a ladder rope. So when

John made his final prayer that night he said, "Lord I got to go, because I've only got fifteen minutes before my execution."

So they said, "Okay John, you'll have to come by way of the rope because my chariot is broke."

He said, "All right Lord, let it down, I'm willing to go any way you carry me."

Little boys up in the tree put down the rope, said, "John, put your head in this loop." So they commenced tightening on the rope, and he commenced praying fast.

"O Lord, didn't you say you know everything? Well, don't you know damn well you choking me?"

A Dime For The Sack
(Harrison Stanfill)

Old Boss had all kinds of confidence in John, and said that anything he asked Jesus for he'd sent it to him. John had been a favorite around for a while and Boss was going to give him $100 for his holiday. And he called John in and asked him, "John, you go on down and pray the Lord to send you $100 for your holiday, and if he send that, I'll have all kinds of confidence in you." So Boss-man sacked up $99.90 and give it to two of his little boys. So they saw John going down to the tree that evening and they went along ahead of him and climbed the tree.

John got on his knees and said, "O Lord, I'm praying to you to have a brilliant Christmas, I wants $100." No quicker said than done, the little boys dropped a sack of dough alongside of John. John grabbed the sack and got off his knees and went hopping off to the house and said, "Master I got it, I got it."

So Master said, "You sure, John, you got it?"

"Yes Master, I got it."

"Well now, pour it out on the counter and see how much you got." So John couldn't count but $99.90. "So you can see John, you only got $99.90."

"That okay Boss, he did what he said he did, but he charged me a dime for the sack."

The praying tree is a Motif in folk tales, particularly Black folk tales.

John's Courtship
(Julia Courtney)

John's Boss-man had a boy, and he and John was long together. His Boss-man's boy would go see his girl reg'larly. Last one night John went to see his girl, and the next day he was out in the field plowing. So the boy went down in the field where John was. So John got to the end of the road he (the boy) said,"Hi John. What do you say when you see your girl? (That's what he asked John.)

And John said, "We just play." See John was shamed to tell him what they were talking about. So John axed the boy, "You said you went to see your girl friend last night." Said, "What did you tell your girl friend last night?"

The boy said, "I talked co'tship."

John axed him, "What is co'tship?"

He says, "Man, when I went to my girl's house last night, you know what I told her?"

John said, "No."

He said, "Well I told my girl, 'Good Mo'ning.' (Said) 'Now, sit down.' And I told her, 'Your eyes look like dove eyes. Your cheeks look like a blood red rose. Your teeth look like pearl. Your breath smell like the best thing in the world. And I'm good mind to kiss you.'" So he kissed her.

So that evening commenced to getting late. John had learnt something to tell his girl friend. John couldn't wait till the sun go down hardly. He went to the lot, put his mules in the lot, and went running home. Took him a good hot bath, put his clean clothes on, and lit out to his girl's house in the biggest kind of hurry. John had waited so long till he done forgot what the boy told him. But he didn't think he had. John went on in his girl's house. Before she could get a chance to rest his hat he said, "Hi."

She said, "Hi." (*Sweetly*)

John couldn't sit down before he started to talking. He say "Yo' eyes look like dove eyes. Your cheeks look like a blood red rose." He say, "Your teeth look like garden rakes. Your breath smell like burnt garlic." Then John drawed his hand back and said, "I'm good mind to slap the hell out of you."

That's what he told her. And he hit her. And she quit him.

(That was told in cou'tship. That's a cou'tship story. People couldn't party out in the country like they could in town.)

Jocular Tales:
Tales of haunted houses, ghosts and the frights.

Visibly the Southern Negro possesses a hair-trigger sense of humor. He relishes a joke hugely, meets it more than halfway, and laughs with body and soul at even a simple wheeze. Such at any rate has been my experience on numerous field trips. While the dirty joke travels among Negroes as readily as among Whites, unsoiled jests enjoy great favor with colored people. One special theme for Negro comedy originates in the fear that colored folk feel about spirits of the dead. But if they will run from a ghost or a hant, in the warmth of their homes amid a friendly circle they can roar about the experience, and enjoy fictional incidents involving eerie frights. Favorite scare-tales deal with the dead man who apparently revives, and the series of horrors that confront the hardy soul who stays overnight in a haunted house.

Other miscellaneous jests enter into the Negro repertoire. Southern Negroes retell quantities of jokes about stupid Irishmen, as do the residents of isolated white communities. Another jocular pattern involves the gullible and credulous country Negro who comes to town and sees his first train or streetcar, and reacts in ludicrous fashion. One joke-cycle deals with the different races, usually the Negro, the Jew, and the white man, and accounts with wry humor for the lowly estate of the colored man.

In his selection of European folktales, the Negro again shows a penchant for ridiculous scenes. He delights in those Old World fictions that tell of simple-minded girls and old maids who commit follies in quest of husbands, in preference to well-known Marchen, which rarely appear in the thousand texts I have collected. Fools, simpletons, and numbskulls parade through the various categories of Negro humorous tales.—Dorson

Waiting For Martin
(Julia Courtney)

You see that ghost was named Martin. See it was a hanted house, could no one stay there. And so they put up money to see could they find someone to stay in the house. And so everyone would go to stay in that house couldn't stay there. And so one of the mens went in town, quite natchally was telling about the hanted house. And so the preacher came along. The man said to himself, if anyone could stay in the hanted house, it should be a preacher. So he saw the preacher, and he axed the preacher, was he afraid of a hanted house. And the preacher says, "Why no, everywhere I go I reads my Bible." So this man takes him on back there to this man what owned this house. So when they got there the man told him how much money he had for everyone that stayed in the hanted house. So that night the preacher got his grip and his Bible and went on over to the hanted house. He went on in and he sat down. He opened his Bible, and the preacher began to read. And the verse he was reading was very familiar to everybody. The preacher said, "In those days came John the Baptist preaching in the wilderness of Judea. Repent for the Kingdom of Heaven is at hand." So he read it for a long time. After a while he heard a door squeak. He kept reading his Bible. He read it, "In those days come John the Baptist preaching in the wilderness of Judey."

The spook come on by and just said, "How de do." He kept reading and he never looked up. Way after a while he heard another door open. That

spook come on by. The preacher began reading just a little bit faster.

"In those days come John the Baptist preaching in the wilderness of Judey."

After a while he heard another one. This time didn't no door open, but he heard footsteps. He began reading just a little bit faster.

"In those days come John the Baptist preaching in the wilderness of Judey."

This spook got even with him and stopped. He said, "Mister," he said, "will you be here when Martin come?" The preacher kept reading.

"In those days come John the Baptist preaching in the wilderness of Judey."

He's getting scared.

So way after a while the hant touched him again. He said, "Will you be here when Martin come?"

The preacher kind of looked up slyly and axed, "Who Martin? Sure I'll be here when he come." (He's trying to bluff this spook you see.)

Way after while the preacher began to read faster an' faster. This time he heard the turriblest noises of all. This was Martin. Martin dug on up to the preacher he did. This time the preacher put his finger on the Bible.

"In those days come John the Baptist preaching in the wilderness of Judey."

(See he didn't want to look up.)

Martin stood there and listened at him read. After a while Martin shook him. Preacher kept reading. He wouldn't look up. He kept tetching the preacher on the shoulder, and arter a while Martin wouldn't go away, the preacher looked up. And when he looked and saw Martin's face, instead of reading "In those days come John the Baptist," the preacher begin to tremble. And every which a way he turn Martin was there. The preacher finally couldn't get out the room. The preacher says, "Oh mama." Way arter a while, he was so scared, he hollered, "Oh papa." Martin was chasing the preacher so bad till when he did get a chance he grabbed his Bible and grip and got going. And no one ever saw the preacher again.

(He figgered he'd just take a gait he could hold that was familiar to the spirits.)

On The Cooling Board
(John Courtney)

There was two fellows setting up with the dead. And in the olden times people would go off in a trance and finally come to. So Sam had went off in trance that evening, and had been quite a few people there sitting up. So after a while pretty well all the people had gone and left nobody there but John and Ike. So John and Ike they slept together; it was round about three o'clock Ike woke up. Sam was setting up on the cooling board. Ike wanted to hunch John but John was little too far from him. So Ike say, "Sam, Sam." (*High*) (He was trying to get away all the time.)

Sam was setting there looking at him. So after a while Sam said, "Wake John up."

Ike kept reaching for the door. Ike said, "I'm damn if that's so, I'm going to leave you and John right here."

So when Sam made all that racket, that woke John up. When John woke up, Sam straightened up on the cooling board, and he laid hands on John. And John carried him straight up to the Boss's house.

(John left there like a hurrycane.)

Who Darket De Hole?
(Silas Altheimer)

Sambo and Jim Bungum were straggling through the woods one day looking for muscadines and wild grapes. And finally they came upon an embankment with a ditch below and a large stump up above, where there was high ground, which went down into the hole. And the stump was hollow at the top. So Jim Bungum went down and peeped into the big hole below, and saw some bear cubs. So he decided to go in, to get him one of the cubs. In the meantime the bear at some distance had seen them. The bear came in great haste, and she chased Sambo round and round a good while. And finally the bear quit chasing Sambo, and stuck her head in the stump on the high ground. And she started down the hole from the embankment. And so when she got part way down Sambo grabbed her by the tail and held her.

And so Jim Bungum down below said, "Sambo, who darket de hole?"
Sambo says, "If tail hold slip you'll see who darket de hole."

Dividing Souls
(A. J. King)

Two well-known tales are cleverly intertwined here. The story of the passerby who thinks he hears the Lord and the Devil counting souls in the graveyard enjoys extraordinary vogue; Vance Randolph says he knows fifty persons in the Ozarks who can tell it. . . . Stith Thompson comments on its European and American popularity . . . In United States Negro texts the slave houseboy sometimes carries his crippled Old Marster down to the graveyard, who in fright runs home under his own power . . . Many other variants have been told me by Michigan and Arkansas Negroes.—Dorson

During the period of slavery time Old Marster always kept one slave that would keep him posted on the others, so that he would know how to deal with them when they got unruly. So this slave was walking around in the moonlight one night. And he heard a noise coming from the cemetery. And it was two slaves counting apples, which they had stole from Old Marster's orchard. They couldn't count, so they were exchanging 'em. "You take dis un and I'll take dat un. Dis un's yours and dat un's mine."

So this slave hear them, and he listened, and he ran back to Old Marster. And running he fell over a skeleton head, and he spoke to the skeleton head. "What you doing here?"

And the skeleton head said, "Something got me here will get you here."

So he told Old Marster when he got to the house that the Devil and the Good Lord was in the cemetery counting out souls. "Dis un's yours and dat un's mine, dis un's yours and dat un's mine."

Old Marster didn't believe him, but he went with him to the cemetery. And Old Marster told him, said, "Now if the Devil and the Good Lord ain't counting out souls, I'm going to cut your head off."

Sure enough the slaves had gone and Old Marster didn't hear anything, and he cut John's head off. Then John's head fell beside the skeleton head. Then the head turned over and said, "I told you something that got me here would get you here. You talk too much."

(That's one my daddy would tell us when we were talking too much.)

I'm Going to Fall
(John Courtney)

This story falls under the motif of "Fear Test: staying in haunted house where corpse drops piecemeal down chimney. Dead man's members call out to hero, 'Shall we fall, or shall we not?'" This trait also occurs as an episode in Type 326, "The Youth Who Wanted to Learn What Fear Is," and appears as tale no. 4 in the classic collection of Household Tales by the Brothers Grimm.—Dorson

Some travelers in olden time traveled with a yoke of oxen. So they come to this old house. So they 'cided they'd put up for the night there. They took out everything and got the cook vessels, 'cided they would cook them something to eat. So they cooked the bread. Then John put his meat on. Just about time his meat began to cook, something holler,

"I'm going to fall." [Very high]

They looked around, looked at one another. Say, "What was that?" He just kept hollering,

"I'm going to fall."

So John thought it was some of the boys trying to kid him, said, "That's not none of us, that's up high, whatsever it is." So he hollered again,

"I'm going to fall."

So that made John mad. John hollered back, "Fall then."

That time down he come into that skillet, and down went the skillet, and knocked his meat and fire and everything, and out went the boys. John whirled and got away from there.

Eating Farther Down the Hog
(Rev. Mrs. L. R. Toler)

There was a man named John Ashe, cut wood for a living, usually would accept just a hog head—raised in a country where they grew hogs. So one day somebody gave him a piece of shoulder—tasted pretty good to him, never tasted it before. Passed by one of his old friends, she'd killed a couple of hogs. Children called out, "Mammy, here comes Uncle John."

She called out, "Children, tell Uncle John I'll give him a hog head to cut a load of wood."

Children said, "Uncle John."

He just threw up the back of his hand, wouldn't stop. Finally their mother came out, called, "John, John—give you two hog heads for the one load of wood."

He kept on going, said, "Children, tell your mammy I'm eating further down the hog now."

I'm Sopping My Own Gravy Now
(E. M. Moore)

The Negro worked for the Southern doctor. The doctor would leave home before breakfast every morning and the Negro would carry breakfast to the office. One morning the doctor was sitting looking out the window from his upstairs office. He saw the Negro coming down the street with his breakfast. He took a biscuit from the plate and sopped the biscuit in the doctor's gravy and ate. When he reached the office, the doctor whipped him, told him he was fired. "I don't allow a nigger to sop out of my gravy. Get out and get you some gravy of your own to sop."

The Negro left and moved to Arkansas (from Mississippi). The first year he was in Arkansas, farming was good. He made money, he bought a pair of mules and some plow tools. The next year farming was good. He started buying forty acres of land, paid for his mules, his forty acres of land, bought a horse and buggy and nice clothes. The next year he drove back to the same town in Mississippi. He saw the doctor he had worked for when he lived in Mississippi. The doctor wanted to know who he was driving for when he saw him in the new buggy with the nice horse.

He said, "I'm driving for myself."

He said, "What are you doing now, John?"

He said, "I'm farming."

He said, "Who for, John?"

He said, "Myself."

He said, "Whose buggy and horse is that?"

He said, "They belong to me."
"And you're farming for yourself?"
"Yessir."
"Own your own mules?"
"Yessir."
"Own your own land?"
"Yessir."
"Well John, tell me, what are you doing in Arkansas?"
"Sir, I'm sopping my own gravy."

Informants

Altheimer, Rev. Silas Jenkins. Born in Toledo, Cleveland County, Arkansas, 21 August 1870. His father was a German immigrant, his mother was born of a slave. He was a pastor of the African Methodist Episcopal Church in Pine Bluff, and spent 54 years teaching, 13 at Alcorn A & M in Mississippi and 8 at the AM & N College in Pine Bluff. He heard many stories from his grandmother, a runaway slave.

Cothran, Dr. Tilman C. Born in Hope, Arkansas, 17 November 1917. Professor of Sociology at the AM & N College, with a Ph.D. from the University of Chicago.

Courtney, John. Born 1907, in Drew County, Arkansas. "I used to be a showboy—that Sugarfoot Green Show—from 1925 to 1927. I was a tap-dancer, I was pretty good at the foots." Due to heavy injuries received on the job, John now does only light work.

Courtney, Julia. Born in Drew County, between Helena and McGehee. Married John Courtney in 1931. "My grandfather on my mother's side was mixed with Indian and Creole. I never saw my father but once, when I was seventeen."

Courtney, Tobe. Born in Drew County, Arkansas, 17 December 1879, between Collins and Monticello. "I made ties for the railroad, cut timber for sawmills, herded cattle, chopped, picked, ploughed cotton." Like his son John, he went up North when he was young, just gallivanting. Came to Pine Bluff in 1944.

King, A. J., Jr. Born in Little Rock, Arkansas, on 25 June 1920. Both his parents came from Trinidad. Head teacher at Barnes Elementary School, outside Pine Bluff, a graduate of the AM & N College. Severely wounded in World War II, but now fully recovered.

Moore, E. M. Born in Utica, Mississippi, 23 November 1907. Spent 23 years up and down the levees, excavating and landscaping. Built the football stadium for the AM & N College. His mother was an Indian, his paternal grandfather a white man.

Stanfill, Harrison. Born in Columbus, Tennessee, 30 November 1894. Blind veteran of World War II, living in a rooming hotel apparently with the aid of a pension.

Summers, Maria. Born in Columbia, South Carolina, in 1864. Lives in Barnes Settlement nine miles outside Pine Bluff.

Toler, Rev. Mrs. L. R. Born in Macon, Noxubee County, Mississippi, in 1896. Taught school in Mississippi, Louisiana, and Alabama, was ordained in the African Methodist Episcopal Church, and felt the call for her mission to found a colored Old Folks Home in Pine Bluff in 1942.

CHAPTER 4

ARKANSAS VOICES SING

Singing, like storytelling, has long been a part of man's nature. To the accompaniment of musical instruments, ranging from crude, homemade banjos to today's expensive electric guitars, voices have been raised in song. Man puts into his music all the pain, the joy, the love, and even the hate he feels within his soul. No other mode of expression can offer the solace or reveal the joy as music can. Every gathering will turn to singing before it comes to a close.

The German philosopher Nietzsche wrote, "Without music life would be a mistake." If this be true, the lives of Arkansans have not been mistakes, for music has played a continuous role in their lives. The ballads from the Ozarks enjoy a respected position in the "hill" culture, while the folk tunes and spirituals of Arkansas Blacks maintain an equal position in the Delta country.

Songs of the Hills

The realm of Arkansas literature is once again indebted to Vance Randolph for his extensive collection of Arkansas ballads. Mr. Randolph devoted many years and many miles to driving over the Ozark mountains, capturing authentic ballads and tracing their origins. The following selections, with their sources listed, are but a minute portion of the multitude of ballads which come from the Ozark hills. An attempt has been made to provide only a cross-section of the accumulation of songs collected.

The Cambric Shirt

This is "The Elfin Knight" (No. 2 in Child's collection), beloved of Samuel Pepys in the time of Charles the Second, and still well known in rural England. There is a black letter broadside in the Pepys collection, printed circa 1670.

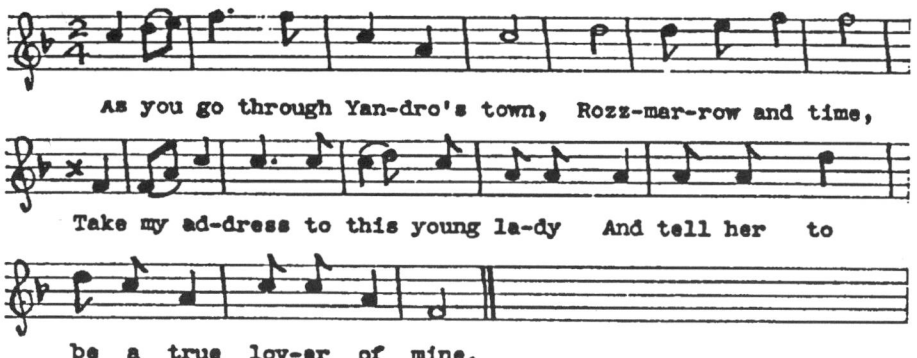

Vance Randolph. *Ozark Folksongs, Vol. I* (Columbia, MO: State Historical Society of Missouri, 1946).

Go tell her to make me a cambric shirt,
Rozz-marrow and time,
Without one stitch of a seamster's work
And then she can be a true lover of mine.

Go tell her to wash it in a dry well,
Rozz-marrow and time,
Where water never was nor rain never fell
And then she can be a true lover of mine.

Go tell her to dry it on a thorn,
Rozz-morrow and time,
Where a leaf never budded since Adam was born
And then she can be a true lover of mine.

Oh it's as you go through Yandro's town,
Rozz-marrow and time,

Sung by Mr. Wiley Hembree, Farmington, Ark., Dec. 29, 1941. Learned from his father, near Farmington, in 1896.

Take my address to this young man
And tell him to be a true lover of mine.

Go tell him to clear me one acre of land,
Rozz-marrow and time,
Between the salt sea and the sea sand
And then he can be a true lover of mine.

Go tell him to plough it with a muley-cow's horn,
Rozz-marrow and time,
And plant it all over with one grain of corn,
And then he can be a true lover of mine.

Go tell him to reap it with an old stirrup-leather,
Rozz-marrow and time,
And bind it all up in a peafowl's feather
And then he can be a true lover of mine.

Go tell him to thresh it against the wall,
Rozz-marrow and time,
And not one grain on the floor shall fall
And then he can be a true lover of mine.

Go tell him to take it to the mill,
Rozz-marrow and time,
And every grain its bushel shall fill,
And then he can be a true lover of mine.

Go tell this young man when he gets his work done,
Rozz-marrow and time,
To come to my house and his shirt'll be done,
And then he can be a true lover of mine.

The Miller's Daughter

This is easily recognized as "The Twa Sisters" (Child, English and Scottish Popular Ballads, 1882-1898, No. 10), which Sir Walter Scott (Minstrelsy of the Scottish Border, 1902 ed., II, p. 352) knew as "The Cruel Sister."

An' next he bought her was a gay gold ring,
Bow she bent to me,
An' next he bought her was a gay gold ring,
The oldest sister not a thing,
I'll be kind to my true love
If you'll be kind to me.

Sis, oh sis, let us walk out,
Bow she bent to me.
Sis, oh sis, let us walk out
An' see the ships a-sailin' about,
I'll be kind to my true love
If you'll be kind to me.

They walked till they come to the salt-cellar brim,
Bow she bent to me,
They walked till they come to the salt-cellar brim,

Communicated by Mr. F. M. Goodhue, Mena, Ark., June 29, 1930. Mr. Goodhue learned the song from a blind woman in the hills near Mena.

The oldest pushed the youngest in,
I'll be kind to my true love
If you'll be kind to me.

Sis, oh sis, hold down your hand,
Bow she bent to me,
Sis, oh sis, hold down your hand,
An' I'll give you my house an' land,
I'll be kind to my true love
If you'll be kind to me.

Sis, oh sis, hold down your glove,
Bow she bent to me,
Sis, oh sis, hold down your glove,
An' I'll give you my own true love,
I'll be kind to my true love
If you'll be kind to me.

Miller, oh miller, yonder swims a swan,
Bow she bent to me,
Miller, oh miller, yonder swims a swan,
A-swimmin' down in your mill pond,
I'll be kind to my true love
If you'll be kind to me.

The miller run out with his fish-hook,
Bow she bent to me,
The miller run out with his fish-hook,
An' he drawed her out of that big brook,
I'll be kind to my true love
If you'll be kind to me.

He took five gold rings off her fingers,
Bow she bent to me,
He took five gold rings off her fingers,
An' pushed her back in that big river,
I'll be kind to my true love
If you'll be kind to me.

The miller was hung by his mill gate,
Bow she bent to me,
The miller was hung by his mill gate,
For drownin' of my sister Kate,
I'll be kind to my true love
If you'll be kind to me.

The miller was hung on a limb so high,
Bow she bent to me,
The miller was hung on a limb so high,
The oldest sister was burnt close by,
I'll be kind to my true love
If you'll be kind to me.

Johnny Randolph

Most Ozark singers know this piece as "Johnny Randolph" or "Jimmy Randolph," but it was originally the old ballad of "Lord Randall" (Child, English and Scottish Ballads, 1882-1898, No. 12) and is still current in England under that title. Cox (Folk-Songs of the South, 1925, p. 23) suggests that the name derives from John Randolph of Roanoke, a Virginia politician who died in 1833. However, it is certain that the name Randolph was somehow connected with this song in the Old World. Sir Walter Scott (Minstrelsy of the Scottish Border, 1902 ed., III, p. 51) thinks it "not impossible that the ballad may have originally regarded the death of Thomas Randolph, or Randal, Earl of Murray, nephew to Robert Bruce, and governor of Scotland. This great warrior died at Musselburgh, 1332 . . . . Our historians obstinately impute his death to poison."

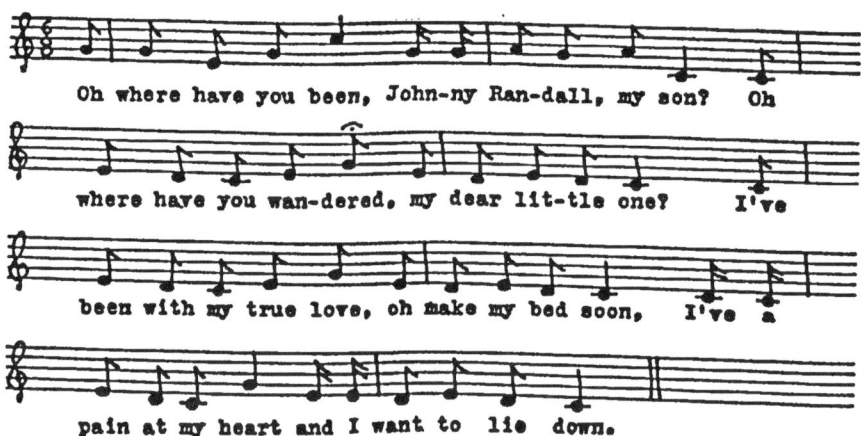

Contributed by Mr. R. H. Clayton, Lanagan, Mo., Nov. 14, 1928. Mr. Clayton learned it from his mother, about 1885.

Where have you been a-ridin', Johnny Randall, my son?
Where have you been a-ridin', my own sweet pretty one?
A-ridin' a-courtin', mother, make my bed soon,
For I'm tired of ridin' and I fain would lie down.

What will you have for supper, Johnny Randall, my son?
What will you have for supper, my own sweet pretty one?
A cup of cold poison, mother, make my bed soon,
For I'm tired of ridin' and I fain would lie down.

What will you will to your sister, Johnny Randall, my son?
What will you will to your sister, my own sweet pretty one?
My trunk and fine jewels, mother, make my bed soon,
For I'm tired of ridin' and I fain would lie down.

What will you will to your brother, Johnny Randall, my son?
What will you will to your brother, my own sweet pretty one?
My horse and fine saddle, mother, make my bed soon,
For I'm tired of ridin' and I fain would lie down.

What will you will to your sweetheart, Johnny Randall, my son?
What will you will to your sweetheart, my own sweet pretty one?
A rope for to hang her, and a knife to cut her down,
I'm tired of ridin' and I fain would lie down.

Barbara Allen

Perhaps the most popular of all the traditional ballads, "Barbara Allen" dates at least to the middle of the seventeenth century. It is mentioned in Pepys' Diary *(Jan. 2 and 6, 1666), and is included in Percy's* Reliques, *1765. The poet Goldsmith, about the same time (3rd* Essay, *p. 14), refers to a dairy-maid who sang the ballad of "Barbara Allen's Cruelty," Child (*English and Scottish Popular Ballads, *1882-1898, No. 84) collected many British versions. Reed Smith (JAFL 28, 1915, p. 203) reported fifty texts from the United States, and many others have since come to light (JAFL 29, 1916, p. 160; 30, 1917, p. 317; 35, 1922, p. 343). Beveridge (*Abraham Lincoln, *1928, I, p. 69) tells us that Abe Lincoln sang "Barbara Allen" as a boy in Indiana. Dolph (*Sound Off! *1929, p. 491) says that the song was well known in America in Colonial days, and that during the Revolution the tune was borrowed for a long-winded ballad called "Sergeant Champe," about an unsuccessful attempt to capture General Benedict Arnold.*

Twas' in the very month of May,
When the green buds they was swellin',
Sweet William on his death bed lay
For the love of Barbra Allen.

He sent his servants into town,
An' there unto her dwellin',
Sayin' Mosso's sick, an' sent for you,
If your name is Barbra Allen.

So slowly, slowly she got up,
An' slowly she went to him,
She drawed the curtains from Willie's pale face,
Sayin' young man, you're a-dyin'.

Don't you remember the other night,
A-settin' in the tavern,
A-drinkin' wine with the ladies all,
An' you slighted Barbra Allen.

Sung by a young woman in Joplin, Mo., July 4, 1924. A native of rural Arkansas, this singer requests that her name shall not be printed in any "hillbilly" book.

Oh yes, I remember the other night,
A-settin' in the tavern,
A-drinkin' wine with the ladies all,
But I never seen Barbra Allen.

So slowly, slowly she got up,
An' slowly she went from him,
She hadn't went but a mile or two
Till she heard the death bell tollin'.

She looked to the East an' she looked to the West,
She seen the chariots a-comin',
With two gray horses a-workin' in the breast,
An' Willie's corpse behind 'em.

Oh mother, oh mother, go dig my grave,
An' dig it both long an' narrow,
Sweet William died for me today,
I'll die for him tomorrow.

They buried her in the old church yard,
An' they buried him beside her,
An' out of his breast grew a red rose bush,
An' out of her'n a brier.

They grew an' they grew to the top of the church,
Till they could not grow no higher,
They linked and they locked in a true love knot,
For all true lovers to admire.

On the Banks of Sweet Dundee

The English broadside version of this song is known as "Undaunted Mary," and it is published in several popular songbooks.

Her uncle had a plowboy that Mary loved quite well,
All down by her uncle's garden a story of love did tell,
There were a wealthy squire-o who came all her to see,
But Mary loved the plowboy best on the banks of the sweet Dundee.

Sung by Mr. Wiley Hembree, Farmington, Ark., Dec. 12, 1941. Mr. Hembree learned it from his father, about 1900.

Her uncle came to her bedside at the dawning of the day,
Saying raise you up, my Mary, a lady you shall be,
Saying raise you up, my Mary, a lady you shall be,
For the squire-o now is a-waiting for you on the banks of the sweet Dundee.

You may have all your squire-os and other dukes likewise,
For Willie he is to me like a diamond in my eyes,
Bid all you . . . little creatures . . .
For I intend to slay fair Willie on the banks of the sweet Dundee.

Oh when they came upon him they found him all alone,
He fought brave for liberty, but they were six to one,
Saying kill me, oh kill me, since the blood has flowed so free,
For I intend to die for Mary on the banks of the sweet Dundee.

One day as Mary were a-walking remaining for her love,
She chance to meet the squire-o all down by her uncle's grove,
Saying stand back, don't cry, Mary, a downsel you shall be,
And the trigger she drew and the squire she slew on the banks of the sweet Dundee.

Her uncle heard the noise and a-hasting to the ground,
Saying since you've killed the squire-o I'll give you your death wound,
Saying stand back, don't cry, Mary, a downsel you shall be,
And the trigger she drew and her uncle she slew on the banks of the sweet Dundee.

Her uncle went for a physician, likewise a lawyer still,
Likewise a lawyer that he might sign his will,
He . . . sealed to Mary for fighting manfully,
And he closed his eyes nevermore for to rise on the banks of the sweet Dundee.

The Pretty Mohee

This song is a chastened American version of "The Indian Lass," a piece common in English broadsides. There are several American texts (JAFL 35, 1922, p. 408) in which the name "Mohee" passes into "Momee" or "Maumee" (Belden, Song-Ballads and Other Popular Poetry, 1910, No. 52). Broadley (Harper's Magazine 130, 1915, p. 906) thinks that the song may have been written in colonial times, and suggests that "Maumee" conserves a memory of the Miami Indians. Combs (Folk-Songs du Midi des Etats-Unis, 1925, p. 98) says that it was well known during the period of colonization, but that "son histoire est vague et on ne sait rien de son origine et de son antiqué."

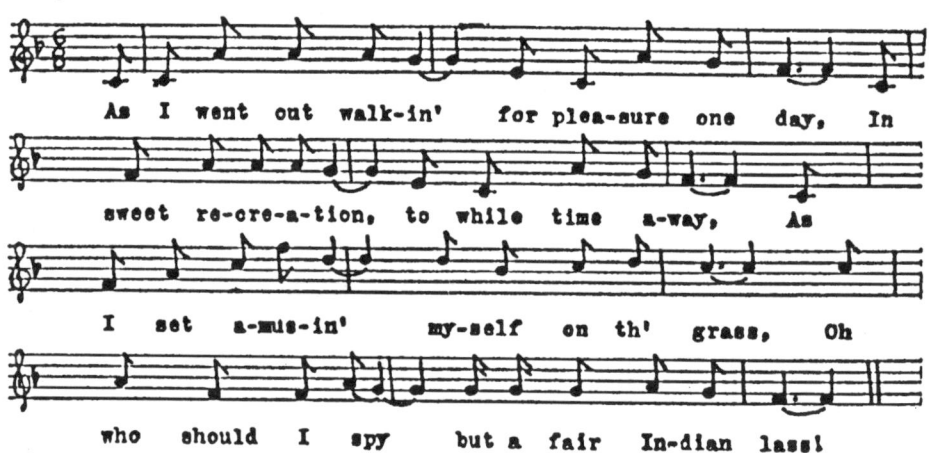

As I went out walkin' for pleasure one day, In sweet re-cre-a-tion, to while time a-way, As I set a-mus-in' my-self on th' grass, Oh who should I spy but a fair In-dian lass!

Contributed by Professor F. M. Goodhue, Mena, Ark., Feb. 5, 1930, from the singing of Mrs. Emma L. Dusenbury, also of Mena.

She stepped up beside me, and taken my hand,
She says you are a stranger, not one of our land
But if you will follow you are welcome to come
And share with me in my snug little home.

The sun was fast sinking beneath the salt sea,
I walked and I rambled with the little Mohi,
We walked and we rambled, and together we roamed
Till we come to the cottage in the coconut grove.

As I rose the next morning to go on my way,
The fondest expression to me she did say,
If you will consent and stay here with me,
I will teach you the language of the little Mohi.

I'll tell you, pretty maiden, that never can be,
I have afar a true love in my own country,
I would not forsake her sweet company
For she's just as true as the little Mohi.

The last time I saw her she was down on the sand,
And as the boat sailed past her she waved me her hand,
Saying when you get over to the girl that you love,
Just think of the Mohi in the coconut grove.

It's now I am safe landed on my own native shore,
Young friends and companions, gather round me once more,
As I look all around me, there is no one I see
That I can compare with the little Mohi.

The Blackbird

The following stanza is quoted as part of "an old Irish Jacobite song" in a serial called "Spanish John" by William McClennan (Harper's Monthly Magazine *95, Oct. 1897, p. 677):*

He's all my heart's treasure, my joy and my pleasure,
So justly, my love, my heart follows thee;
And I am resolved, in foul or fair weather,
To seek out my blackbird wherever he be.

Apparently it was Bonnie Prince Charlie who was called the Blackbird, but according to Frey (Sobriquets and Nicknames, *1895, p. 44) it was Charles II who was alluded to as the Blackbird, in Allan Ramsay's ballads, etc.*

A ten-stanza text is printed in Wehman's Irish Song Book No. 1 *(New York, 1937, p. 12).*

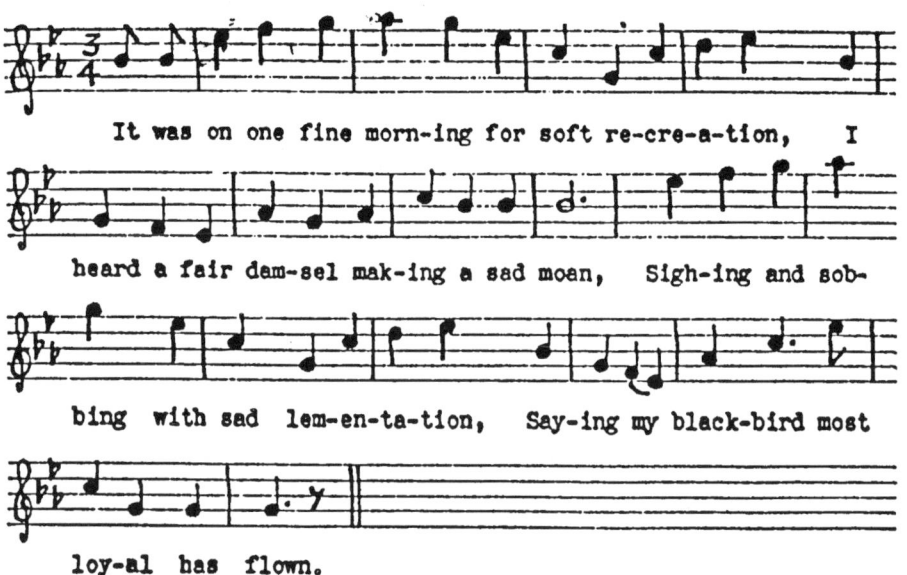

It was on one fine morn-ing for soft re-cre-a-tion, I heard a fair dam-sel mak-ing a sad moan, Sigh-ing and sob-bing with sad lem-en-ta-tion, Say-ing my black-bird most loy-al has flown.

Sung by Mr. Booth Campbell, Cane Hill, Ark., Dec. 24, 1941.

My thoughts they deceive me, reflection it grieves me,
And I am o'erburdened with sad misery,
But if death should blind me, as true love inclines me,
My blackbird I'll seek out wherev-er he be.

Once in fair England my blackbird did flourish,
He was the chief flower that in it did spring,
Fair ladies of honor his person did nourish
Because he was the true son of a king.

But oh that false fortune has proved so uncertain,
That caus-ed the parting between you and me,
But if he remains in France or in Spain
I'll be true to my blackbird wherever he be.

And if by the fowler my blackbird is taken,
It's sighing and sobbing I'll be all the time,
But if he is safe and I'm not mistaken
I'm sure that I'll see him in May or in June.

Oh he is my treasure, my joy and my pleasure,
He's justly beloved, though my hearst follow thee,
How constant and kind, and courageous of mind,
Deserving of blessing wherever he be!

The Frog's Courtship

*The history of this old English song has been worked out in great detail by Kittredge (*JAFL 35, 1922, p. 394*) and by L. W. Payne (*Texas Folk-Lore Society Publications 5, 1926, pp. 5-48*), who prints sixteen texts and tunes and says that the song has been in continuous use for 400 years. Scarborough (*On the Trail of Negro Folk-Songs, 1925, p. 46*) quotes Hyder E. Rollins who claims that it has been traced back to "A Moste Strange Wedding of the Frogge and the Mouse," dated 1580.*

The frog went a-courting and he did ride, uh-huh,
The frog went a-courting and he did ride
With a sword and pistol by his side, uh-huh.

Sung by Mrs. Irene Carlisle, Fayetteville, Ark., Sept. 30, 1941.

He rode up to Miss Mousie's door, uh-huh,
He rode up to Miss Mousie's door
Where he'd often been before, uh-huh.

He got down and he went in, uh-huh,
He got down and he went in
To see Miss Mousie card and spin, uh-huh.

He took Miss Mousie on his knee, uh-huh,
He took Miss Mousie on his knee
And said my dear, will you marry me, uh-huh?

Oh no, sir, I can't say that, uh-huh,
Oh no, sir, I can't say that
Till I see my Uncle Rat, uh-huh.

Uncle Rat came a-galloping home, uh-huh,
Uncle Rat came a-galloping home,
Says who's been here while I've been gone, uh-huh?

A nice young gentleman here has been, uh-huh,
A nice young gentleman here has been
Asking me to marry him, uh-huh.

Uncle Rat laughed and shook his fat sides, uh-huh,
Uncle Rat laughed and shook his fat sides
To think that Miss Mousie would soon be a bride, uh-huh.

Where shall the wedding supper be, uh-huh,
Where shall the wedding supper be?
Way down yonder in a hollow tree, uh-huh.

What shall the wedding supper be, uh-huh,
What shall the wedding supper be?
Three butter-beans and a black-eyed pea, uh-huh.

First come in was a flying wasp, uh-huh,
First come in was a flying wasp
Bringing in the table-cloth, uh-huh.

Next come in was a big black snake, uh-huh,
Next come in was a big black snake
Bringing in the wedding cake, uh-huh.

Next come in was a bumble-bee, uh-huh,
Next come in was a bumble-bee
With a fiddle on his knee, uh-huh.

Next come in was a sly old cat, uh-huh,
Next come in was a sly old cat
And says I'll put an end to that, uh-huh.

Miss Mousie she went up the wall, uh-huh,
Miss Mousie she went up the wall,
Her foot slipped and she caught a fall, uh-huh.

The frog went swimming across the lake, uh-huh,
The frog went swimming across the lake
And he got swallowed by a big black snake, uh-huh.

Songs of the Black Folks

Fred Allsopp, in preparing his Folklore of Romantic Arkansas *in 1931, included a section devoted to spirituals and folksongs of the Black citizens of Arkansas. Since it offers the most comprehensive collection of early Black ballads and songs, it is printed in its entirety, including Allsopp's notes and introductions. As was seen earlier in a comparison of the Black tales and the Ozark tales, both traditions enjoy long and illustrious backgrounds. Like the tales, the songs of the Black people stem from the oral tradition and reflect a culture of the past. The spirituals mirror a faith, which has since the beginnings of recorded time sustained an oppressed people. Men of all ages and all races have clung to a Being, higher than they, when the toil of life has come close to being unbearable. So it is with the Black spirituals, many of which are still sung today. The folk tunes of the Blacks express a spirited courage and a delightful gaiety, replete with rhythm and laughter.*

Fred W. Allsopp. *Folklore of Romantic Arkansas*, Vol. II (Grolier Society, 1931).

Here is a Negro hymn which is said to have been sung by the washerwoman to the accompaniment of soap-bubbles and the rub-de-dub of the washboard sixty or more years ago. It is taken from an article in *Harper's Magazine* of 1878:

> Soul shall shine lak a star in de mornin',
> Soul shall shine lak a star in de mornin',
>   Oh, my little soul's gwine to rise an' shine,
>   Oh, my little soul's gwine to rise an' shine.
>
> I'll see me mudder in de new burryin' groun',
> Watin' to honnah de Lord,
> As I pass by de gates o' hell,
> I'll bid ole satan a long farewell,
> Holy, holy, holy, my Lord!
> Holy, holy, holy, blood of de lam'.

During the old days of slavery the happy-go-lucky Negroes were noted for their cabin and field dances, their jig tunes and fiddle songs. Some of their original plantation and shouting songs were handed down by word of mouth from African ancestors. Some were improvised, and others were brought with them from other southern states when they came to Arkansas with their "marsters" and "missuses." One well-known old song is:

Swing low, sweet chariot—comin' fer to carry me home,
Swing low, sweet chariot—comin' fer to carry me home.
I looked over Jordan, and what did I see—comin' fer to carry me home?

Then there is the "Soldier of the Cross" Spiritual—

I stahted out fo' heaben in de ahmy ob de Lawd,
I stahted out fo' heaben in de ahmy;
An' I'm boun' to be a soldiuh in de ahmy ob de Lawd,
O, I'm boun' to be a soldiuh in de ahmy.

In de kingdom,
Wid my Redeemuh,
Got salvashun
To bring me ovah, etc.

The Negro becomes very emotional when influenced by religion. Anyone who hears him shout "Hallelujah! hallelujah!" when the spirit moves him at an all-day Sunday or all-night meeting, or when he is "ducked" in the water at a baptizing at the river, could well believe he would never rob another hen roost, but the religious ecstatic spell usually wears off as quickly as it came. The Negro women put a great deal of plaintive feeling into such reiterative lines as the following verse of a lengthy song:

Nobody knows my trubles like de Lord,
Nobody knows my trubles like de Lord,
Nobody knows my trubles like de Lord,
Nobody knows but Jesus.
Sister won't you pray for me,

An' help me drive ole Satan away?

It is not the words, but the inflection that is given to the characteristic refrains and the repetitious verbiage that gives them a charm all their own. Here is another old Spiritual, which professional minstrels have been heard to sing:

> Where, Oh, where is Elijah?
> Where, Oh, where is Elijah?
> Where, Oh, where is Elijah?
> 'Way over in de promised lan'.
>
> He went up in a fiery chariot,
> He went up in a fiery chariot,
> He went up in a fiery chariot,
> 'Way over in de promised lan'.
>
> By and by we will go an' see him,
> By and by we will go an' see him,
> By and by we will go an' see him,
> 'Way over in de promised lan'.

The old-time song called the *Moanish Lady* has been heard often in Negro barber sh*ops:*

> Oh, there was a *moanish* lady,
> Lived in a moanish land,
> She had a moanish daughter
> Could moan at the Lord's command.
> Moanish lady and you shall be free
> Moanish honey, and you shall be free
> When the good Lord shall carry you home.

The Negro sings or chants the simplest words with the greatest intensity. Most of them have good voices. In the cotton fields or elsewhere they accompany all their work with song, and one envies the enjoyment that these simple folk get out of life, when, with mouth wide open they sing a folk-song or a "reel," perhaps to the patting of feet or the accompaniment of a mouth-organ or banjo, played by ear. A Negro song often heard in the early days was "Root, Hog, or Die":

> The greatest ole nigger that I eva' did see,
> Looked like a sick monkey up a sour apple tree;
> It don't make a bit of difference to either you or I,
> Big pig, little pig, root hog, or die.
>
> *Chorus*
> Chief cook and bottle washer, Captain of the waiters
> Stan' upon your head while you peel a bag of 'taters.
>
> I come from Alabama with a pocketful of news,
> I'm wofh forty dollars a-standin' in my shoes;
> Doesn't make a bit o' difference to either you or I,
> Big pig, little pig, root hog, or die.
>
> *Chorus*
> Chief cook and bottle washer, Captain of the waiters,
> Stan' upon your head while you peal a bag of 'taters.

Here is a plaintive, more modern Negro song which voices his indifference to politics. It is reproduced from a file of the old Arkansas Traveler, published in the '80's by Opie Read:

> De nigger ain't er keerin' er who's de president,
>   Take kere my soul, good Lawd;
> One way er tuther 'twon't 'feck him er cent.
>   Take kere my soul, good Lawd;
> De constertution says dat de nigger is free,
>   Take kere my soul, good Lawd;
> Dat's de sorter doctrine whut allus fits me,
>   Take kere my soul, good Lawd.

> Oh, de white men growl,
> > Oh, de white men fight,
> Oh, de polerticians howl,
> > Oh, dey strain wid der might,
> But gin ter de po' man de chance ter work an' lib,
> An' yer's dun gin all whut er Sabyer coul' gib,
> Oh, Lawd, Mars' Abraham, lissen ter de call.
>
> Po' man ain't gwine fur ter git no gain,
> > Take kere my soul, good Lawd;
> Out o' de 'publican er dimocratic reign,
> > Take kere my soul, good Lawd;
> White man it seems is er workin' fur hisse'f,
> > Take kere my soul, good Lawd;
> Wid him de wooly head is allus on de she'f,
> > Take kere my soul, good Lawd.
>
> > Oh, de white man laugh,
> > > Oh, de white man grin,
> > Oh, de nigger is er ca'f,
> > > Oh, de sinner man'll win,
> But gin Mars' Jacob, de weaker man er show,
> Yer's p'inted out dey way whut de lowly man mus' go,
> Oh, Lawd, Mars' Abraham, he'p us frum de fall.

Miss Phebe Parke, of Fort Smith, communicates some lines of a folk-song which she heard sung in a Negro church when she was a child. It runs thus:

> There was a maiden, young and fair,
> Who died in sin and dark despair.
>
> On Monday she went to her bed,—
> Her eyes were rolling in her head.

There is a verse for every day in the week, and in the last one the girls asks if she can be saved, when the preacher answers:

> Alas! Alas! yo' time is spent,
> It is too late that you repent.

"Old Rob Ridley" is a typical song which the Arkansas darkies who came from Alabama used to sing in the '60's. It went something like this:

> Now w'ite folks I'll sing yer a ditty,
> I'se frum home, but dat's no pitty.
> O, to praise myse'f it am a shame,
> But Robert Ridley is my name.
>
> O, Bob Ridley, ho; Oh, ho, ho!
> O, Bob Ridley, ho; Oh, ho, ho!
> Robert Ridley, ho!
>
> De fus' time dat I eber got a lickin',
> 'Twas down at de forks ob de cott'n pickin';
> Oh! it made me dance, it made me tremble,
> Oh! golly, it made my eye-balls jingle.
> Oh, Bob Ridley, Oh, ho, ho!
>
> Oh, w'ite folks, I hab crossed de mountain,
> How many mile, I didn't count 'em.
> Oh, I'se lef' de folks at de ole plantation,
> An' cum down here fer my edication.
> Oh, Bob Ridley, Oh, ho, ho!

Like the song, "It ain't Goin' to Rain No Mo'," there are a hundred and more verses to some of these old melodies.

A lullaby that the old black mammies used to sing as they rocked the children to sleep, was:

> Hush a bye an' don' yo' cry,
> Hush a bye, li'l baby;

> Yo' sweetheart'll come bime-by,
>   Hush a bye, li'l baby.
> When he comes dressed in blue,
>   Hush a bye, li'l baby.
> Then you'll know his love is true,
>   Hush a bye, li'l baby.

Then there were such songs as, "Dese Bones Gwine To Rise Ag'in," "The Mules in the Bottoms," "Old Man Moon," "'Possum Fat and 'Taters," "Zip Coon," "Turkey in the Straw," "The Old Gray Mare Came Tearin' Out de Wilderness," "Old Black Joe," "Massa's In De Col', Col' Ground,'" etc., sung by the darkies, with gesticulations, and contortions, and the stamping of feet and the clapping of hands. And here is a verse of a song which has gone the rounds of whites and blacks since the little boll-weevil pest began to devour the cotton crop of the south to cut down production:

> Fus- time I seed de Boll-Weevil,
>   He wuz a-settin' on de squah.
> Nex' time I seed dat Weevil
>   He wuz litin' ever 'whar,
> Jes' a-lookin' foh a home—lookin' for a home.

There are several versions of "Dixie," which is of course not in the class of Spirituals, but sometimes one hears the original "Walk-around" version, which is said to be:

> I wish I was in de land ob cotton,
> Cinnamon seed and sandy bottom;
>   Look away, look away, away,
>   Dixie land.
> In Dixie land where I was born in
> Early on one frosty mornin',
> Look away, look away.
>
> Den I wish I was in Dixie,
>   Hooray! Hooray!

In Dixie land I'll take my stand,
    To lib an' die in Dixie,
Away, away, away down south in Dixie.

Ole Missus marry Will, de Weaber,
William was a gay deceiber;
When he put his farms aroun' 'er,
He looked as fierce as a forty-pounder.

Hooray! Hooray! etc.

His face was sharp like a butcher's cleaber,
But dat did not seem to greab 'er.
Will run away—Missus took a de cline, O!
Her face was de color ob bacon shine, O!

Hooray! Hooray! etc.

While Missus libbed, she libbed in clober;
When she died, she died all ober.
How could she act such a foolish part, O!
An' marry a man to break her heart, O!

Hooray! Hooray! etc.

Buck wheat cakes an' stony batter,
Makes you fat or a little fatter;
Here's a health to de nex' ole Missus,
An' all de gals dat want to kiss us.

Hooray! Hooray! etc.

Now if yo' want to drive away sorrow,
Come and hear dis song to-morrow,
Den hot it down an' scratch de grabble.
To Dixie land I'm bound to trabble.

Hooray! Hooray! etc.

We claim Dixie as a southern song, but it is still a question whether it really was of southern origin. Dan D. Emmett, who had been a northern soldier, is credited with its authorship, and it is claimed that Dixie's Land, or the Negro's Paradise, was on Manhattan Island or Long Island. When the slaves were moved from the north and carried south, they pined for their old homes, as represented in the song. This was also the case with the song, "Carry Me Back to Old Virginny."

A writer in the *Little Rock Democrat* in 1861, said he remembered some fifteen or twenty years back when a favorite game of the boys in Virginia was called "Dixie Land." Each boy would get on a piece of ground, representing a square or circle, which was marked out, and "Dixie" took his stand in the middle of it. Each boy as he stood there would sing:

"I'm on Dixie Land,
And Dixie ain't at home;
Dixie's men have run away,
And Dixie's wife has gone."

If Dixie succeeded in touching him, he became one of Dixie's men and helped to catch the others till all were caught and the game ended. That writer thought the song originated in some such way as this, first being a rude ditty, chanted by exiles, and then gradually assuming its present form.

On his monument in Ohio, Daniel D. Emmett is credited with authorship of the famous song, and although he popularized the song by singing it, it is doubtful whether he was the author of either the song or the music, or even was capable of composing it. James H. Malone, a distinguished Memphis lawyer, wrote an article which was published in the *Arkansas Gazette* May 8, 1928, in which he said:

> The usual story is going the rounds, attributing the authorship of both the melody and the words of that inspiring war song, "Dixie," to Daniel D. Emmett, often called "Uncle Dan." These articles usually state it was left for a Union soldier to write this inspiring song for the south. President Roosevelt said to me while in Memphis that it was the most inspiring air he had ever heard. A monument has been erected to Emmett at his former home in Ohio, on which the authorship is

This reference is obviously to President Teddy Roosevelt

attributed to him, nevertheless it is not true. That Emmett, as a member of a side show with a popular circus, aided in bringing the melody to public notice, is true, but I believe it has been shown beyond a reasonable doubt that this is the full extent of his achievement, and that its introduction came from men of the South. Mark, the claim is now made specifically that on a rainy Sunday, September 18, 1859, Emmett composed both the words and melody of "Dixie."

The overwhelming evidence shows that the melody now called "Dixie" was an old folklore song, and had been sung in the South long before 1859, when it is claimed Emmett composed it. In addition, Colonel T. Alston Brown, a soldier of the North, and the dramatic editor of the New York *Clipper,* stated that in 1861 Emmett admitted to him that he based the music on an old English nursery song, and he called his production "Dixieland," not "Dixie." No one pretends, so far as I know, that the words he composed so late as 1859 were used in the South by the army or Southern people.

The truth is the song was sung in the South long prior to 1859, and that in 1857 or 1858 D. P. Faulds, a music dealer and publisher of Louisville, Kentucky, received from a New Orleans house a sample sheet of music called "Dixie," which struck his fancy, and he called two young clerks, Will S. Hays and Charlie Ward, showing them the music and suggesting that they compose a song from it, when Hays wrote the words for "Dixie" and Ward arranged for piano the music to suit the words. Faulds sold thousands of copies of "Way Down South in Dixie" (the name Faulds gave the song) long before Emmett is supposed to have composed it.

This is not all. Our fellow townsman, Professor Thos. J. Firth, a Confederate veteran, aged eighty-five years, was first appointed brigade bandmaster by Brigadier-General Preston W. Smith of Memphis, who was killed at the battle of Chickamauga, after which he was successively appointed to the same position by Brigadier-General Geo. W. Gordon, with the rank of Captain. It is almost needless to say that his band played "Dixie" throughout the Civil War. Professor Firth states of his own personal knowledge that in the spring of 1858 Professor John R. Millen of New York came to La Grange, Tennessee, and formed a cornet band of sixteen members. Firth being one of them, that Millen wrote with his own hands the music he was to teach, including "Dixie," furnishing each member a book with the name of the member and the year 1858 thereon. Firth now has in his possession not only his book, but six others, showing that the melody is the same as that which is claimed to have been originated by Emmett on September 18, 1859. Firth also says that Will S. Hays never claimed to have composed the melody, but is equally emphatic that Hays was the author of the words sung in the South to that melody, and it is well and widely known that Hays was the author of many poems and songs, among them "Molly Darling," which, no doubt, all the old-timers will recall with mixed feelings of pleasure and pathos.

This is a lengthy quotation, but it would seem to be of too much interest to be confined in a newspaper article. The universality of the appeal of this tune is emphasized by the fact that Lincoln is said to have greatly enjoyed "Dixie" and clapped his great hands whenever he heard it. The piece was played at a White House serenade just after the surrender of Lee, and it is noteworthy that Lincoln remarked that it was captured from the Confederates "and is legitimately ours."

There have been many versions of "Dixie," two of which are credited to Arkansas. The "Western Dixie," was written by Mrs. Virginia Smith during the war, and the majestic lines of Albert Pike at the same period.

The Musical "Quill"

"Interest in Negro folk-songs and spirituals has brought to light a crude reed instrument used by some of the older darkies on eastern Arkansas plantations," says a writer on the *Arkansas Gazette*. "Said by students of Negro melodies to have been widely used in the old slavery days, the instruments, which the old Negroes call 'quills,' have been gradually discarded.

"A lover and student of Negro folk-songs found one of the instruments on an Ashley County plantation. He brought it to Little Rock and from him a story of the 'quill' was obtained.

"Made of joints of cane, bound together and tied with string, the instrument has the appearance of a child's toy. Eight joints of the cane, cut to different lengths, to give forth different notes, are used in making it. This gives the Negro musician one octave.

"There are no sharps and flats. These are obtained by the peculiar manner, half singing and half blowing, which the player uses in bringing forth harmony from the reeds. In the hands of an expert, real melodies are produced, and the instrument gives forth a weird, eerie music, similar to no other instrument in the world.

"Musicians and students of musical history say the the 'quill' is the Negro's imitation of the ancient 'Pipes of the Great God Pan.' Old Negroes tell how the instruments first were made by the tribes in the heart of Africa, and were brought into America by the slaves. The eerie music of the reeds, the Negroes say, was played as an accompaniment to the drums of the medicine men, and many of the savage dances of the African tribes were executed to the strange music of the 'quill' and drums.

"The instruments of the Africans were made of carefully seasoned reeds, cut, turned, and highly polished. They were bound together with thongs of tough leather, taken from the hides of wild animals. The instruments used by the plantation Negroes today are patterned after those of the native tribes, but lack the workmanship and polish of those made by the real Africans.

"Likewise, the music of the Negroes today, though sometimes having the throb and beat of the savage, is for the most part the soft, crooning lullabies, or the deep, fervent chant of spirituals. Probably the instrument described was never used for more martial airs than, 'I got shoes, you got shoes, All ob God's chillun got shoes,' and the last air the old Negro played before he turned the 'quill' over to the collector of Negro melodies and instruments was, 'Swing Low, Sweet Chariot, Comin' fer to Carry Me Home.'"

CHAPTER 5

The Poetic Voice of Arkansas

No collection of literature, whether it be large or small, would be complete without some representative poetry. Some emotions and experiences are always best described through the medium of verse. In Arkansas, as in all other regions, there have been sensitive individuals who turned to rhyme and meter for expression. The magnificence of the mountains, the loveliness of the seasons and the little ordinary Arkansan have been exalted in native poetry. Arkansans can be proud of their poets; some have gained national and even international recognition, while others have produced works which are rather obscure even in their own locale. Regardless of their destiny, the poets of Arkansas have compiled vast numbers of poetical reflections. The items chosen for this chapter come from those who constitute the finest among the poets of Arkansas —the early poets as well as the modern ones, the frequently published as well as the private poets. In this revision of the volume, I have included some of Arkansas' developing poets as well as the established ones.

Creative Writing Programs in nearly every institution of higher learning are actively producing writers of tomorrow in Arkansas. Many high schools also provide some outlet for creative writing. The nurturing of poets is vital for the artistic future of the Arkansas culture. To include such youthful examples in an anthology is not without its pitfalls and dangers; however, it constitutes an exciting and encouraging portion of this revision. Poetry and poets are alive and well in Arkansas today. While many serious young poets are practicing their art in the state, all of them cannot be included, and therein lies the danger of this addition. Submissions from several of the Creative Writing Programs were solicited, and selections were made from these submissions. No doubt there will be some disagreement on the selections and some fine efforts will be omitted. Still I take great pleasure in presenting some of the "newcomers."

Albert Pike

Editor, soldier, lawyer, poet—this was one of Arkansas' favorite sons. Albert Pike came from a distinguished family in the history of the United States. Among his forebears is Nicholas Pike, the author of America's first published arithmetic book and the planter of the famed liberty tree which stands today in Boston. Zebulon Montgomery Pike, the trailblazer of the old west who named Pike's Peak, is another member of this eminent family.

Albert Pike, born in Boston on December 29, 1809, had a variety of careers and he achieved success in all of them. He arrived in Fort Smith, Arkansas, in 1832, where he became a teacher in a small school near Van Buren. While engaged in this position, he entered the journalistic field by contributing a series of political articles to the Little Rock Advocate. *In October of 1833 Pike became associate editor of this Whig organ, which he purchased in 1835.*

In the field of law, he again found success. After having instructed himself in the legal profession, he was licensed to practice law in the state of Arkansas. He was admitted to the bar of the United States Supreme Court in 1849 along with a young lawyer of Illinois who was destined to become the sixteenth president of the United States—Abraham Lincoln.

As a military leader, Pike received special honors from General Zachary Taylor during the Mexican War and served with the Confederacy during the War Between the States. During the latter conflict, he organized a Confederate force of Cherokee Indians who engaged in several battles for the South. Pike also proved to be a diplomat of stature when he consummated the first treaties ever made with the wild Commanche and Apache Indians.

His poetry, which romanticized the Indians and affectionately pictured his home state of Arkansas, received much notice, though it seems to be better known today than during his own time. His poem "Ode to the Mocking-bird" holds the distinction of being the first poem of America to be published in a foreign publication. It appeared in Blackwood's Magazine *at Edinburgh in 1836.*

Albert Pike. *General Albert Pike's Poems* (Little Rock: Fred W. Allsopp, pulisher, 1900)

Ode to the Mocking-bird

Thou glorious mocker of the world! I hear
    Thy many voices ringing through the glooms
Of these green solitudes; and all the clear,
Bright joyance of their song enthralls the ear,
    And floods the heart. Over the sphered tombs
Of vanished nations rolls thy music-tide:
    No light from History's starlit page illumes
The memory of these nations: They have died:
None care for them but thou; and thou mayst sing,
    Over me, too, perhaps, as thy notes ring
Over their bones by whom thou once wast deified.

Glad scorner of all cities! Thou dost leave
    The world's mad turmoil and incessant din,
Where none in others' honesty believe,
Where the old sigh, the young turn gray and grieve,
    Where misery gnaws the maiden's heart within;
Thou fleest far into the dark green woods,
    Where, with thy flood of music, thou canst win
Their heart to harmony, and where intrudes
    No discord on thy melodies. Oh, where,
    Among the sweet musicians of the air,
Is one so dear as thou to these old solitudes?

Ha! what a burst was that! The Aeolian strain
    Goes floating through the tangled passages
Of the still woods; and now it comes again,
A multitudinous melody, like a rain
    Of glassy music under echoing trees,
Close by a ringing lake. It wraps the soul
    With a bright harmony of happiness,
Even as a gem is wrapped, when round it roll
    Thin waves of crimson flame; till we become,
    With excess of perfect pleasure, dumb,
And pant like a swift runner clinging to the goal.

I cannot love the man who doth not love,
    As men love light, the songs of happy birds;
For the first visions that my boy-heart wove,
To fill its sleep with, were that I did rove
    Through the fresh woods, what time the snowy herds
Of morning clouds shrunk from the advancing sun,
    Into the depths of Heaven's blue heart, as words
From the Poet's lips float gently, one by one,
    And vanish in the human heart; and then
    I revelled in such songs, and sorrowed, when,
With noon-heat overwrought, the music-gush was done.

I would, sweet bird, that I might live with thee,
    Amid the eloquent grandeur of these shades,
Along with Nature!—But it may not be:
I have to struggle with the stormy sea
    Of human life until existence fades
Into death's darkness. Thou wilt sing and soar
    Through the thick woods and shadow-chequered glades,
While pain and sorrow cast no dimness o'er
    The brilliance of thy heart; but I must wear,
    As now, my garments of regret and care,
As penitents of old their galling sackcloth wore.

Yet, why complain? What though fond hopes deferred
    Have overshadowed Life's green paths with gloom?
Content's soft music is not all unheard;
There is a voice sweeter than thine, sweet bird,
    To welcome me, within my humble home;
There is an eye, with love's devotion bright,
    The darkness of existence to illume.
Then why complain? When Death shall cast his blight
    Over the spirit, my cold bones shall rest
    Beneath these trees; and from thy swelling breast
Over them pour thy song, like a rich flood of light.

1834

Sunset in Arkansas

Sunset again! Behind the massy green
    Of the continuous oaks the sun hath fallen,
And his last rays have struggled through, between
The leaf-robed branches, as hopes intervene
    Amid gray cares. The western sky is wallen
    With shadowy mountains, built upon the marge
Of the horizon, from Eve's purple sheen,
And thin, gray clouds, that insolently lean
    Their silver cones upon the crimson verge
Of the high Zenith, while their unseen base
    Is rocked by lightning. It will show its eye
When dusky Night comes. Eastward, you can trace
    No stain, no spot of cloud upon a sky,
        Pure as an angel's brow.
    The winds have folded up their swift wings now,
And, all asleep, high up in their cloud-cradles lie.

Beneath the trees, the dusky, purple glooms
    Are growing deeper, more material,
In windless solitude. The young flower-blooms
Richly exhale their thin, invisible plumes
    Of odor, which they yield not at the call
    Of the hot sun. The birds all sleep within
Unshaken nests; save the gray owl, that booms
His plaintive cry, like one that mourns strange dooms;
    And the sad whip-poor-will, with lonely din.
There is a deep, calm beauty all around,
    A heavy, massive, melancholy look,
A unison of lonely sight and sound,
    Which touch us, till the soul can hardly brook
Its own sad feelings here.
    They do not wring from the full heart a tear,
But give us heavy thoughts, like reading a sad book.

Not such thy sunsets, oh New England! Thou
    Hast more wild grandeur in thy noble eye,
More majesty upon thy rugged brow.
When Sunset pours on thee his May-time glow
    Gray granite mountain, rock and precipice,
Crowned with the white wreaths of the long-lived snow;
On sober glades, and meadows wide and low;
    On wild old words, gloomy with mysteries;
On cultivated fields, hedged with mossed rocks,
    And reening with the husbandman's young treasure;
On azure ocean, foaming with fierce shocks
    Against stout shores, that his dominion measure;
        On towns and villages,
And environs wealthy with flowers and trees,
Full of gray, pleasant shades, and sacred to calm leisure.

When Sunset radiantly unfolds his wing
    Upon thy occident, and fills the clouds
With his rich spirit, while the laughing Spring
Leans towards the arms of Summer, like a king
    He treads the West, and sends in glittering crowds
    His flocks of colors forth upon the river
Of the blue sky, there spirit-like to cling
To the cloud-cliffe and waves, there wandering
    And circling westwardly the world for ever.
Thy sunsets are more brilliant and intense
    But not so melancholy or so calm,
As this that now is fast retreating hence,
    Shading his heavy eyes with misty palm,
        Lulled to an early sleep
By Thunder, from the western twilight's deep,
Under the far horizon muttering a stern psalm.

1833

Night on the Arkansa

> The author spelled Arkansas without the final "s," as it appears here, in this privately printed volume of poems, and it seems to have been the customary spelling then.

Night comes upon the Arkansa with swift stride,—
    Its dark and turbid waters roll along,
Bearing wrecked trees and drift,—deep, red, and wide.
The heavy forests sleep on either side,
    To the water's edge low-stooping; and among
    The patient stars the moon her lamp has hung,
Lit with the spirit of the buried sun.
No blue waves dance the stream's dark bosom on,
    Glittering like beauty's sparkling starry tears;
No crest of foam, crowning the river dun,
    Its misty ridge of frozen light uprears:
    One sole relief in the great void uprears:
A dark, blue ridge, set sharp against the sky,
Beyond the forest's utmost boundary.

Not so wast thou, O, brave old Merrimac!
    As I remember thee; as thou art seen
By the Soul's eyes, when, dreaming, I go back
To my old home, and see the small boats tack
    On thy blue waters, gliding swift between
    The old gray rocks that o'er them fondly lean,
Their foreheads scarred with lightning. There, around
Grim capes the surly waves whirl and bound;
    And here and there grave patriarchal trees
Persuade the grass to clothe the reluctant ground
    And frowning banks with green. Still villages
    Sleep in the embraces of the cool sea-breeze:—
Ah, brave old stream!—thou seemest to infold
My heart within thy waters, as of old.

Fay Hempstead

Fay Hempstead was born in 1847 in Little Rock, where he spent most of his life as a highly respected citizen. His greatest contribution to Arkansas literature lies in the field of history. His Historical Review of Arkansas *consists of several large volumes which are extremely comprehensive. A less detailed history,* The School History of Arkansas, *was used for many years in the public schools. His poetry, however, is a noteworthy addition to the native literature. Hempstead published his first volume of poetry in 1878. A* Complete Edition *appeared in 1922. At Chicago, in 1908, he was crowned poet laureate of Freemasonry.*

Hempstead was an avowed disciple of Tennyson and much of the latter's metrical facility, high ideals, and abundant sentiment is reflected in the poetry of Hempstead.

A New Bethesda

(The Hot Springs of Arkansas. The Indians from very early times evidently had a knowledge, though crude and imperfect, of the virtues of these waters.

Dark Hills that hold the secret flow
    Of rills that break and wimple down
    In curving channels, green and brown,
To meet the stream that winds below;
Whence is thy source of hidden might?
    What mystic powers in thee contend:
    To charge thy chemic floods, and send
Their volume flashing into light?

Unnumbered ages have ye stood,
    Mayhap, and emptied ceaseless tides,
    Fire-likened, down thy rugged sides
Girt by the silence of the wood;
When denser grew the forest line,
    And over thee no sound was fixed,

Fay Hempstead. *Poems* (Little Rock: Allsopp and Paul, 1898).

Save plashings of thy waters, mixed
With sighings of the mountain pine.

Unused thy open fountains lay,
    And wasted down their broken falls,
Till stumbling o'er thy tufa walls,
Wild hunters of an early day,
Drank of thy streams and, startled, found
    A marvel springing at their feet;
    Clear streamlets seethed of hidden heat,
That gushed and bubbled from the ground.

And bringing here their stricken, these,
    Plain Nature's children, made the test
    What worth thy waters held to wrest
The strength from sickness and disease;
And so they came to be
    In ruder fashion famed and known,
    Till widening outward heat thou grown,
To be the World's Infirmary;

Where not alone the first that laves—
    As in the Charmed pool of old
When by the Angel stirred and rolled—
Finds healing in its magic waves;
But to the utmost of the race;
    In Earth's far numbering the last
    To seek thy favor, shall be cast
The tokens of returning grace.

So vast and ceaseless in thy flow.
    Thou markest well the gracious deed
    Of him who fixed for human need
So great a balm for strokes of woe;
Like as within our little length,
    He placed the stream that, who therein

Doth wash, shall cast the shards of Sin,
And rise from weakness unto strength.

Flow upon full streams! that rush and leap
As glad to do a kindly thing:
To brighten here and there, and fling
A solace when the forces sleep.
Flow on forevermore! to be
The ease and rout of hopeless pain,
That myriad soul may turn again,
And bless the hand that ordered thee.

Flow on! thy tides with healing filled!
And ye, dark hills, that frowning seem
To bid the sunlight cease to gleam
Upon thy summits, many-rilled:
Live till thy craggy points are hurled
And scattered, and thy boulders strewn,
By shocks through which the signs are shown,
That mark the closing of the world.

Ichabod

(The subject of this sketch is a well-known village of Arkansas, now entirely deserted. It is said that upon one occasion during a session of the Legislature in early times, this village came within one vote of being designated as the State Capital.)

Calm sleeps the valley by the river,
Where groves of oak and aspen shiver.
And trailing onward far below,
The water windeth, brown and slow.

And for the waste-land outward pushes,
Thick sown with feathered sedge and bushes.

Rank vines drawn upward clasp and seize
The blackened trunks of giant trees.

And here mid fields devoid of tillage,
Stands grouped the remnant of a village,
Where Commerce once, with busy mien,
And bustling pride of life, was seen.

Yon moss-grown building, long forsaken,
Hath in its time been rudely shaken,
When came the trader with his bales,
With barter, and the din of sales.

Yon vacant roadway, leading by it,
That lies in rarely-broken quiet,
Once saw the time when o'er its breast,
The tide of travel hourly pressed.

No friendly hail of passer calling;
No voice of song or music falling;
But on the place there lingereth,
The presence of a living death.

Yet this dead spot, so runs the story,
Once stood this near a higher glory;
That in grave legislative hall
One only voice she lacked to call

Her forward, in her bold ambition,
To hold the Capital position;
When statecraft, simple and sedate,
Had marked the boundaries of the State.

One only voice she lacked to enter
Time's annals as a new land's center,
And thence to broaden and to grow,

To what proportions, who may know?

Ah, thus our lives stand close to pleasures;
And thus the world's chief valued treasures
Slide past us, waiting eager there;
And Fortune builds her otherwhere.

Ah, thus the Good approacheth nigh us,
But coldly turning passeth by us.
While other wears the gloried wreath,
We pine in silence underneath.

The Night-Watch

(The following poem was suggested by the guard duty done by the writer, over the body of Chief Justice E. H. English, as it lay in state in the Senate Chamber at Little Rock, on Saturday night, September 6, 1884.)

Dim lights in yonder chamber high,
That looks with all its Eastern side
To where the river stretches wide,
   And outward to the naked sky;
   What see ye, lights, that faintly flame
With softened radiance o'er the scene,
In stillness, such as might have been
   Ere Nature into motion came?

And thou, O moon, that risest large,
And flingest out a line of light
Upon the waters, smooth and bright,
   Where curves the river's broken marge;
   That peepest through this window wide,
With thy clear sheen and open glare;
What see'st thou, as through the air
   Thou pourest down thy silver tide?

Alas! ye look on all that is
Of one who filled a noble space.
The strength of wisdom and of grace,
   The strength of purity was his.

Who held his course serene and mild
Through paths that sloped to higher ground;
Yet he who had his friendship found
   Him simple as a guileless child:

   With freedom in his heightened thought
For all that men should think and hold;
And fixed purpose made him bold
   To walk the paths that Virtue taught.

   And so he gathered force and might,
The strength of Truth within his hand,
'Till shineing through the lengthened land,
   He stood a lofty beacon light,

   That men beholding from afar
Should mark, and reverence for his worth.
He spared above the general earth,
   With shineings like the larger star.

   His life was open and was free
From latent baseness of the mind.
His deeds were deeds of Christian kind,
   Benevolence and charity.

   To Need he gave with ready hand:
He kept his scutcheon clear and bright;
As knightly as the highest Knight
   That ever died in Holy Land.

   And we, whatever men may say,

> I speak for those who loved him true,
> We gave to him the reverence due
>   When noble natures pass away.
>
> We gave what feeble honors stood
> Within our reach; and then above
> We gave the homage born of love,
>   As tribute to the wise and good.
> We bore him sadly, and away
> Where yon green hill its slope inclines,
> We laid him by the sighing pines,
> To wait the resurrection day.

Fred W. Allsopp

The "Old Lady" and the name Allsopp are synonymous. The success of the Arkansas Gazette *was the success of Fred W. Allsopp, who was born in England on June 25, 1867. His family migrated to Prescott, Arkansas, where Allsopp received his meager education. At the age of 17, he gained employment at the* Gazette *as a mailing clerk. As a result of his industrious and capable ability, he was later advanced to the position of advertising manager. He was, for many years, business manager and part owner of the* Gazette. *Allsopp became active in civic affairs and was engaged in various business endeavors in Little Rock. His poetry reflects the enthusiasm, patriotism, and wit which ruled his life and molded his character.*

Fancy and I

> Fancy and I played truant,
>   On a summer day.
> Strolled we through the Ozarks,
>   Careless of our way.

Fred W. Allsopp. *Rimeries* (Little Rock: Central Printing, 1926).

Joyously I rambled,
    Under Fancy's spell,
Over hills and valleys,
    To where fairies dwell.

While we basked in sunshine,
    Waded through clear streams,
Fancy told me stories—
    Weaved for me love-dreams.

Sitting in the twilight,
    'Neath a kingly oak,
We were serenaded
    By the greenwood folk.

Fancy and I told secrets
    You would like to share—
But we chance to think them
    None but our affair.

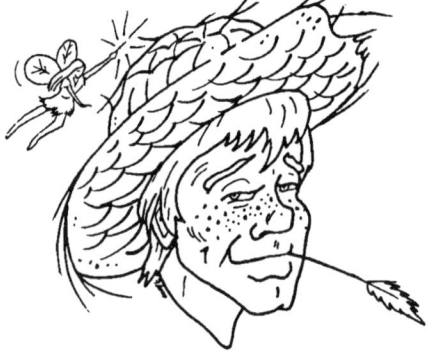

David O. Dodd
The Nathan Hale of Arkansas

Drums were beating, troops were marching,
    'Mid grim war's tempestuous scenes.
Outposts coming to headquarters,
    Brought in a soldier in his teens.

Captured by the Federal minions
    As a hated Rebel spy,
He was brought before the General,
    To be heard—mayhap to die.

"Tell me, boy, whom your notes came from,
    And you gain a prompt release;

Give the name of your informant,
   Then go your way in peace."

Rays of sunshine, gentle breezes,
   Told the youth his life was sweet;
Birds sang to him of his mother,
   Whom his heart craved sore to meet.

Yet he answered, "Never, General,
   I am not afraid to die;"
Then he wrote to that old mother,
   "I will meet you by and by."

Old men wept, he did not falter,
   But obeyed his country's call.
There were protests, but by others,
   When he heard his sentence fall.

As no blind-fold was provided
   For the poor boy's saddened eyes,
"Use my handkerchief!" he bid them,
   As he told them kind good-byes.

When the cruel drop had fallen,
   Dangled yet his form in breath,
And the soldiers pulled and jerked him
   'Till they strangled him to death.

In a grave in old Mount Holly
   Lie the bones of David Dodd,
Who to serve his friends—his country,
   Gave his spirit back to God.

Lines to the "Old Lady"

Illustrious Arkansas Gazette,
'Tis many years since we first met,
   Yet well do I remember
When I approached your sanctum first,
Adventure, knowledge, work athirst,
   One day in fair September.

Revered Gazette, bright morning star,
What fond remembrancer you are,
   Of golden days of beauty—
When Fancy whispered to my ear,
When proud ambition silenced fear,
   And printing was sweet duty.

I was a simple little boy,
Who deemed it would be endless joy
   To serve a dame so royal;
So I resolved to be your knight,
Forever in your cause to fight,
   With heart sincere and loyal.

No Don Quixote ever fought,
Or favor of a princess sought
   With sentiments more knightly,
Then those I joined your busy crew,
   When youth's clear fires burned brightly.

It gratified my soul to find
Your potent power to sway mankind;
   With words at times resistless,
You opened wide my eyes to truth,
And helped to smooth my ways, uncouth,
   My great and noble mistress.

'Tis true I heard you called a hag,
Inclined behind the times to lag,
   By those unduly jealous;
Some smiled when you would advocate
Or criticize affairs of state,
   Believing you o'er zealous.

But no one could malign the name
Of such a high and worthy dame
   Nor charge her with deeds shady,
Without provoking show of fight
From one who was the valiant Knight
   Of Arkansas' Old Lady.

'Twas royalty that I espoused
A queen my ardent love aroused,
   Long praised in song and story;
At whose high court were noblemen,
Who worked away with brain and pen
   For your eternal glory.

I owe you much, My Lady great,
For influencing my poor fate;
   You made life's problems clearer,
And though you have exacting been,
Your smiles to me were sweet to win,
   As each year found you dearer.

One of Arkansas' most famous legends inspired Fred W. Allsopp to the realm of poetry.

Petit Jean

One of the legends about Petit Jean Mountain is to the effect that the valiant French explorer Cheves was lured by stories to the unexplored coun-

Fred W. Allsopp. *Folklore of Romantic Arkansas*, Vol. I (Grolier Society, 1931).

try of America. Though deeply in love with his fiancee, Adrienne, wavering 'twixt love and desire for adventure he determined at last to sail to the distant land. When Adrienne heard of his decision, she made up her mind, unknown to her lover, that she would also go the new land. Disguised as a cabin boy, she secured passage under the name of Jean on the same ship on which Cheves sailed. Because of her small stature, the sailors called her "Petit Jean."

<small>Thwaites says that the Petit Jean tributary of the Arkansas was named for Little John, a Frenchman of small stature, who was killed on its banks by the Indians and that the mountain may have taken its name from the stream.</small>

Reaching the mouth of the Mississippi, they sailed up that river to the Arkansas, and landed at the foot of a mountain, where they found the Indians friendly, the country beautiful, and the climate delightful. It was so much like fairyland that Cheves ordered his crew to go no farther, and a settlement was thus made in what is now Arkansas. The Indians adored Petit Jean, and regarded her as a being from another world. They brought her offerings of fruits and flowers, and strove in every way to express their love. Still ignorant of her identity, Cheves announced one day that he proposed to return to France, to bring his fiancee to the new land. Petit Jean fell seriously ill, and the news of his departure made her worse. Fearing that she would not recover, she called Cheves to her side and disclosed her identity. His grief and woe were indescribable. Broken-hearted, he nursed her, but she expired in his arms, and, in accordance with her request, was buried in a beautiful spot on top of the mountain which was given her name.

The Indians used to say that her spirit guarded the grave. They saw her among the tree tops swaying in the breeze; they saw her rowing on the river in her canoe; they saw her wandering gaily in the forest, and ever shedding a blessing over the mountain they called Petit Jean.

Petit Jean

'Twas in France, where men of fashion
    Drank and gambled to excess,
At a time when swords and pistols
    Were accoutrements of dress.

Dainty was young Jean's appearance,
    From the headdress to the toes,

No one still showed greater valor
    When an exigent arose.

Marquis Pierpoint was attracted
    To this youth of undersize,
But, though strange, he ne'er suspected
    That his friend posed in disguise.

Gaming instincts—ardent natures—
    Of these men had not been changed
By their entering the forest,
    Far from former ties estranged.

One clear night with dice they gambled
    On a nameless river's brink;
There arose a bitter quarrel,
    And men fought, while crazed by drink,

Pierpoint's sword had left its scabbard,
    And with madness in his eye,
It seemed certain in a moment
    His antagonist would die.

Quickly two soft arms were circled
    Firmly 'round the swordsman's neck,
An unerring thrust was thwarted
    Ere it caused a human wreck.

Marquis Pierpoint dropped his weapon,
    But in fury turned around,
And dispatched the interposer
    In the river to be drowned.

As the form strove in the water,
    He exclaimed, "O, God!" and reeled.

He was sobered in an instant
    By a mystery revealed.

Marquis Pierpoint, skillful swordsman,
Loved a Calais social queen,
    And the maiden shared his passion
    With the fervor of sixteen.

But the Marquis fought a duel,
    And his enemy cut down;
When, to keep from being punished,
    He was forced to leave the town.

Hasty was the lovers' parting,
    As of luckless fate they wailed.
Then across the English channel
    And to New Orleans he sailed.

Constant was his sweet enchantress,
    And suspense ere many weeks
Left its impress on fair features,
    Paled the roses on her cheeks.

After months of dissipation,
    Brought on by his mind's distress,
He engaged with fellow Frenchmen
    To explore the wilderness.

Into Arkansas they ventured,
    As they sought in vain for gold,
And the young and haughty Marquis
    Made a leader staunch and bold.

All this time the fair French maiden
    Suffered from an aching heart,
Which induced a resolution

To perform a daring part.

In a year came other Frenchmen
To that sparsely settled zone,
   And among them was a person
Who as Petit Jean was known.

Sweet, reproachful glances told him
   It was Adrienne, his love.
Vain were his attempts to reach her,
   Vain his pleas to powers above.

Tears that stood in eyes of sadness,
   Once so radiantly blue,
Showed him that his love of Calais
   To the end had proven true.

Now he knew that his old sweetheart
   And his comrade in strange lands,
Were one and the selfsame person,
   Doomed to perish at his hands!

With a love supremely constant
   She had come to him from France,
And through his unruly temper,
   He had ended their romance.

Love for her, his sense of justice—
   Native chivalry, were shocked.
When he felt what fate had dealt him,
   Doubt not that his reason rocked.

Vainly did he dive and wander
   Up and down the stream all night,
Not to find the stiffened body
   Till the morning gave forth light.

Far up in a mountain fastness
    There was dug a lonely grave,
    Where in grief he hid the treasure
That he would have died to save.

Near by it he built a cabin,
    To live ever by her side.
Petit Jean men named the mountain
    And the river where she died.

Allsopp's poem is based on a story told by Col. M. L. Davis

John Gould Fletcher

John Gould Fletcher, a Pulitzer Prize winner in 1939, was born in Little Rock in 1886. He attended Phillips Academy and Harvard University and was awarded an honorary doctor of laws degree by the University of Arkansas in 1933. He occasionally served the University in the capacity of visiting professor and consultant. Fletcher was an enthusiastic member of the Imagist school of poets and was heralded by some as its leader at the death of Amy Lowell. In 1934 he was listed in Who's Who of America as one of the five foremost contemporary poets. A famous French critic once termed Fletcher "the great dreamer of contemporary American poetry." After residing in England for a number of years, he returned to his native state to spend the remainder of his life at Johnswood, his home in Little Rock.

    Fletcher's poetry is beautifully descriptive and reflects the strong mysticism peculiar to the Imagists. The following selections come from his 1939 Pulitzer Prize winner and are the poet's favorite works. Selected Poems *and Fletcher's autobiography have been reprinted by the University of Arkansas Press. His other works are in the process of being reprinted.*

Late Summer

Against the sky, a cloud-white bowl of flame,
The trees stand out, in masses of dark green;
Dizzy sunlight, fainting shadow,

John Gould Fletcher. Selected Poems (New York: Farrar & Rinehart, 1938).

To the distance dimly seen.

Great billows of haze rise up, slowly uncoil
Their heavy folds in silence. Underneath the leaves
The heat consumes the dew. A swallow darting
Skims, brushing the brown eaves.

Weedy gardens rank, neglected, smoulder
With ragweed, thistle, purple and scarlet flowers:—
Like gypsy girls they are staring
Through eyes unquiet and sombre,
Down the long hollow silences of the hours:—

Seeking for something long ago vanished and forgotten,
Something that time has now taken away, and fate no more will bring;
The hour before the blossom of life fell and the apple of earth went rotten,
The passionate, shrill, riotous hour of the waking of the spring.

Spring

At the first hour, it was as if one said, "Arise";
At the second hour, it was as if one said, "Go forth."
And the winter constellations that are like patient ox-eyes
Sank below the white horizon at the north.

At the third hour, it was as if one said, "I thirst";
At the fourth hour, all the earth was still.
Then the clouds suddenly swung over, stooped, and burst;
And the rain flooded valley, plain, and hill.

At the fifth hour, darkness took the throne;
At the sixth hour, the earth shook and the wind cried.
At the seventh hour, the hidden seed was sown;
At the eighth hour, it gave up the ghost and died.

At the ninth hour, they sealed up the tomb;
And the earth was then silent for the space of three long hours
But at the twelfth hour, a single lily from the gloom
Shot forth, and was followed by a whole host of flowers.

The Swan

Under a wall of bronze,
Where beeches dip and trail
Thin branches in the water,
With red-tipped head and wings,
A beaked ship under sail,
There glides a great black swan.

Under the autumn trees
He goes. The branches quiver,
Dance in the wraith-like water,
Which ripples beneath the sedge
With the slackening furrow that glides
In his wake when he is gone:
The beeches bow dark heads.

Into the windless dusk,
Where in mist great towers stand
Guarding a lonely strand
That is bodiless and dim,
He speeds with easy stride;
And I would go beside,
Till the low brown hills divide
At last, for me and him.

Glenn Ward Dresbach

Glenn Ward Dresbach—banker, poet, lecturer—was born in Lanark, Illinois, in 1889. He settled in Eureka Springs from 1944 until 1952. His poetry was repeatedly sold to a large number of magazines and newspapers. He published eleven collections of poetry, several of them in foreign languages. Among his many awards are the Poetry World Prize in 1930 and the Hamlin Garland Memorial Prize in 1940. Mr. Dresbach was named Arkansas Poet of the Present in 1953.

An Old Mill

The road to its sagging doors
    Is tangled in wild grape vines,
But through the sycamores
    The brook beside it shines.
Old timbers, mellowed long,
    Stand firm below the hill—
But here is silence after the song
    At last is still.

Artists, in autumn, pause
    To sketch the old mill caught
In soft lights, and because
    Of something others brought
To it, we take away
    Some richness from its bins—
For where dreams were, on another day
    A dream begins.

Where some need ends, at last
    Another happens by . . .
This old mill, holding fast
    Its place against the sky,
Grinds, with no turn of the wheel,
    The hard shell from the kernel

Of thoughts—until the grists reveal
   Something eternal.

I Would Build Myself A House

I would build myself a house
   On this mountain-top today,
Not to shun the World, or feel
   It was shutting me away,
   But that I might come at times
   Little things had baffled me,
And look out, at set of sun,
   On immensity.

A Vagabond At The Gates

What is this strife and worry all about,
   This building up and tearing down of things?
I know a wood where birds flit in and out,
   And the west winds sings.

What of the sobs and hate-words that I hear,
   This shouting and mad barter in the street?
I know a calm hill where the stars seem near
   And the airs are sweet.

What of the power that passes in a breath,
   This digging for the buried gates of Doom?
I know a vale where echoes laugh at Death
   And the wild flowers bloom.

I Have Always Said I Would Go

I have always said I would go sometime in the autumn
    Away from the bare boughs and the fallen leaves,
Away from the lonely sounds and the faded colors,
    And all the ancient sorrow, and change that grieves.

I have always said I would go—and now it's autumn—
    To an island where the wild hibiscus grows
And parakeets flock to the groves at twilight
    And fragrance drifts from bays where the moonlight glows.

But there would be the vasty sound of breakers
    Come in to toss their pearls upon the sand.
All through the night—a longing of great waters
    Trying to make the vastness understand.

I have always said I would go sometime in autumn
    Away from the lonely sounds and change that grieves—
But here in my heart is the sound of a distant ocean
    And here in my heart is the sound of these falling leaves.

Mail Box

Someone had left the mail box by the road
That is a road no longer, overgrown
With weeds and berry bushes. Nothing showed
Of name, if name were there, to make it known
Before the cabin roof had sagged below
Its weight of silence, and the fallen door
Let in the wind. A vine that chanced to grow
Beside the box, put in one bloom it bore.

What better message could be left at last
For anyone to turn from work and find?

What carrier, unseen, unheard, had passed
And left such warmth of color for the mind?
I doubt, since then, that, given rain and sun
There is no address to oblivion.

Rosa Zagnoni Marinoni

Rosa Zagnoni Marinoni was born in Bologna, Italy, in 1891. As a child, she came to America with her family and settled in New York City. In 1908 Mrs. Marinoni moved to Fayetteville, where her husband served as chairman of the Romantic Languages Department at the University of Arkansas. She resided at Villa Rosa, her home in Fayetteville, until her death. Mrs. Marinoni began her writing career in 1925 and became a prolific and widely published writer. Her literary achievements lie in the areas of the short story, children's stories and verses, witty epigrams, and most assuredly in the realm of poetry. She was appointed Poet Laureate of Arkansas. Throughout her life she was an active participant in literary circles, political affairs, and charitable projects. The brief introductions accompanying these poems were supplied by the poet.

The Reservation Mountains, flanking Central Avenue in Hot Springs, Arkansas, are sanctuaries of memories.

Hot Springs

Rosa Zagnoni Marinoni. *The Ozarks And More Of Its People* (Privately pub., 1956).

Though I have climbed the Alps where eagles fly,
And walked the seven hills encircling Rome,
I've never felt more kindred to the sky,
Than on these reservations you call Home.
To this Main Street, a mystic hour glass,
Through which life and the mystic waters flow,
I have returned to watch the old year pass,
And the new year advance through veils of snow.

In April I have come to welcome Spring,
When the magnolia blossoms burst in bloom,
And lent my ear to nightingales that sing
Along the race track to a Summer moon.

These hills are altars to which I must return
To light a candle, and to watch it burn.

This winter snap shot was taken on the way to Devil's Den State Park. We stopped at the picturesque log cabin, and the old lady invited us inside to warm ourselves. She was kind. It was a

Winter Dusk in the Ozarks

Slow . . . silent . . .
The snow flakes have covered the orchard.
The trees droop heavily.
Each branch an arched bow
Straining beneath the unaccustomed burden.
A crackling staccato is heard at intervals,
As sap-frozen branches snap.
Fluffed sparrows
Huddle in close community
Along a barbed wire fence
Like birds strung on a spit to broil.
A rabbit hops diagonally across the snow,
Making shadowless half circles
Above the white expanse.

A woman with a brown shawl
Wrapped around her shoulders,
Stands in the doorway of a log cabin . . .
A kitten in her arms.

Standing Chimneys

From *Timberlline* (Cedar Rapids: Torch Press, 1954).

Out of Rogers, after enjoying Lake Atlanta, if you decide to visit Monte Ne, to see the Coin Harvey Pyramid, you will find many Standing Chimneys. And if you happen to be there at sunset, you may see this:

> The chimney stands among the yellow weeds,
> Rising against the sunset, grim, alone.
> What purpose prompts the voice that intercedes
> With time and wind to spare this ghost of stone?
> I asked myself. And then from out of nowhere,
> There came the answer I might not have heard
> Had I walked on in silence. Through the air,
> I heard the whir of wings, the cry of bird.
> Through wind-swerved trees and tangled underbrush,
> Rising and circling in their nightly guest,
> Into the chimney throat with chirps that hush
> As each small creature finds its perch and nest,
> A swarm of chimney-sweeps drop out of sight
> Like penny change inside the bank of night.

The poor can not only be found in crowded cities, but also in places rich with space . . . We have them here in the hill country . . . Like most people poor in worldly goods, they are rich in love, and they prove it when it's

Christmas in the Ozarks

> The sky is gray.
> Gray like the thin mare nosing above the grassless field.
> Gray as the unpainted shack and its hingeless door,
> And its cardboard-patched windows too.
> Gray as the dusty road, the barren trees
> And the blackberry bushes.
> The corn stubble nodding in the wind is also gray

Like the cowless barn that slants northward revealing its ribs.
The headless scarecrow is gray,
And the snow, fast-frozen in the useless trough, is gray.

But at the east window,
The only one with a glass pane in it,
There hangs a bright Christmas wreath
Made of red-paper stars caught on a twisted wire.

If some dawn you find yourself on Highway 62, on your way to Eureka Springs (Ark.), stop at Inspiration Point and you may see this . . .

Native

We came upon it suddenly. The sun
Shone brightly on the mountain ledge. Below,
Trapped in the valley where the river curled,
Spread the dawn fog—an ocean white as snow,
From which like islands rose the humps of hills
Purple and black beneath the yellow sun.
Above us drops of light from tall pine trees
Dripped silently through blue space one by one.
Binoculars and cameras in hand,
We stood as poised between the earth and skies,
Well conscious chance had led us to trespass
Upon a sight not meant for mortal eyes.

A mountain lad in rags, his large feet bare,
Leaned to a tree. The surging pride that stills
The eager lips spoke through his eyes the words:
"This is My valley . . . these my native hills!"

Edsel Ford

"My ambitions are twofold—to write good poetry, and to write it in, and of Arkansas." So said Edsel Ford about his creative efforts. Born in Alabama, Mr. Ford came to Arkansas as a child and with his family settled in the Ozark hills near Rogers. He was graduated from Rogers High School in 1947 and earned his Bachelor of Arts degree in 1952 from the University of Arkansas. He began writing while still a high school student; his first published works appeared while he was a student at the University. From 1952 until 1954, he served with the United States Army in Germany, where he contributed to the Army magazine Stars and Stripes. A pamphlet entitled, "This Was My War," containing poems of this period, was issued in 1955. Before his death, Mr. Ford was the recipient of many honors and awards for his poetry and won a secure position in the literary circles of America, particularly in the South and Southwest.

Everyman

Edsel Ford. *Looking for Shiloh* (Columbia, Mo.: UP Missouri, 1968).

Who will remember what the causes were
When, washed by history's impersonal tide,
We mellow to the madness and the stir
Which broke our hearts when headlines opened wide
To take us in, to say that on July
The twenty-third, in nineteen fifty-nine,
Or some such date, a man whom you and I
Knew well, fell, or was felled; and we knew why.
But in the course of days we sleep, we dine,
We catch the bus for work. Injustices
Are daily bread; and we forget his face.
We wonder, sometimes, where (or if) he is;
And tell each other, There, but for the grace . . .

And wake up knowing he is in this place.

White River Float

Translating summer into another tongue,
The boat lisps through the cold emerald
Water, through the onyx deeps and the crystal riffles,
Spinning late fallen leaves into yellow chapters
And red oak volumes.

The thermal-knit fisherman flicks ice from his line,
Casting and reeling from bank to boat.
Somewhere a bass is lurking; somewhere a jack
Noses a pebbled recollection of the sporting summer.

Here the long fingers of willows write on the water;
Here the log deciphers the cryptic pool;
The wintering river glosses its margins with meaning.
High on a naked hill the symbolic staccato
Of a yellowhammer shatters the frozen hush.

It has been a long time since the last geese flew.
It will be a long time before they fly again.
But this boat moves north, for the river runs that way:
Summer or winter, this river runs north.

And the fingers of the willows write on the water.

Contingent

In water as we wind we shape
Our arms around familiar bodies.
Beds know the way we are;
Chairs turn to living shells.

The runner finds earth
First fact of his running;

The medium of the flier
Is air, his coexistent.

Man the Upright is a lie.
Something is always there
To cradle him; water,
Earth, fire, or air.

At the Museum Again

Fashion be hanged, he said, the dinosaurs
Seemed much too thin this year; they rattled about
With bow legs bared. This philosophical look
Disquieted him. He thought, with Rabelais,
What a sad end it is when one is buried
With a tall erection, wondering about life.

It was ten tedious years since he had been
(A visitor) to the Museum of Natural History.
He had been giddy as the blind goose he was,
Strayed in from the bayou country of the Lowlands,
Poking anatomical slights at outmoded creatures
Whose centuries were rodded up for ridicule.

But then he had not imagined how extinct
One can become in a decade, nor how the world ends
Somewhere somehow with every turn of second;
That, coming again, the terrible juveniles
From P.S. 28 would look on his contemplating
With puzzlement, and whisper among themselves
That he *belonged* here, a part of the exhibit.

Obligingly beneath their curious eyes
He turned to stone; and an attendant came
To hang a temporary tag on him

Until he could be classified and placed
In the catalog, along with his own kind.

Low Tide At Fire Island

It is ourselves we mourn when tides recede
To leave our bleached bones balanced on the ripples
Of sand and foam. We are the only cripples
In evidence; all other things are freed
By ebb and flow. In our insatiable greed
We tied the farmhouse down, the crib, the stables,
The rickrack fence, the doghouse, picnic tables . . .
Even the wind's denied the tethered steed.
So these are our bones, left from other summers.
We grieve among them, choosing what we will
To put ourselves together from the grave;
But the tide departs, erasing half the numbers,
And, uninstructed, we have not the skill
To make us whole with these few parts we have.

Booker T. Jackson

Booker T. Jackson was born in Center Point, Arkansas, on March 6, 1929. After completing high school in Memphis, Mr. Jackson entered Philander Smith College in Little Rock, where he received a Bachelor of Arts degree in 1956. He began writing in 1948 and has continued to write while pursuing a career with the Federal government in North Little Rock and Little Rock. His poetry has been published in more than sixty different publications, including South and West, Swordsman Review, Contemporary Poets of Arkansas, The Arkansas Gazette, The Denver Post, The Kansas City Star, *and* Voices International. *Among his awards are* South and West *Poet of the Year in 1969; a citation from the World Poetry Society; Select Poem, "Hymn to Martin Luther King" in World Brotherhood 'Poet' of July, 1969; listing in* Who's Who in Poetry, *1970, and Directory of British and American Writers.*

Of People and Power

People talkin' 'bout power
Like you never heard or seen.
They talkin' 'bout power
Colored black and white and green.
Some folks blabbin'
For black color scheme,
And some whinin' for white.
If power is gonna be white or black,
Then what color is gonna be right?

Theme for Dignity

A long time ago, on this old land,
The Lord took some dirt, and in His hands;
He did, He did what no one else can,
He made the original woman and man.
A many years have gone by since then,
The world is full of women and men;
But still, but still, ha, no one else can,
Can make the original woman and man.
Sometimes, as I wander, from place to place,
Sometimes, yet I'm looking, from face to face;
And you know what I think? What a world this would be,
If every man and woman had dignity.
Guess it's gonna take many years more,
For this human race to just ignore
The colors of skin, let each one stand:
A dignified original woman and man.

Soul Democracy

I can't hide my heritage
And I can't hide my skin
Now I can't go back inside
I can't be born again.
I am what I am
So please give a damn
I'll give a damn for you
You give a damn for me
And brother that is true
Soul democracy.
You are you and I am me
But we can do our thing
Now we can get together
And help make freedom ring.
You can't change your skin to black
And I can't change mine to white
There's a lot we still can do
There's wrong that we can right.
I can't tear the whole world up
I got a life to live
Now both of us must learn to love
We both must learn to give.

The Crisis of 57

There was a crisis in our land,
On that September day;
Nine children started out to school
And Daisy led the way.
The law was passed the year before,
To some it was a jest;
But when they came to enter school,
The news went East and West.

Daisy Bates, a civil rights leader in Arkansas

The guard was called to bar their way,
While insults poured from mouths;
And ugly words were spat at them;
The news went North and South.
The word had reached our President:
Defiance of the law;
And soon the world began to watch
The state of Arkansas.
The President sent in the troops,
With bayonet and gas,
With orders to protect the Rights
Of the kids who wanted to pass.
The crowd grew angry at the troops
Whose presence hurt their pride.
Somehow—perhaps a miracle—
Through it all, no one had died.
Nine children entered school that year;
No blacks had gone before;
An Army had to lead the way
To get them through the door.
The crisis came, the crisis went,
The state of Arkansas,
Had shown itself, had shown the world,
Its ugly human flaw.
But flaws in men that yield to time,
Are beautiful to see;
The flaws that fail to yield are ones
That cause the misery.
There was a crisis in our land,
That came from hate in hearts;
But tolerance and love correct
the flaws when hate departs.
Nine children went to school that day,
And history was made;
Little Rock, your card was marked—:
You got a passing grade.

Richard Hudson

Richard Hudson is a well-read, widely traveled individual who has developed a keen sense of literature and the creative process. A native of Arkansas, he earned his B.A. degree at Hendrix College, his M.A. degree at the University of Arkansas, and completed his course work and language requirement for a Ph.D. at Vanderbilt University. His teaching career began at Little Rock Central High School, followed by five years at the University of Arkansas at Monticello, and finally at the University of Central Arkansas in Conway, where he currently holds the position of Associate Professor of English.

His interest in poetry has led him into discussions with such poets as John Crowe Ransom, W. H. Auden, Stephen Spender, and John Ciardi, who contributed to his awareness of poetic style and sensitivity. Although not heavily published, Professor Hudson is an authentic voice, an Arkansas voice, one with important links to the past and one who demonstrates considerable poetic merit.

He recently founded a poetry journal entitled Slant *which publishes contributions from well known poets like Maxine Kumin and Gwendolyn Brooks as well as lesser known but equally talented poets, nationwide.*

Kite

While I warned too small
His field of grass, too tall
That bordering limit of trees in spring,
His lofting breeze too slight, he paid out string.

And his dark eyes and his small hands closed tight,
Clinched evidences calling from his far kite.

Theoretical Problems of the Piano

A wispish boy, boy of fluid hand,
Widening span, this side prodigy,

Intently probes, at his over-sized grand,
Through slight keys a fragile harmony,
Sudden resurrection of ancient mystery.

A circle of sage composers
Long dead, listening. Mozart.
Brahms.

And Wagner mute.

On Going to the Wars

That Marine, lank in glittering gold,
Here yesterday, lightly
kissed her lips, and again
Her eyes,
Here.

Today up-stream rain gorges
The stilted river Gulf-ward
Through glaring, sunwashed pylons,
Here, where faint lingering fragrance
Recoils under the diesel's shuddering horn.

But he kisses her tears away here,
While terrible wheels, groaning under tank
And infantry, pound those arching tracks west,
Irresistably to go from their brief space
And that embrace.

Telegraph Road
"On Pea Ridge"

1

What mute markers point the battle now,
That raged along the road? What place allow
Their arranged arms, in dust remembering death?
Leathers crazed, gaunt uniforms' smell,
A watch clogged, handless, eying, tell

The soldiers rose into view, corps by corps.
They marched, half heedlessly, with weapons more
Than steel, cresting their march to the vistas of truth.

2

Their sun revealed,
Below, a spreading field
At least, so green to the advancing youth
As to stagger sight;
And the bursting air so bright
So fair,
As to hear infinity whisper there
And to burn with the sucked-in breath.

3

That day
They lay,
Down rows along a sun line,
Doubtfully set;
But bravely met,

Nameless under echoing cannon blast,
The last flashing bayonet, the last

Reverberating cry of pain
From the slayer and the slain

4

And strangers in a strange country. There
Beneath the blue air,
Beneath the grey rock,
Their phantom shock

Marches again on a telegraph road
In the dust of implacable boots, to pass
Arms and regimentals, smartly along the road,
Yet easily ordered, rumoring the hour—not to yield
To any wept warnings of the red crest and field.

5

The column scattering fantail, in silence falling
Where wind gusts shining ripples calling,
Met forever to bleed at the deepest roots.

There you strike at the last through the loam,
Strike through the waving world of grass,
Brightly there
Through time and air,
Your phantom missile home.

Retreat to Calico Rock

From earth's heart out rose this rock,
Giddy lava dreaming overlook bluffs, grim
Hub of autumn's wheel, broken, gone blue at the rim.

Along a border of trees at the foot, the river runs,

Leaf-green, momentously meandering, hinting cold,
Spangled where winds shower silver leaves and gold.

And stretching away wait hills, hidden and old,
Where road turns lane, turns trail, turns track,
Calling, to kinship of creatures, pure hunters back.

About, about the mountain ridge
The track is a darkling way,
Where moonshine fathoms light an eye,
And tune the far sweet song of hounds at bay.

And the cabin waits, clinging to outcropped rock,
Outweathering ancient fathers, ghosts across the floor,
Eyeing hound and hunter and banked leaves at the door.

    Tune up the fiddle, resin the bow,
    Strum a guitar to a fleet banjo;
     One, take a look, take a smell, take a taste;
    Two, feel the moonshine; three, go.

And the bluetick guitar bays a banjo wing,
With a fluttering wed to bone;
When heart's desire is keen,
Along the hill echoes still sing
The leafways of our dreams.

Here fire draws together beast and friend
In a chorus of remnant dreams;
A plain table gathers us to meat and bread,
A cup or two, and all is as it seems.

For a brief space here, we spin the tales we know,
Believe those worlds where we make one;
The lamp again between us glows
To tell upon our faces tracks of hunting done.

Maya Angelou

Maya Angelou lived her childhood years in Stamps, Arkansas, with her grandmother. The rest of her life has been spent in California, where she has developed her numerous talents. She studied dance in San Francisco, has toured Europe and Africa for the State Department in Porgy and Bess, *and has taught dance in Rome and Tel Aviv. Ms. Angelou has served on the faculty of the University of Ghana, has written for newspapers in Cairo and in Ghana, and has directed feature films for the Public Broadcasting System. She is the author of the best-selling* I Know Why the Caged Bird Sings, *an autobiographical novel, and several collections of poetry, including* Gather Together in My Name *and* Just Give Me a Cool Drink of Water 'fore I Diiie.

I Almost Remember

Maya Angelou. *Oh Pray My Wings Are Gonna Fit Me Well* (New York: Random House, 1975).

I almost remember
        smiling some
years past
        even combing the ceiling
with the teeth of a laugh
(longer ago than the
                smile).
Open night news-eyed I watch
channels of hunger
        written on children's faces
        bursting bellies balloon
in the air of my day room.

There was a smile, I recall
now jelled in
a never yester glow. Even a laugh
that tickled the tits of
heaven
(older than the smile).
In graphs, afraid, I see the black

brown hands and
white thin yellowed fingers.

Slip slipping from the
ledge of life. Forgotten by
all but hatred.
Ignored
by all but disdain.

On late evenings when
quiet inhabits my garden
when grass sleeps and
streets are only paths for silent
mist.

    I seem to remember

        Smiling.

Southeast Arkanasia

After Eli Whitney's gin
brought to generations' end
bartered flesh and broken bones
Did it cleanse you of your sin
    Did you ponder?

Now, when farmers bury wheat
and the cow men dump the sweet
butter down on Davy Jones
Does it sanctify your street
    Do you wonder?

Or is guilt your nightly mare
bucking wake your evenings' share

of the stilled repair of groans
and the absence of despair
        over yonder?

My Arkansas

Maya Angelou. *And Still I Rise* (New York: Random House, 1978).

There is a deep brooding
in Arkansas.
Old crimes like moss pend
from poplar trees.
The sullen earth
is much too
red for comfort.

Sunrise seems to hesitate
and in that second
lose its
incandescent aim, and
dusk no more shadows
than the noon.
The past is brighter yet.

Old hates and
ante-bellum lace, are rent
but not discarded.
Today is yet to come
in Arkansas.
It writhes. It writhes in awful
waves of brooding.

Still I Rise

You may write me down in history
With your bitter, twisted lies,
You may trod me in the very dirt
But still, like dust, I'll rise.

Does my sassiness upset you?
Why are you beset with gloom?
'Cause I walk like I've got oil wells
Pumping in my living room.

Just like moons and like suns,
With the certainty of tides,
Just like hopes springing high,
Still I'll rise.

Did you want to see me broken?
Bowed head and lowered eyes?
Shoulders falling down like teardrops,
Weakened by my soulful cries.

Does my haughtiness offend you?
Don't you take it awful hard
'Cause I laugh like I've got gold mines
Diggin' in my own back yard.

You may shoot me with your words,
You may cut me with your eyes,
You may kill me with your hatefulness,
But still, like air, I'll rise.

Does my sexiness upset you?
Does it come as a surprise
That I dance like I've got diamonds
At the meeting of my thighs?

Out of the huts of history's shame
I rise
Up from a past that's rooted in pain
I rise
I'm a black ocean, leaping and wide,
Welling and swelling I bear in the tide.

Leaving behind nights of terror and fear
I rise
Into a daybreak that's wondrously clear
I rise
Bringing the gifts that my ancestors gave,
I am the dream and the hope of the slave.
I rise
I rise
I rise.

Jack Butler

The son of a Baptist minister, Jack Butler grew up in the rural South, which has provided many subjects for his verse. He began writing at an early age and has developed a noteworthy reputation as both a poet and a writer of fiction. From 1968 until 1971, he was associated with the Writers' Workshop at the University of Arkansas. He was for three years Writer-in-Residence at Henderson State University and Ouachita Baptist University in Arkadelphia. He is married to Jayme Tull, Director of the Arkansas Artists' Registry, and is currently Assistant Dean at Hendrix College.

He has published two collections of poems and one collection of short stories. His first novel Jujitsu for Christ *appeared in 1987, and his second novel will be published in the spring of 1989.*

The Ant-Hill

The ant-hill's now untenanted
that festered like a boil all summer
just where a visitor to the shed
(whether old-timer or new-comer),
stepping back down, would plant a foot,
one hand on the doorjamb to prevent
a twisted ankle. Where the ants went
I don't know, and I don't know why.
It's only, lying here in the sun,
I noticed an irritant was gone.
And a lift and a pull on my amber home-made
to that. But what? Did the queen die?
Did they get tired of being stirred
by a boy poking with a stick?

— What image for anger would you rather?
The idle or the curious thrust
to open the almost cranial crust —
the sudden seething and the quick
reciprocal boil of disgust:
one day when I was one or two,
they found me worked into a lather,
screaming, stomping, and covered with ants.
They washed me off and changed my pants,
they say, and the next thing they knew,
there I was on the hill again,
stomping, screaming, and turning blue.

So I don't have much ground to stand on,
trying to balk my young nephew's
natural shivering abandon
at ants crawling some gobbet of refuse.
a still-living grasshopper, say.
But he didn't drive these ants away.

Something no doubt was over with,
a battle lost or just a path
to convenient food-supplies.

And though I drop with round fat water
and even when I shut my eyes
cannot shut out a bloody blaze,
somehow a moonlit vision occurs:
one night everything that is ant
knows it is time to leave, and stirs
in a ghostly rustle, a murmur or armor
and whisper of spiracle and vent,
and frays off into the infinite jungle
beneath our notice in the roots,
along a highway beaten flat
by ants' feet only, to commingle
each tiny lunar silhouette
with wilder shadow yet.

Three

I

Weeds of all sorts,
but two I mention—
the weeds of neglect
and the weeds of attention.

One ragged and rank and sour,
the other a wild and vivid flower.

II

from experience

Paranoia, I opine,
is just a very
distant
early
warning
line.

III

last light

a leaf can be a turtle
a turtle can be a stone
a stone can be a nameless fear
at sunset, alone—

The Frustration of Simple Desires

How many times have I set out after
what I wanted
only to have it change to water
in my hands, and so amaze me
I let it slip through my fingers
before I knew I was thirsty?

How many times
have I jumped out of sleep to answer
a voice that a moment later
I couldn't swear I had heard,
calling me —
and I wanted so badly to answer.

—And you, spilling my name in droplets
all day long
and I never notice?

Jack Butler. *The Kid Who Wanted to be a Spaceman And Other Poems* (Little Rock: August House, 1984).

How many times have I told you
how they gave me to God like Samuel
before I was born?

How many times have I opened the closet
to find the one coat
that will make me a man and yet gentle
and put on the same grey jacket?

And how many times have I wanted
a lover's mouth to open
only to find I teetered
like an inch-high dwarf with no sense of balance
on the edge of the keys of a grand piano?

How many times
have I studied the theory of numbers
till late in the evening
and stood the next morning in line for breakfast
despairing and stubbled,
unable to figure my change,
and begging the god of small favors
to cross my pockets with silver,
spare me the minor hassle, the register girl's
friendly forgiveness?

And how many times have I drunk to forget
or swallowed a tab
to wander a mystical animal
in the church of the world's stained light
and wound up shaking all night
under Orion?
And how many times have I thought
that words somehow on paper
would ease a man's pain, or my own?

Oh how many times have I set out after
what I wanted
only to have it change to water
in my hands, and so amaze me
I let it slip through my fingers
before I knew I was thirsty?

In Love's Way

A dog can see love.
He sees it raw and flowing, real as water.

So when you pet the other dog
or hug your wife,
that's why he's in the middle jumping. Yuk,
you say, don't lick, and whack him.

Which must be puzzling to a dog,
how There it goes you see it
and Here I am you go there
but Wham is what you get.

We could explain it to him, subtle,
so subtle as we are,
so versed
in object and observer, uncertainties.

He has no doubt it's there.

James Whitehead

James Whitehead, a member of the creative writing program at the University of Arkansas in Fayetteville, is the author of a novel, Joiner, *as well as a book of poetry,* Domains. *Professor Whitehead is a Guggenheim Fellow and his volume of poetry won the Robert Frost Fellowship in Poetry of the Breadloaf Writers Conference. Several of his poems have appeared in periodicals, and he is currently working on a new volume.*

Domains

James Whitehead. *Domains* (Baton Rouge: LSU Press, 1966).

1

Sometimes I find it hard to concentrate
On politics
And the rugged Brotherhood of Man—
I mean to be a Populist
Who goes according to a good reformer's plan
With all the races for a swim . . .
And the local union gets my dues . . .
But still the pamphlets, tracts and speeches bring the blues
And dreams of flight
To Red and Yellow, Black and White
Who tumble on the common beach
And by wild water where
The common terror will be shared.

2

This is the way a young man has to learn . . .
Making love to economics and the faithless moon.

3

One great-great-grandfather died
At twenty-seven of rotten meat that carried worms
In the Civil War
For the Union—

But on the other side
Dr. Bourland suffered Vicksburg
Lived to write a book to state the wisdom in his life
And cried when his eyes went out.

4

I stagger with my banner everywhere
Toward a better state
But always lovely hair
Long limbs negotiate
To turn my mind from taxes
And jack the old reflexes.

5

It is all death in time I would obliterate
And rigorous confusions of the noble dead—
But be it flesh, or memory,
Or present justice in a rout,
God, give me strength to nervously admit
I am not fit
To serve at once
Two dying bodies with equal wit.

Tornadoes (for H.R.T.)

Mine wasn't as extraordinary as
My grandfather's. His came down from higher,
A classical shape, hung from the Kansas sky.
Mine stooped over the woods, a squatty cloud.
Grandfather's, like a cornucopia
Gone haywire—sucking horribly, not spilling
Plenty (unless you grant the stories it left
A bounty)—came and beat his town down flat.

Hysterical naked women were in the streets;
Fortunes like his own were thrown across
The tragical Kansas plain, his jewelry store
A blasted treasure-trove.
                Every acre
In Kansas a sullen Populist demanding
His share—a pair of broken glasses, a diamond—
The grasses grown suddenly filthy rich,
And laughing—naked women howling all night—

His town become a waste on that rigorous land.
And he told that story each year, in still weather,
Until he died: Weeds! Diamonds gone!
And the neighbor's daughter turning around and around . . .

Mine came buckling over the trees and fell,
For a moment, to lift up one dog, and that was all,
A helpless old dog swung up in an awkward squall,
And nothing was beaten flat to raise a tale.

The Opinion of an Interesting Old Man

It's plain damned hard to lose yourself these days . . .
or at least you can't the clean way you once could . . .
gone for a week with boiled water and food,
then turning up in town misunderstood

with the whole place mad because they'd planned to say
nice things when sure you wouldn't come their way
again. It's a crying shame the way they're rude
enough to hunt you down within a single day

and just before you get that taste of fear
and just before you feel you're about to pray.
You hear them thrashing through the brush, when you're nude

with love of being lost. They think you're crude

if you plead you'd like to stay. They always intrude
like parents who are appalled by curious play,
and they trade with the oldest lie: "It's for your good,
dear friend. We've come to help you out," they say.

And out you go. Be sure they knew you would.
Be sure they'd rather have you alive than dead.

Miller Williams

A native of Hoxie, Arkansas, Miller Williams has earned a reputable position among the contemporary poets of the world. His poetry has been published in Saturday Review, Atlantic Monthly, Poetry *and other literary magazines. Among his books are translations, anthologies, and criticisms, as well as five volumes of poetry.*

He is currently serving as editor of The University of Arkansas Press and holds the rank of Professor of English. Since joining the faculty at the university, he has served as co-director of the creative writing program, executive director of the Arkansas Poetry Circuit, director of the Arkansas Poetry-in-the-Prisons program, and director of the U of A translation program.

Professor Williams has been the recipient of numerous poetry prizes, including the Henry Bellaman Poetry Prize, the Bread Loaf Fellowship in Poetry and the American Academy of Arts and Letters' Prix de Roma. *He the only Arkansan ever to receive the* Prix de Roma.

Main Street

We came here to live in a small town.
Already the bypass half-encircles us,
the three-story houses on Maple Street are gone
except for one which is a funeral home

Miller Williams. *Distractions* (Baton Rouge: LSU Press, 1981).

with sad blue blinking letters over the porch.

The streets are guarded by two-headed parking meters
which doesn't matter since half the stores closed down
after Sears and Penney's moved to the mall.

Now something neither town nor city takes over.
The hospital adds a wing. The census swells.
The city limits signs of six towns
move toward each other like suspicious children.

Our children whom we meant to raise as hicks
come strangely into the house and bring new words.
They are well-bred and come from good stock.
They join us always for breakfast. We see in their eyes
and in their smiles they are patient and willing to wait.

The News

When we saw the guerrilla get shot in the head
his face flattened as if a fist had hit it.
He collapsed like clothes left standing empty
by a street magician suddenly disappeared.

I saw a woman once come out of her window
and fall with a flower pot for twenty floors,
her panties horribly public. Her long fingers.

And houses floating and people sliding off.
School books and jackets scattered half a mile.
Trains turned over and turtles laying eggs.
Most every day I see the president.
And all those people in pain, dying in pain,
or facing the camera saying, "I beg your pardon."
A woman jumping at last. Goodbye. Goodbye.

I also have my books and good music.
I have a bottle of cold white wine.

My grandfather saw in all his eighty years
one gunfighter go down in a street in Kansas.

I understand the difference in death and art.
I understand the woman out of the window
was giving all she had in a hard performance
so far as I could see from curtain to curtain;
those who watched her go in the good flesh
have seen plain death and some will dream about it.
Art is not life, but what it is it is.
We've seen figures run across the moon,
hostages released and mad kings.

He told me he could smell the gunpowder still.
He said the man was lifted off the ground.

He was eighty-three years old when he told me this.

For Rebecca, For Whom Nothing Has Been Written Page After Page

We have a language that serves us more or less
for the earth and air and fire and the earth's water,
that sort of thing, for hydrogen and tin.

What phrase explains, what simile can guess
a daughter's daughter? We half know who you are,
moment by moment, remembering what you were
as you grow past, becoming by quick revisions
an image in the door.
What matters when all the words are written and read
is what remains not said, not said,
which is what long silences are for.

About the Airplane, Then

Looking out the window, across the room,
I saw a plane heading toward the west.
I thought as I often do when I see a plane
of who might be on board and what they wish
they'd said before they left or not said,
those they love and those they meant to love.
The plane seemed so small at such a distance,
and seemed to move so slowly, it might have been
some little creature crawling across the screen.
It stopped as if to consider that a while,
changed directions slightly and crawled on.

Inside my head two hundred and seventy people
including a crew of eleven disappeared
leaving no trace but only vacancies
at typewriters, bedtime and breakfast. It came so fast
nobody had a hint of what was coming
except for one especially perceptive
flight attendant who seemed to be startled
about something just at the last moment.

Normandy Beach

Miller Williams. *The Boys on Their Bony Mules* (Baton Rouge: LSU Press, 1983).

The waves on the Normandy coast jump heavily toward us.
Somewhere above the rolling, ocean-thick air
soldiers are lining up in a rising light.
The name we have come to find is whitely there.

We stand awhile above the ragged beach
where the German gunnery crews held hard
and spread the beach with bodies that still sprawl,
appearing and disappearing. A silent charge

comes out of the lifting fog, vague visions of men,
some of them drowning, some digging holes in the sand,
some lying on the sand with waves washing their boots.
We watch as the bodies fade away in the sun.

We find his name, Lieutenant, Arkansas.
To leave you there alone I turn around
to a curving monument, The Spirit of Youth
Rising Out of the Sea, what might be found

as frontispiece in a book of Romantic verse.
It must have suggested solace to someone:
arms that might be wings, and flowering waves,
what Shelley as a sculptor might have done.

I watch the statue standing over the stones
and think of what the living do to the dead.
Then suddenly what you came to do is done.
We stop in a dark store for cheese and bread

and a bottle of wine. We find that famous room
where tapestry runs like a frozen picture show
the slow invasion that went the other way
over eleven hundred years ago,

princes and knights and horses in feathers and metal
changing the names of things. An iron cross
leans from an iron gate at the foot of a hill
where careful Germans step out of a touring bus.

I don't want to make a bad metaphor here
and everything is suddenly metaphor.
We head the Fiat south in a sundown light
and follow the back roads. Beside a river

we make the wine outlast the food and sit still

and watch the water run. Thought after thought
comes into my head and goes. Lonely companion,
there's something I have to tell you but I don't know what.

The Muse

Driving south on U.S.71
Forty miles from Fort Smith
I heard a woman speak from the back seat.
"You want a good idea for a closing line?"
I recognized the voice.
"Where did you come from?"
"I wiggled in back there when you stopped for gas.
You'd better pull over."
She knew about the cards I kept in my pocket
to scribble on whenever she came around.
We'd been through this before.
I bumped down from the blacktop and stopped the car.
Between a couple of oaks and a yellow line,
above the howl and sizzle of passing traffic,
she said some words. I waited. She looked out the window.
"Well?," I said. "Is that it?"
"It's all I have," she said. "Can't you do
anything for yourself?"
"I listen," I said. "That's what I'm supposed to do."
She took a slow breath and got out of the car.
"I'll try to get you something.
I'm going to walk around for a little while.
If you leave me here I'll forget I every saw you."
"I won't leave you," I said. So I'm sitting here
between the darkening road and pin oak trees,
a 3 x 5 card in one hand, a pen in the other,
beginning to feel vulnerable and foolish
like a man waiting for more toilet paper
thinking he may have been left there and forgotten.

Rebecca at Play

She lies in the grass and spreads her golden hair
across the grass, as if for simple joy
in being what she is, quietly aware
that she is not a tree or horse or boy.

Lily Peter

Miss Lily Peter, current Poet Laureate of Arkansas, makes her home on her cotton and soybean plantation at Marvell. Besides being a worthy poet, she is one of the state's most generous philanthropists. Her concern for the arts has resulted in music scholarships at several institutions of higher education, the installation of a fine organ in the Lily Peter Auditorium of the Fine Arts Center in Helena and the engaging of the Philadelphia Orchestra for a performance in Little Rock. She also has a keen interest in conservation and takes an active part in projects designed to protect the natural resources of Arkansas. Miss Lily is active, it seems, in everything in which she is associated. Her tireless energies, her constant encouragement of artistic talents, and her genuine love of the arts have become one of Arkansas' greatest assets.

Her volume of poetry The Green Linen of Summer, *published in 1964, received the Distinguished Alumni Award from Vanderbilt, and her volume* The Sea Dream of the Mississippi, *published in 1973, was selected as one of the important books of the United States Bicentennial in 1976.*

The Green Linen of Summer

I wrap my thoughts of the summer
    Against the terror of the dragon wind,
And pray that the linen may not too soon be thread-bare
    Its texture thinned.

Lily Peter. *The Green Linen of Summer and Other Poems* (Nashville: Robert Moore Allen, 1964).

For by and by I know will come November
> With its wintry blast;
And what is there to keep body and soul from freezing,
> If the linen do not last?

For an Autumn Night

The fever of drought burned up the year's fresh
> beauty,
and when the fever was gone, came the deadly chill
of the frost. Now the white corpse of the November
> night
lies on the marshland, wraith-like, composed and
> still.

The white haze reaches from the garden, where the
> chrysanthemums
lean stiffened and white, to where Aldebaran,
white in the sky like the sunken eye of a ghost
of an autumnal universe, stares balefully down.

In the dead clematis vines on the trellis, a wind
too faint to be felt, plucks at the brittle leaves,
as if Death, insatiate, had come from the tomb
to clutch at the treasured memories of one who
> grieves.

There are death-fires to the east along the bayou,
where a careless brand that lit the late briers and
sedge
dwindled and flared until it made of the gaunt timber
funerary torches on the dark water's edge.

Do not speak to me of love on a night like this—

I fear this incredible fever and frost and flame!
This moonlight is too malign—it could undo us!
Tonight let our love be a secret we do not name.

From: **"The Cypress Bayou"**

XI

Delta Rain

Across the brown delta loam
the thin green cotton rows run to the woods along
    the bayou,
where the bullfrogs bellow among the cypress knees
in the cool dimness of the cloudy May afternoon.
A finger of lightning reaches down to the treetops
where the south wind whips up the leaves like ivory
    lace
against the hyacinthine blue of the rain clouds,
and the rain follows with its silver shadow.
The treetoads call to each other from the China
    trees;
a mockingbird trills from its nesting place in the cedars.
In the rain-sweet air drifts the fragrance of road-
    side honeysuckle.

The May rain lasts but an hour, yet this remembrance
will refresh a scorched season of August drought.

XIII
Cypresses

The cypresses, darkly aristocratic,
rearing their stately armorials of green lacework
a hundred feet above the black marsh water,

lift up their heads to look over the edge of the world.
Their friends are the white crane,
the hawk and the horned owl—
they foregather with none beneath their dignity.
Last of their great dynasty,
disdainful of men, clannish,
they dwell in bands and companies in the swamps
    and bayous,
and a cypress tree alone and far from its kindred
is an exile in an unhappy country.

Terry Wright

Terry Wright is one of Arkansas' promising poets and is quite active in literary circles of the state. His poems have appeared in several reputable literary magazines. He is currently on the faculty of the English Department at The University of Central Arkansas.

Narcissus

I don't feel like
looking at myself
today
because I see
self-portraits, refractions
in which I appear realistic
& break

the line
here I mean there
then suffer seven years
of no voice or verses.

I look just like myself.

No. That's not what
I have to say. I want
to yell
have less
obsession or
an image may flower, a bloom
superimposing your face over mine—

you prefer your image?

I can't imagine your
point of origin or
read your body
language for intent
when you black out
my double in water.

You use force & call
it form.

After much reflection
I spy my I.

WELL,

I do think it's nice to know that
according to the *National Inquirer*
ALIENS ARE COMING SOON TO RELIEVE ALL OUR MISERY
so the supermarket must be safer
than it was yesterday. I grab a cart
with a broken wheel. I hate life when
things like this happen   usually
but not today because I know I won't

suffer for long. Surely the coming space
beings will unstick my simple problems. I'm so
happily tranquilized by this thought I never notice
the hamburger meat has turned into wood shavings --
the spiral macaroni has become steel shavings --
the produce section is "under reconstruction."
It is not until I enter the express lane
that I observe I now push a wheelbarrow.
The checkout clerk wears a hardhat. In fact,
the walls have vanished & between the exposed
skeletal beams I can see the parking lot where
the cars have changed into flying cement mixers.
The cash register crackles in a mechanized monotone
Do   not   be   alarmed   human.
This   entire   area   is   under   new management.

The small print on the front page reads
Blind Date With A Life Form: See Page Seven.
Red lights blink behind the sacker's pupils.

From **Recording**

I sigh in relief as expiring
satellites shed skin & tumble
from space. Their fiery tails
streak over & trash kilometers
of once blue ocean. A sadder call
on the monitor beats a membrane
or head clot. I remember robots
lifting off, coming down. Orbit
is curves on a screen & malfunctions
make me deeply sleepy after millions
of TV murders. I stare blankly.
Soon, kids with swollen guts will
fill a field. *No clear message*
replies every answering machine.

*

> We think coroners are very busy
> cutting. No glider or parachute
> bloom materializes for two blue-
> faced skydivers. A political bomb
> blast is at fault & results in
> deflated cabin pressure & lungs.
> Slapped by atmosphere   & out
> of a peeled jagged steel hole
> a bloody child & mother emerge as
> double or nothing breech births.
> The air hurts. Our fear is not
> what was said or seen or felt
> but is instead the anticipation
> of arriving to no embrace.

*

> We might need a briefing, a panel
> after making light of our human
> status. Seeing more freeze frame
> clips could help. The experts are
> machines & comforted by replays—
> tape loops of ghosts. A burnt
> black box records facts, moments,
> fragments between descent & impact.
> All we want to know is what
> each victim thought or felt
> but each repeats small talk
> & routine checks like frantic
> distress signals. We hold hearings,
> or we talk in tongues to spirits.

*

I should stop   stop watching
replays of the rocket booster
blast off & blow up *Challenger*.
I feel cheap. My heart hurts.
I know the crew is cheated but
friends in grandstands must wait.
I see Krista's mother now knows
the hardest lesson but her father
is still smiling & hasn't seen
the cuckold cloud. That's when
I do stop   stop watching
& rewind. The shuttle drops
to its pad & the crew disembark.
They're waving   glad to be back.

*

I hear they were maybe alive.
A clear separation transforms
metal from crew cabin to meteor—
not golden, but active & hollow.
What's said before splashdown?
I'd like to think   nothing.
Perhaps people sit still as
group photographs   or move near
portholes for a better view of blue
sky or water   & wait for news-
casters to cough, run more clips.
The fireball liberates rather
than chars but descent is filmed
in super super slow motion.

*

>We sit, watch salvage boats
>dredge for hard copies & seek
>the buzzword for photos & bones—
>"remains." We tuck glop into
>ambulances, ship goop to doctors
>& computer analyzers. *Is it
>human or marine?* We'd watch our
>own autopsies if we could. Machines
>on call maintain we suffer then decay
>as a mold for even more recycled
>bits of information age victims
>hardens into chromosomal chains.
>The running lights are absent.
>The cargo holds are not vacant.

William Mills

William Mills is one of the South's most prolific poets and enjoys a wide reputation for his work. While he is not an Arkansan, he visits the state frequently, and the poem included here is so uniquely Arkansas that it required inclusion in this volume. The most recent expression of his interest in the region is The Arkansas: An American River.

Rituals Along the Arkansas
For Robert Lowrey

By the first hour we knew the day's luck
Would leave us time to think about each fish.
Not a day when even the unskilled
Pulls fish after fish into a thoughtless boat.

William Mills. *The Meaning of Coyotes* (Baton Rouge: LSU Press, 1984).

Mindful, we worked the rock jetties
Dragging our baits through the waters
Of a fast Arkansas.
Sometimes it was a rock bass,
Sometimes a white.

But it was the final fish
We held out for—the black,
His barrel of a mouth
Waiting like a mine.
We moved to the pools at the river's edge,
Full of tangle, full of food.
We knew he waited to eat there
Or be eaten.

The priests of do, we sat patiently,
Working our rods with solemnity
And form and always hope,
The idea of Fish large in our minds
Awaiting its marriage to fish.

We brought only water to keep it simple,
The beer was for another time.
Lowrey caught the biggest and should have.
His study has been longer.
This black seemed not to want to leave his world below.
But he rose up and danced the bottom of the boat.
That brought the morning to a proper end.

We lay each glistening bass,
Rock, white and black,
On the cleaning board at the boat's side
And prepared their bodies for our use.
First the great heads with their lidless eyes
Were slipped overboard, and then the skin and the bones,
Set to drift through the live waters

Feeding the underworld.
There on the wooden board I poured water
Over the mound of luminous white meat.
As I laid my hands on the meat
To pack it away Lowrey looked up river.
"Looks like Canadians flying."
The sight of the big birds
Lining toward us made me forget my duty.
As they drew nearer we knew
We had read the signs wrong.
"Pelicans, white pelicans," he cried.

The line turned into a great spiral of birds
Riding thermals above us:
The utterly no sound, no bird cry,
Only whisper of their outstretched wings
Above our boat, above the Arkansas.
There in the high summer sun
Their great helix of white
Drew fish and man with them.
We are wedded to what we use,
What we love, what we find beautiful.

Mike Nichols

Mike Nichols has written poetry for a number of years and exhibits a promising talent. He has participated in the creative writing programs at The University of Central Arkansas, the University of Arkansas and Oklahoma State University. He is currently Techinical Director of the Arkansas Repertory Theater.

"For Grandfather's Want To Go Up Home"

Marking time by supper and baseball games
you suffer life like a failing heart.

Children, chickens and the good farm gone,
left only with the woman
whose dark eyes and strong back
made you whole,
you lived that solitary joy left behind
by growing up and the super highway.

With joy called home, the days are long
and nights are what no one
ever could have made them.
Full of dark, you amble the small rooms.
Photographs of the fully grown and fully gone
snatch your eyes to the walls
and held there they hurt
for all you knew.

Be gone, man, away from here.
Your woman needs you now
and calls you to her like dust.
Be gone and in your going blessed
as the day that brought you here.

"Untitled"

The old man
Left a creak in this rocking chair,
A reminder of his brittle bones,
A legend of his joints that cracked
Like dry twigs beneath a dog's weight.
He used to sit like a prophet
Drinking Yellowstone whiskey and
Telling hometown lies and booger stories
To wide eyed white boys like me
Drop mouthed and knock-kneed on the grass.
He left a whittle mark

On the right arm of this chair.
No initials, just a mark
As if to say he'd been here.
I remember the sound of your barlow
In white pine, in piss-elm twig.
Your bones creak in the rockers
As I allow my blade to slip.

NEWCOMERS

The following selections were solicited from Creative Writing Programs in the state's colleges and universities. They constitute proof that poetry is alive and well in Arkansas. All of these young poets show promise, I think, and I am delighted to include them in this volume. If there appears to be a propensity of students and former students from The University of Central of Arkansas it is only because I had greater access to their work and very little discipline to the selecting process. I appreciate the cooperation of Professors Michael Hefferman at Fayetteville, V. J. Coleman at Pine Bluff, Nebo at Russellville, and J. Patrick Adcock at Arkadelphia for sending submissions.

Flatrock Creek

Early morning mist mingles
With filtered sun through leaves of ash, birch,
And green maple,
Falling in rays
Against the wood framed Flatrock Creek.

Fed by springs and springtime snows
Surging sensually over falls
Splashing, foaming
White and misty
Smoothing into a cool deep pool.

Rocks, first jagged and piercing,
Flattening into layers hiding
Crevices where
Fish swim safely
Then leave to seek the filtered sun.

Dorothy Jones
Arkansas Tech University

Beds

My favorite bed is not mine
But my lover's,
It is soft and warm
And feels quite like no other,
Especially when I am
Not alone.

> Judd Mann
> Arkansas Tech University

Aerobics Class

Open thighs pulsing with the throb of rock music—
Straining, holding, flexing then
Pumping quickly.
Forty legs spread high, it's a gynecologist's
Dream . . . or nightmare.
Standing up, I gloat—

The woman in front has her green butt in my face.
I can see the dimpled fat
Like cottage cheese
Straining against glimmering nylon. Next to her
I'm lean and hard, a
Sexy animal . . .

Until I see the vixen in designer tights
With a tight ass and a loose
Shake laughing at
Me in the mirror. So what if I'm wallowing
In my own sweat like
A huffing sow? I

Glance the other way so I don't have to "donkey
Kick" her head in. Gloating bitch.
I am sinking
Beneath the wave of good health. I am tired. I want
To go home. I want
A chocolate shake.

       Tammy J. Marshall
       Arkansas Tech University

Traffic

One week before Christmas, but I need
An oil filter. The toy department
Is empty except for the two new
Grandmas (this is baby's first christmas)
Four rows right fighting for the last pink
Fluffy Dog. I get wedged at the head
Of the automotives aisle between
Shopping carts and gray and balding heads.
I have no cart. A fat lady with
Twins blocks the upper end. Just behind,
An Oriental woman trying
To maneuver her cart to head back
This way. Ludicrous. We're clogged up, too.
I remember where the bathroom is—
in back of domestics—and need it.
There is a break at the parts chart. I
Cheat, move between carts, get rammed in the
Rear, but ignore it. (No cart is a
Dangerous advantage.) The big twin
Sneezes and the row ripples backwards
But I still have the chart. I'll find my
Number. Burry brows and thick glasses
Are on my left shoulder. "You lookin'

At Mercury? Mazda on that page?"
I keep the chart long after I find
Fram PH8A. Can't move from my
Floor tile yet anyway. I see the one
I need by the French bun lady's purse,
(It's aluminum and matches her
Cart.) I get three and won't have to come
Back for nine months or nine thousand miles,
Smuggle them as far as the wiper
Blades before Burry brows thrusts his butt
In the way looking at a tire
Gauge. He spits a brown wad in a white
Cup I thought held Coke and measures the
Display golf cart tire. The twins
And Moma find their plugs and unstop
The upper end. I see freedom there
And lean into a fast, "Pardon me,"
Burry drops his cup, Fix-a-flat falls.
I break out. Three Frams. PH8A.

                                        Jennifer Miller Methvin
                                        Arkansas Tech University

Tiny Infant

Tiny infant
Cradled there
A perfect untouched rose.
(Petal soft,
    fragile,
        sweet—
Pure, yet to unfold)

Child of children
Born too soon

(You'll pay
    for their mistakes.)
Learn too soon
The how and what.
(what ''bastard'' means,
How cruelty can manifest.)

Tiny infant
Nurture seeking
Lives on mother's milk.
Grows too soon
Needs too much,
(Security, affection,
        dreams).
Denied so much
The child
Soon withers,
Withdraws
Into himself.

Like the shaded rose
Denied the sun,
Somehow doesn't die
But fades, fades,

Yet to unfold,
Hangs listless
On the stem.

Deedre Colquitt
Henderson State University

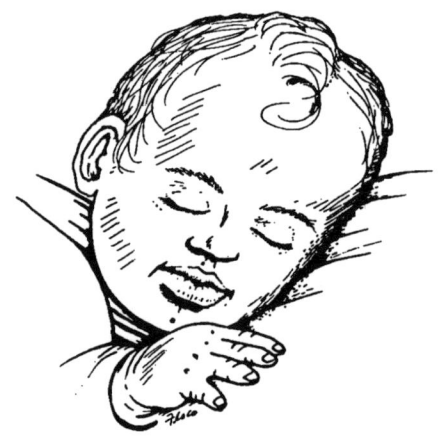

False Faces

He, she,
You and I,
We all see the world's awry
To those who seek the fountain of youth,
Searching forever for beauty and truth,
Looking for something to take from the shelves
Of natural elixer for cosmetic selves.

Bottles of cream for instant beauty,
Powders and paints for cover-up duty.
Vials of perfume and decanter of waters,
Eyebrows and lipstick for mothers and daughters.
Lips and hips, eyes and thighs, hair black, hair back,
Bleaches and dyes, keep it all youthful, truthful,
    and tight.

Jerri Hutcheson
Henderson State University

Frustration

Performing gymnastics in an atmosphere
without gravity.

Talking against the music
of a chain saw.

Walking a dog
that has only three legs.

Trying to sit quietly
while suffering from hemorrhoids.

Driving on the Interstate
while sleeping soundly.

Reading a novel
with dry contacts in the eyes.

Strumming the guitar
with raw and swollen fingers.

Singing to the rhythm
of a jackhammer.

Combing human hair
with a steel dog brush.

Walking against the force
of a moving bus.

Staring at Twinkies
while trying to stay slim.

Eating a club steak
without teeth.

Praying to God
against the sound of a bomb.

Mark Overton
Henderson State University

Pursuits

Old Trey, Dog of mine,
You struggle up on arthritic
Legs and wobble your Badger

Body to me.
With your geriatric, gravelly
Voice you welcome me home,
But I have been deceived by
Time itself, for you, the Father
Of my youth are no longer
Rising up on limber legs to greet
Me, but have taken up with
Old Dog in his pursuits.

                Trudy Walker
                Henderson State University

The Unicorn

She prances about the field,
                head held high.
Twilight cradles her body,
                sleek and pure.
A silver line hangs on air,
                lingering.
Ivory hair trails on the breeze;
                her path glows.

Nostrils flare and then relax,
                soothing her.
A sweet perfume of springtime
                surrounds her
As her forest's creatures grow—
                new life thrives.
A scent engulfs her forest. . .
                enchantment!

                Elizabeth West
                Henderson State University

The Wedding Guest

(Previously published in *The Wedding Guest*. Ptarmigan Chapbooks: Fayetteville, Arkansas, 1987)

At noon I part the curtain to so much sun
It's like slashing
A sack of grain.
Toward dawn the wedding rout retired
The searing fiddle,
Left the wine
To brood in its cask.
Now the heart muscles the dull blood
Into my temples,
And I recall
The bride leading us through the hall upstairs,
Her candle
Wavering on the bedroom's threshold,
And the mahogany
Seraphim of her wardrobe
Opening its wings to furious satins.

I didn't hear
The rooster crow,
Or see the sun fire one opal in the dew.
The white cake
That rose on a simple note
Is a ruin of shattered scroll and fluting.
Tonight the groom
Will snore in his boots,
A cricket ring its flinty spur on hardwood.

Floyd Collins
University of Arkansas
Fayetteville

Skinny Dipper

At first I saw her shoulders, then her spine,
delicate as the band of a woman's watch,
her waist which curved down to the water line
and long dark hair, floating as she bobbed
up and down, up and down again.
A boy of twelve, I hid behind a tree,
afraid to breathe for fear she'd find me there
and dive down deep and never come again
back to the surface. Her hand touched the water
and rippled her oblique reflection, dipped
and brought clear water to her mouth. She turned.
I drew my head back from her view but saw
her wet breasts glimmer and dip down again.
Her every curve was a geometry
I longed to study. I had never seen
a woman nude before, and I was stirred,
and my whole body reached for hers. I touched
myself, then quickly tore my eyes away
and brushed rough bark with both my hands and prayed
and promised God I would not look at her
and looked at her again.

> Julia Guernsey
> University of Arkansas
> Fayetteville

Henry Samuel Chesser Tours His Farm

This old windsock does its job
and the roosters, they do theirs.
The windmill works and the wife
makes good gravy—it's an art,
her gravy—makes the day start out right
A man can forget what he's got to wade through

if the gravy's good, and I've been through
some bad cotton in my time, had some jobs
made my knuckles bleed, jobs I'd have quit outright
if it hadn't been for something driving from inside. There's
no telling where this life ends ups. You start
with a craving. Pretty soon, you got a wife.

I could have done worse, could have got a wife
who screams or paints her face or looks through
catalogues all day. Mine's a quiet one. But I start
any kissing on her neck or ears, and she's got jobs
for me—the sink, the yard. Different with women—theirs
isn't need that wakes them up. Theirs is complications. Right

when I'm dying for it, she'll say something like: "Now get this right.
A man has to learn his soul and tempers. That's why he's got a wife."
Once she patted my head and said, "There, there,"
like I was her little pup. I got so mad I threw
the butter bowl against the wall and said: "A wife's job
is to damn well finish what her husband starts."

She cried when I took her dress up and that made me start
to bite. It was like having the sky pull me right
through God's eyes when she stopped fighting long enough to say, "Your job
is to stop the ache," and she whispered it from her throat, this wife,
this woman who never gave it back. I was done for. Through.
We went there that day. And I mean There.

She loved me the way I knew. Women. I love all they are.
And the butter hung on to the wall. My mind starts
that day again when I see the butter spots come through
the new coat of paint. "We got it right,"
is what I said to her and she kissed my eyes. My wife.
Now, when I'm not working this place, I do my job:

I think of ways to start the ache up in my wife—
tonight I'll wait to touch her right, there.
And the windmill will creak through the dark. That's its job.

>	Judy Ruiz
>	University of Arkansas
>	Fayetteville

If I Should Live a Thousand Years

If I should live a thousand years,
I owe my living to forces three: to
Him, whose breath of life strengthens
me, to her, whose milky breasts
nourished me, and to you, whose
tender love revitalizes me.

>	Japhet N. Makia
>	University of Arkansas
>	Pine Bluff

Remembering Highways

I walk the gravel in June
to take away the chill—
Slower than before
and looking back.

The rusting frame
of a '28 Ford slumbers
behind the barn.
I sit with drawn up legs
on the sun warmed steel
while he chops weeds

around the chicken yard to chase
away corn snakes and racers.

81 last fall, he's
worn from too many miles,
like the wheeled scrap of metal beneath me:
Remembering highways.

Driven, he moves
(he can't warm up he says).
When June warms
and school doors close behind me
we walk the lane below the house
and I see it isn't the chill
he fights, but the stillness.

Moving, he was alive.
Till the stillness
sprouts brambles through
his mile-rattled frame.

Tony Gifford
University of Central Arkansas

Coma

Last fall
The porch rocker was left lonely
To creak and quarrel
With the whispering winds . . .
As he muttered away
To search for soft visions of sleep
That brought portraits
of the nightmare woman
Streaming into his temple.

Like a shadow
That had chosen
To take its own shape,
She would appear
On the window sash
To rock soft and moon-framed
Against a Lucifered sky.
Pulling her mane
Back from the wind,
She would gently
Weave and plait
Him into her hair
To let him share
Her wet jasmine, incense
And sweat.

One morning
In late fall,
He awoke—
Touched the wrinkled face
At his side . . .
And closed his eyes again.

Bob Child
University of Central Arkansas

Compelling Little Moments of Forward Motion Vertigo

As if my feet were
Clenched fists at the Idiot's
Table. They rise and fall in
The rhythm of demands.
Rise and fall with
A pounding on the table which

The Nurse provides with
Heaping spoons of
Life which he can no longer see in
His quickening tempo, his
Frenzied tap-dance, his
Whining starvation with
Blind eyes thrown back he slowly starves.

                              E. E. Eller
                              University of Central Arkansas